LIBERTY,
PROPERTY,
AND
PRIVACY

Edward Keynes

LIBERTY, PROPERTY, AND PRIVACY

Toward a Jurisprudence
of
Substantive Due Process

The Pennsylvania State University Press
University Park, Pennsylvania

For Josie, Marvin, and Their Family

Library of Congress Cataloging-in-Publication Data

Keynes, Edward.
    Liberty, property, and privacy : toward a jurisprudence of substantive due process
/ Edward Keynes.
        p.   cm.
Includes bibliographical references and index.
ISBN 0-271-01509-8 (cloth)
ISBN 0-271-01510-1 (paper)
    1. Due process of law—United States. 2. Right of property—United States. 3.
Privacy, right of—United States. 4. Civil rights—United States. 5. I. Title.
KF4765.K49   1996
347.73′05—dc20
[347.3075]   95–12709
                                                                           CIP

It is the policy of The Pennsylvania State University Press to use acid-free paper for
the first printing of all clothbound books. Publications on uncoated stock satisfy the
minimum requirements of American National Standard for Information Sciences—
Permanence of Paper for Printed Library Materials, ANSI Z39.48–1992.

Contents

Acknowledgments   vii

Introduction   ix

1. The Core Constitutional Values: Life, Liberty, and Property   1
    The Core Values
    The Evolution of Substantive Due Process
    Preconstitutional Development
    The Bill of Rights
    Case Law and Commentaries

2. Antecedents of the Fourteenth Amendment's Core Values   31
    Congressional Antecedents
    The Freedman's Bureau Bill
    The Civil Rights Act of 1866

3. Framing the Fourteenth Amendment   55
    The Substance of Due Process
    Bingham's Early Draft
    The Search for a Compromise
    The Debate and Adoption

4. Congressional Protection of Fundamental Rights in the   75
    Reconstruction Era
    The Enforcement Act of 1871
    Drafting the Ku Klux Klan Act
    The Public Accommodations Act of 1875

5. The Supreme Court, the Public Interest, and Economic   97
    Liberty, 1873–1921
        The Rise and Evolution of Substantive Due Process
        Substantive Due Process—Public Monopolies and Businesses
            Affected with a Public Interest
        Economic Liberty and the Apotheosis of Substantive Due
            Process
        Property Rights and Substantive Due Process
        Property Rights of Public Utilities and Businesses Affected
            with a Public Interest
        Liberty of Contract: The Free World of *Lochner* and
            Coppage
        Congressional Power, Substantive Due Process, and
            Economic Liberty

6. The Much-Acclaimed Demise of Substantive Due Process,   129
    1921–1991
        The Court and the Emerging Welfare State
        The Court and Substantive Due Process, 1921–1937
        The Premature Burial of Substantive Due Process,
            1941–1969

7. Liberty and Privacy—Marriage and the Family   154
        Family Privacy and Individual Autonomy
        Parents, Children, and the Nuclear Family
        Procreation, Marriage, and Family Relationships

8. Reproductive Liberty and Individual Autonomy—   181
    Contraception and Abortion
        Contraception and Individual Autonomy
        Abortion and a Woman's Right to Decide
        The Challenge to *Roe* v. *Wade*
        Casey and the Promise of Liberty

Epilogue   211

Table of Cases   219

Index   223

About the Author   239

Acknowledgments

Although I cannot express my gratitude to all who contributed to this book, I want to thank my friends and colleagues Vernon V. Aspaturian, Evan Pugh Professor Emeritus; Trond Gilberg, Professor of Political Science at the National University of Singapore; and Werner Kaltefleiter, Professor of Political Science at the Christian-Albrechts University, Kiel, Germany, for their encouragement. I also want to thank the Alexander von Humboldt Foundation for its generous support, which has allowed me to complete this work and begin a new study. I also thank Larry Scaff for facilitating my sabbatical leave, which permitted the completion of this book.

The intellectual history of this book began in a joint seminar with my close friend and thoughtful critic Phillip E. Stebbins, Associate Professor of History at the Pennsylvania State University, to whom I owe a special debt. I am also indebted to my friends and former students Randall K. Miller and David L. Tubbs, who offered their suggestions for improving the manuscript. To James W. Ely Jr., Professor of Law and History, Vanderbilt University; Lewis Fisher, Senior Specialist, Congressional Research Service, Library of Congress; and Paul Kens, Professor of Political Science, Southwest Texas State University, a special thanks for their careful reading and thoughtful criticism of the manuscript. It is a great pleasure to publish again with Penn State Press, and to acknowledge the important role that Sandy Thatcher, director of the press, and Peggy Hoover, senior manuscript editor, played in publishing this book.

I thank my colleagues Deborah Cheney, Kevin Harwell, Helen Sheehy, and Ruth Senior of the Documents and Interlibrary Loan departments of the Pennsylvania State University Libraries for their continuing cooperation and professional assistance in completing the research for this book. Finally, I thank James L. Hollis, who contributed to this book by proofreading the manuscript, and Andreas Beckmann, who assisted in preparing the manuscript for publication. Of course, I assume responsibility for any errors that appear in this book.

Our Constitution is a covenant running from the first generation of Americans to us and then to future generations. It is a coherent succession. Each generation must learn anew that the Constitution's written terms embody ideas and aspirations that must survive more ages than one. We accept our responsibility not to retreat from interpreting the full meaning of the covenant in light of all of our precedents. We invoke it once again to define the freedom guaranteed by the Constitution's own promise, the promise of liberty. *

* Joint opinion of Justices O'Connor, Kennedy, and Souter, *Planned Parenthood of Southeastern Pennsylvania* v. *Casey*, 112 S.Ct. 2791 (1992), 2833.

Introduction

Since 1965, U.S. Supreme Court decisions concerning marriage, the family, contraception, and abortion have kindled a national debate about the role of the judiciary in a democratic society. The Court's critics have argued that it is beyond the competence of the federal judiciary to make policy in these areas. The Court's advocates have responded that questions of marital privacy and reproductive liberty implicate constitutional rights that federal judges are eminently suited to decide. As the Supreme Court's decision in *Planned Parenthood of Southeastern Pennsylvania v. Casey*[1] reveals, judicial intervention in the abortion controversy has evoked passions that will not die and that often obscure basic issues of jurisprudence and constitutional law that underlie the public debate.

Although this book examines the Supreme Court's role in a constitutional democracy, it is about the development of the fundamental-rights philosophy and jurisprudence that affords constitutional protection to unenumerated liberty and property rights. Since the 1880s diverse justices, including Stephen Field, Joseph Bradley, Rufus Peckham, James Clark McReynolds, John Marshall Harlan (II), and Harry Blackmun, have inferred unenumerated fundamental rights from the due process clauses of the Fifth and Fourteenth Amendments. Foremost among the Supreme Court's critics, Raoul Berger insists that due process is exclusively a guarantee of judicial fairness. The due process clauses ensure that the state and national governments cannot deprive individuals of life, liberty, or property, except by established judicial procedure. Berger and other proceduralists deny that due process imposes substantive limitations on the power of Congress and the

---

1. 112 S.Ct. 2791 (1992).

state legislatures to enact policies that are otherwise within their constitutional competence.[2]

The thesis of this book is that due process includes a substantive as well as a procedural component. In the United States, due process is a guarantee against arbitrary governmental deprivation of life, liberty, and property. Although the due process clauses are a broad promise of liberty, they do not define the specific liberty or property interests that are encompassed. The due process clauses express the core substantive values that are the raison d'être of constitutional government—the protection of life, liberty, and property, but the framers of the Fifth and Fourteenth Amendments left the definition of specific liberty and property interests to Congress and the courts. Congress has the primary authority to define specific rights and remedies, but the courts can employ their power of constitutional review to restrain legislative deprivations of fundamental rights. This joint exercise of authority promotes a dialogue that inhibits both judicial overreaching and the abandonment of individuals' rights to intemperate legislative majorities.

The language of the Constitution suggests that the due process clauses are conditional, rather than absolute, guarantees of life, liberty, and property. Neither the Fifth nor the Fourteenth Amendment was intended to frustrate the legitimate exercise of governmental authority to promote the public's health, safety, morals, or welfare. They were designed to prevent government from depriving people of fundamental rights without a justification rooted in the public interest. As a conditional promise of protection, the due process clauses require that a judicial arbiter decide in individual cases when public policy invades a constitutionally protected private realm that is beyond considerations of the public welfare.

Since the late 1880s the Supreme Court has flirted with substantive due process, sometimes affirming, at other times rejecting, the due process clauses as a restraint on the exercise of legislative power. Between 1897 and 1923 the justices employed due process to protect liberty of contract against various economic regulatory policies. After 1937 a new majority repudiated liberty of contract as a limitation on social and economic policy. Speaking for the Court, in 1963 Justice Hugo Black rejected the use of "the 'vague contours' of the Due Process Clause to nullify laws which a majority of this Court believed to be economically unwise."[3]

But just two years later Justice John Marshall Harlan (II) invoked the due

2. See Raoul Berger, *Government by Judiciary: The Transformation of the Fourteenth Amendment* (Cambridge, Mass.: Harvard University Press, 1977), 194–99.

3. *Ferguson v. Skrupa*, 372 U.S. 726 (1963), 731.

process clause of the Fourteenth Amendment to repudiate a Connecticut law prohibiting the use of contraceptives.[4] Following *Roe v. Wade*[5] the Supreme Court employed the due process clause to invalidate many state regulations concerning abortion. In 1992 the *Casey* Court explicitly affirmed its commitment to substantive due process reasoning. As the *Casey* decision indicates, due process remains a prolific source of specific rights that the Court has defined within the boundaries of the Fifth and Fourteenth Amendments.

Although the Supreme Court repudiated substantive due process as a protection of economic and property rights, it has derived other personal liberties from the due process clauses. The logic underlying the Court's contraception and abortion decisions is similar to the rationale that informed its liberty-of-contract opinions. As Justice James Clark McReynolds observed in *Meyer v. Nebraska*, the term "liberty" in the due process clause encompasses the right "to enjoy those privileges long recognized at common law as essential to the orderly pursuit of happiness by free men."[6] While he did not provide an exhaustive enumeration of these unenumerated rights, McReynolds did list the right to enter into contracts, to engage in any lawful occupation, to marry, to acquire knowledge, and to rear one's children.[7] In addition to the specific protections of the Bill of Rights, as Justice Harlan (II) noted, the Fourteenth Amendment's due process clause includes unenumerated fundamental rights that limit the exercise of the states' police powers to a valid public purpose.

This book argues that the substantive component of the due process clauses is derived from British and American jurisprudence as well as from general principles of natural justice. The framers of the Fifth and Fourteenth Amendments relied on natural law, social-contract philosophy, and Anglo-American legal history. While natural law and social-contract philosophy provided general principles, the common law offered specific rights and remedies in defining the substance of due process. Drawing on this rich legal tradition, the framers developed a conception of fundamental rights that encompasses the protection of life, liberty, and property. They understood these rights as co-equal and integrally related to one another. Together, they form the foundation of human happiness and good government in a well-ordered civil society.

4. See Harlan (concurring), *Griswold v. Connecticut*, 381 U.S. 479 (1965).
5. 410 U.S. 113 (1973).
6. 262 U.S. 390 (1923), 399.
7. *Id.*

At the same time, the framers acknowledged that in a republican society Congress and the state legislatures have the primary constitutional responsibility to determine what the public welfare requires. Unless the legislature clearly has abused its power, courts should defer to legislators' fact-finding and judgment. In a republican society, the justices cannot determine the wisdom of public policy, but they can inquire into the factual premises of legislation. Does the record support the legislature's ostensible purpose? What are the policy's foreseeable legal consequences? Does the policy serve a valid public purpose?

Although the Supreme Court has a duty to decide whether laws burden fundamental rights without clearly advancing a public purpose, it is not a roving commission with authority to set aside legislative policies of which it disapproves. As Justice Harlan (II) once commented, if the Court decides that a specific right is protected, it must exercise reasonable and sensitive judgment in deciding whether the government's stated objectives justify abridging an individual's liberty.[8] Despite Harlan's warning, since the 1960s the Court has intruded on the states' exercise of policymaking authority and imperiled its own authority to protect fundamental rights. While the Court attempted to correct the course in *Casey*, it adheres to a fundamentally flawed balancing methodology that invites judges to act like legislators who weigh competing interests and allocate scarce resources.

This book attempts to illuminate the origins, evolution, and application of substantive due process as an important source of contemporary liberty and property interests. It seeks to engage students, practitioners, scholars, and jurists in a dialogue about the possibilities and dangers of employing the due process clauses as a limitation on the policymaking authority of the people's elected representatives. Although some scholars allege that the Supreme Court used substantive due process solely to defend entrenched economic interests, the Fuller Court (1888–1910) employed the due process clause to define and protect economic liberty. More recently, the Court has used the due process clauses to protect other personal liberties of Americans from governmental intrusion. In an age that offers government the technological capacity to invade Americans' personal lives, due process remains a vital protection of personal dignity and autonomy, which are core values in a constitutional democracy.

As Chapter 1 argues, by the 1850s there was a substantial body of jurisprudence and philosophical literature that advanced constitutional theories

---

8. Harlan (dissenting), *Poe v. Ullman*, 367 U.S. 497 (1961), 543.

compatible with substantive due process. Derived from the British common law and legal commentaries, as well as from natural law and social-contract philosophy, the American understanding suggests that due process protects individuals from governmental interferences with life, liberty, and property interests that are not justified by a public purpose. American jurisprudence before the Civil War implies that due process guarantees fundamental fairness in the judicial process and restrains the exercise of legislative and executive power vis-à-vis the individual's fundamental rights. But there is no direct link between pre–Civil War judicial decisions and later cases invoking substantive due process.

Chapters 2 and 3 examine the evolution and framing of the Fourteenth Amendment's due process clause. As the debates on the Freedman's Bureau Extension Act, the Civil Rights Act of 1866, and the Fourteenth Amendment indicate, many moderate and Radical Republicans in the Thirty-ninth Congress (1865–66) articulated views that are compatible with substantive due process. Congressional Republicans believed that the Fourteenth Amendment imposed on the states a broad affirmative duty to protect the individual's fundamental rights of life, liberty, and property. Although the privileges or immunities clause does not define the specific interests that are encompassed, even the narrowest interpretation would include the individual's physical security, personal liberty, and property rights. However, the Fourteenth Amendment's framers left the definition of specific rights to Congress, and to the courts in the Reconstruction Era.

Chapter 4 argues that Reconstruction Congresses interpreted the Fourteenth Amendment liberally. In a series of civil rights acts, Congress expanded the federal judiciary's jurisdiction to protect specific life, liberty, and property rights against active deprivation by the states. As the debates suggest, the legislative drafters derived these rights from their understanding of common law, natural law, and social-contract theory. Congress also authorized the federal courts to protect fundamental rights in the event that the states failed to meet their affirmative duties. With few exceptions, congressional Republicans argued that the Fourteenth Amendment prohibited the states from exercising their powers arbitrarily vis-à-vis the individual's life, liberty, and property rights. They acknowledged the states' authority to promote the public welfare, but congressional majorities adopted legislation that limited the states' exercise of their reserved powers under the Tenth Amendment. In the event that the states failed to fulfill their constitutional duty, Congress made the federal courts a custodian of the individual's fundamental rights.

Chapters 5 and 6 examine the Supreme Court's evolution of economic liberty and property rights under the due process clauses. Initially, after the Civil War the Court was deferential to the states' exercise of their police, tax, and eminent domain powers in order to accommodate rapid growth and technological change. By 1888, however, the justices began to restrain the states' interference with vested property rights and the individual's liberty to make labor contracts. Under the influence of Justices Stephen Field and Joseph Bradley, the Supreme Court embraced liberty of contract as a fundamental right. Between 1897 and 1905 a majority of justices accepted the view that liberty of contract is indispensable to the individual's pursuit of happiness.

Although the Taft and Hughes Courts acknowledged the states' authority to promote the public welfare, between 1933 and 1936 the justices voided such congressional legislation as the National Industrial Recovery Act of 1933 and the Bituminous Coal Conservation Act of 1935 as an impermissible exercise of the power to regulate interstate commerce. These decisions precipitated a conflict with the Roosevelt administration that reached a crescendo in 1937. Subsequently, the justices began a strategic retreat, abandoning the field of economic and social policy to Congress and the state legislatures. By 1941 the Roosevelt Court's doctrine of presumptive validity shifted the burden of proof to individuals and corporations attacking social and economic policy as a deprivation of liberty or property without due process of law. The Supreme Court's new doctrine ensured that few attacks on social and economic policy would survive judicial review.

At the same time, the Court resurrected the fundamental-rights, substantive due process reasoning of *Lochner* to expand constitutional protection for noneconomic personal liberties. Applying strict scrutiny and a compelling-interest standard to legislation that implicates unenumerated privacy rights, for example, the Supreme Court has struck down various state policies that promote otherwise valid public purposes. However, as Chapter 7 argues, the justices have failed to develop a coherent theory or set of principles for identifying which unenumerated rights are fundamental and therefore constitutionally protected. The Court also has failed to provide a rationale for affording unenumerated privacy rights greater protection than unenumerated economic liberty and property rights.

As the Supreme Court's management of the abortion controversy suggests, the justices have failed to resolve the basic conflict between competing claims of private rights and the public interest. Although the Court has abandoned Justice Harry Blackmun's trimester approach to the regulation of abortion, it adheres to a balancing methodology that is basically flawed. As long as the Court treats unenumerated rights as indivisible values and the public welfare as divisible goods, it cannot balance them on the same scale. But the justices can array such dignitary rights as "life" and "privacy" in an ordinal scale to resolve conflicts of rights. Implicitly, the justices have adopted such an approach by arguing that at the point of viability the right of the fetus to live outweighs all but a woman's right to preserve her own life and health. By articulating a more permissive approach, the *Casey* plurality has steered the Court away from a serious controversy with Congress and the states, without resolving the basic dilemma.

Chapter 8 argues that the Court should abandon efforts to weigh the relative importance of unenumerated rights and public interests in regulation. Instead, it should recognize that due process was never intended to shield individuals from regulations that are directly related to a valid public purpose—that is, an objective that is within the constitutional authority of Congress or the states. As Stephen Field, Joseph Bradley, Thomas M. Cooley, and other nineteenth-century jurists argued, the due process clauses protect individuals from purposeless restraints, from restrictions that do not serve a constitutionally valid public purpose. Due process is a guarantee against partial or class legislation that promotes a particular group's interests or imposes its values without serving the public welfare. As nineteenth-century exponents of constitutional limitations understood, the best way to protect unenumerated fundamental rights is to clarify the boundaries between the public and the private realm, however difficult that task may be.

In a constitutional democracy that limits the exercise of governmental power over the individual, the due process clauses are a bulwark against arbitrary and capricious government. Of course, the danger exists that judges might overreach their power, frustrating the legitimate efforts of the people's representatives to enact policies that advance the public interest. While judges should be careful to avoid deciding the wisdom of policy, they have a duty to protect the individual's fundamental rights against unwarranted intrusions—that is, policies that are not clearly related to a valid public purpose. As Justices Sandra Day O'Connor, Anthony Kennedy, and David Souter have observed, the Supreme Court has an obligation to invoke the due process clauses "to define the freedom guaranteed by the Constitution's own promise, the promise of liberty,"[9] against unjustified governmental intrusions.

9. *Id.*, 2833.

The problem with the Court's contemporary jurisprudence of liberty is its free form or lack of explicit standards, which creates the potential for judicial interference with valid legislative policymaking. Properly understood and applied, the common-law tradition and police-power jurisprudence offer a promising approach to reconciling conflicts between claims of individual liberty and the public welfare. By defining specific rights and remedies, the common law gives explicit meaning to the broad contours of due process and restrains the freewheeling jurisprudence that Justice Black criticized. Police-power jurisprudence provides a standard for upholding public policies that promote a well-ordered society. An enlivened common-law, police-power jurisprudence could afford protection for fundamental rights and provide government with ample opportunity to demonstrate that regulations regarding property and liberty are clearly related to valid public objectives.

1

The Core Constitutional Values:

Life, Liberty, and Property

In *Ferguson* v. *Skrupa*[1] Justice Hugo Black proclaimed that the Supreme Court had abandoned substantive due process as a restriction on legislative power to enact economic regulatory policy. He denied that the "vague contours" of the due process clause authorize courts to set aside legislative policies that judges believe "unwise or incompatible with some particular economic or social philosophy."[2] Black rejected the view that the due process clauses contain substantive guarantees of life, liberty, and property limiting a legislature's authority to enact legitimate policies to protect the public health, safety, welfare, and morals. Without indicating why he believed the due process clause to be vaguer than other constitutional limitations, Black stated simply that the Court would not "sit as a 'superlegislature to weigh the wisdom of legislation.'"[3]

1. 372 U.S. 726 (1963), 726–27. The statute forbade all but lawyers in the course of their regular practice from making contracts with debtors to collect money periodically and distribute this sum among their creditors.
2. *Id.*, 731–32. Black rejected the natural-right and substantive due process philosophy that had informed the Supreme Court's decisions in such cases as *Lochner* v. *New York*, 198 U.S. 45 (1905), *Coppage* v. *Kansas*, 236 U.S. 1 (1915), *Adkins* v. *Children's Hospital*, 261 U.S. 525 (1923), and *Burns Baking Co.* v. *Bryan*, 264 U.S. 504 (1924).
3. 372 U.S., 731.

A little more than two years later, in *Griswold* v. *Connecticut*,[4] the Supreme Court employed both the Ninth and the Fourteenth Amendments to strike down a Connecticut statute that made it a crime to prescribe or use contraceptives. Although Justice William O. Douglas rested his opinion on the concept of penumbral rights emanating from various provisions of the Bill of Rights,[5] in a concurring opinion Justice Arthur Goldberg argued that the concept of liberty in the due process clause is broad enough to encompass a fundamental, unenumerated right to privacy.[6] Also concurring was Justice John Marshall Harlan, who concluded that the Connecticut statute infringed the "concept of ordered liberty" implicit in the due process clause of the Fourteenth Amendment.[7] Concurring separately, Justice Byron White agreed that the statute, as applied to married couples, deprived them of their liberty without due process of law.[8]

In a stinging dissent, Hugo Black, along with Justice Potter Stewart, objected to the vague right to privacy employed in the majority and concurring opinions. Black warned the majority against returning to the natural-law and substantive due process philosophy of *Lochner*, which the Court had rejected in many subsequent opinions.[9] He argued that the *Lochner* philosophy, "based on subjective considerations of 'natural justice,' is no less dangerous when used to enforce this Court's views about personal rights than those about economic rights."[10] While Black's criticism is well taken, such nineteenth-century judges as Stephen J. Field employed common-law and police-power jurisprudence, as well as natural-law principles, to define substantive due process rights.

4. 381 U.S. 479 (1965).

5. Indeed, Douglas explicitly declined the invitation to use *Lochner* as a guide, arguing that the Court does not "sit as a super-legislature to determine the wisdom, need, and propriety of laws that touch economic problems, business affairs, or social conditions" (*id.*, 482). However, Douglas argued, this law was different because it touched on the intimate private relationship between husbands and wives. His critics suggested that the Court had returned to the discredited line of reasoning in *Lochner*, *Coppage*, *Adkins*, and *Burns*. See Black (dissenting), *id.*, 522–23.

6. *Id.*, 493–94.

7. *Id.*, 500.

8. *Id.*, 502. A majority agreed that the due process clause encompasses a right to privacy that includes a married couple's decision to use contraceptives.

9. *Id.*, 514–16. See also *Nebbia* v. *New York*, 291 U.S. 502 (1934); *West Coast Hotel Co.* v. *Parrish*, 300 U.S. 379 (1937); *Lincoln Fed. Labor Union* v. *Northwestern Iron & Metal Co.*, 335 U.S. 525 (1949); *Day-Bright Lighting, Inc.* v. *Missouri*, 342 U.S. 421 (1952); *Williamson* v. *Lee Optical Co.*, 348 U.S. 483 (1955); and *Ferguson* v. *Skrupa*, 372 U.S. 726 (1963).

10. 381 U.S. (Black dissenting), 522. Black failed to indicate why economic rights were less personal, fundamental, or important than other liberties.

In the 1860s Thomas McIntyre Cooley, John Appleton, and other jurists derived constitutional protections of liberty and property from English customary and common law as well as American state practice. From their perspective, the Anglo-American legal tradition gave explicit definition to the meaning of due process in specific historic contexts. Thus common-law precedents provided guidelines for judges to fashion rights in confronting new legal controversies. Adherence to precedent, common-law rules of construction, and established remedies restrained judges, inhibiting them from intruding on the legitimate functions of legislatures while affording protection to fundamental rights.

Although scholars have paid considerable attention to the natural-law and social-contract basis of unenumerated rights, they have until recently ignored common-law and police-power jurisprudence in defining the scope of these rights. If natural justice is an invitation for judges to roam indiscriminately across the political landscape, common-law and police-power jurisprudence bridles the temptation to abandon accepted legal canons. The two legal traditions complement rather than conflict with one another.[11] Moreover, neither Stephen Field nor the framers of the Fourteenth Amendment and the civil rights acts drew a bright line between the common and natural law.

Field and Bradley believed that the Fourteenth Amendment embodied historic limitations, derived from common and natural law, on the states' authority to burden life, liberty, and property. Only reasonable police-power legislation—that is, measures clearly adopted for a public purpose—could justify restrictions of fundamental rights.[12] As the Supreme Court's recent

11. However, some recent revisionist historians argue that the natural-law, social-contract philosophy played only a minor and insignificant role in the development of American constitutionalism and legal thought. John Phillip Reid states that American revolutionaries relied on traditional English conceptions of rights. They turned to common and customary law in their struggle with Parliament. American constitutionalists relied on the British constitutional tradition before the Glorious Revolution, a historical tradition that was older than the Magna Carta. See, for example, John Phillip Reid, *The Concept of Liberty in the Age of the American Revolution* (Chicago: University of Chicago Press, 1988); John Phillip Reid, *Constitutional History of the American Revolution*, vol. 1, The Authority of Rights, and vol. 2, *The Authority of Legislation* (Madison: University of Wisconsin Press, 1986 and 1991).

12. Thus partial or class legislation—that is, measures that favor a particular interest—are not valid police regulations. Field, Cooley, and Appleton opposed exclusive franchises, monopoly grants, and tax subsidies as a misuse of the police, tax, and eminent domain powers to the advantage of one group over another at the public's expense. See Charles W. McCurdy, "Justice Field and the Jurisprudence of Government-Business Relations: Some Parameters of Laissez-Faire Constitutionalism, 1863–1897," 61 *J. Am. Hist.* 970–1005 (1975), 979–82 (hereafter McCurdy, 61 *J. Am. Hist.*); Alan R. Jones, *The Constitutional Conservatism of*

abortion decisions demonstrate, the Court has not abandoned the concept of substantive due process that emerged in the 1870s as a restriction on social and economic regulatory legislation. But it has jettisoned the standards and restraining influence of the common-law and police-power jurisprudence in reconciling private rights and the public welfare.

Since 1923 the Court has expanded the concept of personal liberty to encompass a broad range of unenumerated, fundamental rights, including a woman's decision to terminate a pregnancy. Beginning with *Meyer v. Nebraska*, the Supreme Court has stated that the Fifth and Fourteenth Amendments' guarantees of liberty include more than the Constitution's explicitly enumerated rights.[13] Writing for the majority, Justice James McReynolds reiterated:

> Liberty . . . denotes not merely freedom from bodily restraint but also the right of the individual to contract, to engage in any of the common occupations of life, to acquire useful knowledge, to marry, establish a home and bring up children, to worship God according to the dictates of his own conscience, and generally to enjoy those privileges long recognized at common law as essential to the orderly pursuit of happiness by free men.[14]

Although Justice Oliver Wendell Holmes, dissenting, denied that the Nebraska statute was an undue restriction on the liberty of teachers and students, he recognized that an arbitrary or unreasonable law (one that did not serve a valid public purpose) would unconstitutionally burden liberty interests that the due process clause protects.[15]

Thomas McIntyre Cooley (New York: Garland Publishing Co., 1987), 24–25, 40, 155, 158–60, 177–79; and David M. Gold, *The Shaping of the Nineteenth-Century Legal Mind: John Appleton and Responsible Individualism* (New York: Greenwood Press, 1990), 10, 20, 21–22, 124–25, 138–39, 143–45, 147–48.

13. 262 U.S. 390 (1923), 399. The Nebraska statute required that all public and private instruction through the eighth grade be in English. More than fifty years earlier Thomas Cooley had argued that due process is a broad limitation on the states' legislative power. Due process is a shield against arbitrary power that goes beyond specific constitutional limitations. See Thomas M. Cooley, *Treatise on the Constitutional Limitations Which Restrict the Legislative Power of the States of the American Union*, 2d ed. (Boston: Little, Brown & Co., 1871). See also Jones, *Constitutional Conservatism*, 141–46.

14. 262 U.S., 399. Justice McReynolds assumes that the framers of the Fourteenth Amendment embodied common-law conceptions of liberty in the amendment but does not offer any evidence to support his position.

15. See Holmes (dissenting) in the companion case, *Bartels v. Iowa*, 262 U.S. 404 (1923), 412.

While the Supreme Court has given considerable scope to the states' regulation of business, industrial, professional, and other traditional property interests, since the late 1930s it has expanded protection for non-economic liberty interests. The justices have recognized that the concept of personal liberty encompasses the right to marry, to procreate, to rear and educate children, to use contraceptives, and to terminate a pregnancy.[16] The Supreme Court and some state courts have acknowledged that the due process clauses include a so-called "right to die."[17] Despite various jurists' rejection of *Lochner*, the Court continues to articulate and infer unenumerated liberty interests from the due process clause in the Fifth and Fourteenth Amendments.

As the continuing debate over the meaning and scope of the due process clauses suggests, these issues raise significant questions about fundamental rights, legislative power to promote the public welfare, and the relationship of the individual to the state and society. There are also important questions of institutional competence implicit in this debate. Is it appropriate for the Supreme Court to articulate liberty and property interests that the Constitution does not explicitly enumerate? How far can the Court go in protecting these due process interests before it impairs the legislative function and interferes with the legitimate policy judgments of Congress and the state legislatures as representative institutions? The Supreme Court's reliance on substantive due process in the struggle over contraception, abortion, and sexual intimacy suggests that the time is ripe to examine the adequacy of this concept in reconciling individual rights with the public welfare.

The due process clauses of the Fifth and Fourteenth Amendments declare that life, liberty, and property are conditional albeit fundamental rights. Both clauses contain the critical prepositional phrase "without due process of law," which conditions or restricts the meaning of the main clause. The Fifth and the Fourteenth Amendments do not furnish an absolute guarantee of life, liberty, or property, but they do require government to demonstrate

16. *Loving v. Virginia*, 388 U.S. 1 (1967); *Zablocki v. Redhail*, 434 U.S. 374 (1978); *Skinner v. Oklahoma*, 316 U.S. 535 (1942); *Meyer*, 262 U.S. 390 (1923); *Pierce v. Society of Sisters*, 268 U.S. 510 (1925); *Prince v. Massachusetts*, 321 U.S. 158 (1944); *Stanley v. Illinois*, 405 U.S. 645 (1972); *Wisconsin v. Yoder*, 406 U.S. 205 (1972); *Quilloin v. Walcott*, 434 U.S. 246 (1978); *Caban v. Mohammed*, 441 U.S. 380 (1979); *Lassiter v. Department of Social Services*, 452 U.S. 18 (1981); *Santosky v. Kramer*, 455 U.S. 745 (1982); *Lehr v. Robertson*, 463 U.S. 248 (1983); *Michael H. v. Gerald D.*, 109 S.Ct. 2333; *Griswold v. Connecticut*, 381 U.S. 479 (1965); *Eisenstadt v. Baird*, 405 U.S. 438 (1972); and *Roe v. Wade*, 410 U.S. 113 (1973).

17. See, for example, *Matter of Quinlan*, 70 N.J. 10 (1976); 355 A.2d 647; *Cruzan v. Director, Missouri Dept. of Public Health*, 110 S.Ct. 2841.

an important public purpose in restricting fundamental rights. As Justice Harry Blackmun wrote in *Roe* v. *Wade,* the landmark abortion case, "the right of personal privacy includes the abortion decision, but . . . this right is not unqualified and must be considered against important state interests in regulation."[18] Thus contemporary courts attempt to employ balancing tests to determine whether government may burden these rights.[19]

The language and syntax of the due process clauses raise at least three important questions. First, what specific liberty and property interests do the Fifth and Fourteenth Amendments encompass? Second, is due process merely a guarantee of fair judicial procedure—for example, proper notice, a timely and meaningful hearing, and a decision by an impartial judge? Or is it a limitation on the legislative power of government to regulate and restrict the exercise of constitutionally protected liberty, property, or privacy interests in order to promote the public welfare? Third, what judicial standards are appropriate in reconciling individuals' claims and legislative judgments about the public welfare?

The Core Values

The due process clauses recognize the essential obligation of government to protect the individual's physical security, liberty, and right to acquire, enjoy, and dispose of wealth (property), within the limits of the community's duty to protect the collective welfare.[20] Several other constitutional provisions— the Preamble and the privileges and immunities clauses of Article Four and

18. 410 U.S., 154.

19. Michael Perry, for example, suggests that the judiciary performs an important normative function in balancing such competing interests as liberty and the public welfare. Removed from daily political struggles, the courts can take a long-term view. In construing the meaning of such open-ended terms as "liberty" and "the public welfare," the judiciary translates these terms into enforceable constitutional limitations. See Michael Perry, "Abortion, the Public Morals, and the Police Power: The Ethical Function of Substantive Due Process," 23 *U.C.L.A. L. Rev.* 689–736 (1976) (hereafter Perry, 23 *U.C.L.A. L. Rev.*).

20. In the eighteenth century, as Willi Paul Adams points out, liberty was linked closely with property. The close juxtaposition of liberty and property before the Revolution reflected the early eighteenth-century American view that individuals could not be free, independent, or happy without security for their property. However, as Adams notes, during the Revolution the tension between political liberty and property rights was recognized. See Willi Paul Adams, *The First American Constitutions: Republican Ideology and the Making of the State Constitutions in the Revolutionary Era* (Chapel Hill: University of North Carolina Press, 1980), 156–58, 160–63.

the Fourteenth Amendment—also express these obligations. The Preamble proclaims that one of government's essential purposes is to "secure the Blessings of Liberty," as well as promote the general welfare.[21] The close juxtaposition of these two declarations reflects the framers' recognition of the need to reconcile individual liberties and the collective welfare.

Judicial construction of the privileges and immunities clause of Article Four, which protects the rights of interstate travelers, reenforces the states' obligation to protect fundamental liberties. As Justice Bushrod Washington noted in *Corfield v. Coryell*, the privileges and immunities clause comprehends the fundamental rights that belong to "the citizens of all free governments."[22] While Justice Washington denied that these fundamental rights could be cataloged exhaustively, he iterated the most important ones:

> Protection by the government; the enjoyment of life and liberty, with the right to acquire and possess property of every kind, and to pursue and obtain happiness and safety; subject nevertheless to such restraints as the government may justly prescribe for the general good of the whole.[23]

As he emphasized, these rights are conditional, subject to the legitimate exercise of the national government's enumerated and implied powers and the police, tax, and eminent domain powers of the states. Like other early nineteenth-century Americans, Washington recognized "the public ingredient of private property," which justified limiting its use and enjoyment to promote a well-ordered society.[24] Rather than balancing private claims and

21. U.S. Constitution, Preamble. Although the Court does not regard the Preamble as a source of substantive power, "the Supreme Court has often referred to it as evidence of the origin, scope, and purpose of the Constitution." Johnny H. Killian, *The Constitution of the United States of America: Analysis and Interpretation*, S. Doc. No. 99–16, 99th Cong., 1st Sess. (Washington, D.C.: GPO, 1987). See also Harlan (opinion of the Court), *Jacobson v. Massachusetts*, 197 U.S. 11 (1905), 22.

22. 6 F.Cas. 546 (C.C. E.D. Pa. 1823) (No. 3230), 551. It should be emphasized that Washington issued this opinion sitting as a circuit justice. Although the opinion is cited frequently, it does not represent an authoritative or binding construction of the privileges and immunities clauses. It does, however, reflect the social-contract, natural-right thinking that informs the original Constitution, the Bill of Rights, and the Fourteenth Amendment.

23. *Id.*, 551–52. Speaking for the Court in *The Slaughterhouse Cases*, 83 U.S. (16 Wall.) 36 (1873), Justice Samuel Miller virtually emasculated the meaning of the Fourteenth Amendment's privileges or immunities clause, but he did not dispute Justice Washington's definition of the fundamental rights of free citizens. See *Slaughterhouse*, 408–9.

24. See Paul Kens, "Liberty and the Public Ingredient of Private Property," 55 *Rev. of Pol.* 85–116 (1993) (hereafter Kens, 55 *Rev. of Pol.*). Kens questions whether the Constitution

the public welfare, which is a relatively recent approach, Justice Washington attempted to determine whether the policy served a public purpose that was within the state's competence.

The framers of the Constitution, the Bill of Rights, and the Fourteenth Amendment were also familiar with John Locke's *Second Treatise on Civil Government*, which embodied natural-right, natural-law, and social-contract principles. The framers accepted these fundamental moral-philosophical principles as a foundation for limited, constitutional government. Locke's thinking was an important part of the framers' Weltanschauung. As Hadley Arkes has written, the Constitution can "be understood and *justified*, only in moral terms, only by an appeal to those standards of natural right that existed *antecedent* to the Constitution."[25]

In his *Second Treatise*, Locke argues that government is obliged to secure the individual's life, liberty, and property.[26] According to Locke, no rational person would submit to a government possessing arbitrary power over the "Lives and Fortunes of the People."[27] The legislative power, which is the commonwealth's basic power, "in the utmost Bounds of it, is *limited to the publick good* of the Society."[28] Locke regarded personal safety, individual liberty, and security for property to be so fundamental that he recognized the people's supreme power to alter or remove the legislature should it violate its fiduciary duty.[29] Although constitutional government exists to protect life, liberty, and property, Locke also acknowledged government could

---

creates a broad and open-ended restriction on economic liberty and property rights. For a more detailed analysis of antebellum regulations of property and liberty of contract, see William J. Novak, "Public Economy and the Well-Ordered Market: Law and Economic Regulation in 19th-Century America," 18 *Law & Soc. Inquiry* 1–32 (1993) (hereafter Novak, 18 *Law & Soc. Inquiry*).

25. Hadley Arkes, *Beyond the Constitution* (Princeton: Princeton University Press, 1990), 17 (emphasis in the original); see esp. Arkes's introduction, 16–19, and his chs. 2 and 3 for an analysis of the natural-rights philosophy that gives the Constitution meaning and moral authority.

26. John Locke, *Two Treatises of Civil Government*, ed. Peter Laslett (Cambridge: Cambridge University Press, 1967), 368–69 (hereafter Locke, *Second Treatise*).

27. *Id.*

28. *Id.*, 375. Locke also argues that such power, exercised for the public good, should not be arbitrary or capricious, but rather exercised according to established and promulgated laws—that is, the law of the land. *Id.*, 378.

29. *Id.*, 385. "[T]he *Community*," Locke noted, "perpetually *retains a Supream Power* of saving themselves from the attempts and designs of any Body, even of their Legislators, whenever they shall be so foolish, or so wicked, as to lay and carry on designs against the Liberties and Properties of the Subject."

limit the exercise of even these fundamental rights to preserve the community's welfare.

Published in 1689, Locke's *Letter on Toleration*[30] emphasized the duty of the state to protect the civil rights of its citizens. Arguing again that civil society's essential purpose is to secure life, liberty, and property,[31] he stated:

> The commonwealth seems to me to be a society of men constituted only for preserving and advancing their civil goods.
>
> What I call civil goods are life, liberty, bodily health and freedom from pain, and the possession of outward things such as lands, money, furniture, and the like.[32]

According to Locke, protection of "civil goods" is the basis for social peace and political obligation.

Natural law, social-contract philosophy, and English legal history justify constitutional limits on governmental power over the individual. Both the natural-law and common-law legal traditions support a substantive as well as a procedural interpretation of due process. American colonial history, the period from the Declaration of Independence to the Constitution, and certain legal and political developments between 1791 and 1866 indicate that due process was evolving into a restraint on the arbitrary exercise of governmental (legislative and executive) power as well as a commitment to fairness in judicial proceedings.[33]

30. John Locke, *A Letter on Toleration*, ed. Raymond Klibansky (Oxford: Clarendon Press, 1968). Locke first published the *Letter* anonymously in Gouda, while he was living as a voluntary exile in the Netherlands. It appeared at approximately the same time as his *Second Treatise*.

31. *Id.*, 123.

32. *Id.*, 65, 67. The term "furniture" here includes a house or home as well as its contents; see *id.*, editor's note 12, 156.

33. Traditionally, most commentators deny that substantive due process is consistent with an original understanding of the Fifth and Fourteenth Amendments. See, for example, Harry Hubbard, "The Fourteenth Amendment and Special Assessments on Real Estate—*Norwood v. Baker*, 172 U.S. 269," 14 *Harv. L. Rev.* 1–19, 98–115 (1900); Hannis Taylor, "Due Process of Law: Persistent and Harmful Influence of *Murray v. Hoboken Land & Improvement Co.*," 24 *Yale L.J.* 353–69 (1915); and Hugh E. Willis, "Due Process of Law Under the United States Constitution," 74 *U. Pa. L. Rev.* 331–45 (1926). But see Frank R. Strong, "The Economic Philosophy of Lochner: Emergence, Embrasure, and Emasculation," 15 *Ariz. L. Rev.* 419–55 (1973), 420 (hereafter Strong, 15 *Ariz. L. Rev.*), where Strong notes that in England before the American Revolution, from the Magna Carta to the Restoration, due process developed as a limit on royal prerogative. See also Frank R. Strong, *Substantive Due Process of Law: A Dichotomy of Sense and Nonsense* (Durham, N.C.: Carolina Academic Press, 1986).

The Evolution of Substantive Due Process

In addition to natural-law and social-contract thought, the framers of the U.S. Constitution relied heavily on English common and statutory law, English and colonial judicial decisions, and the common-law traditions in their own states. They also drew on such English commentators as Sir Edward Coke and Sir William Blackstone, who represented the Magna Carta (1215) and "The Petition of Right" (1628) as embodying substantive limits on the Crown's authority. Similarly, the Fourteenth Amendment's framers turned to Chancellor James Kent's and Justice Joseph Story's commentaries on American law, which reiterated Coke's and Blackstone's arguments. From this legal tradition, the authors of the Fourteenth Amendment developed a broad conception of fundamental rights that obligates government to protect three core values: life, liberty, and property.

Preconstitutional Development

By 1791, English commentators viewed chapter 39 of the Magna Carta[34] and its many confirmations as evidence of restraint on the Crown, while their American counterparts saw it as a limit on legislative action.[35] Arising from the conflicts between King John and his barons, the Magna Carta (1215) proclaims:

> No freeman shall be arrested, or detained in prison, or deprived of his freehold, or outlawed, or banished, or in any way molested; and

34. Here and throughout, all references are to chapter 39 in the original "Ci" text of the Magna Carta, which bears the king's seal, rather than to chapter 29 of the 1225 text. See J. C. Holt, *Magna Carta* (Cambridge: Cambridge University Press, 1965), 326, 327.

35. Robert E. Riggs, "Substantive Due Process in 1791," 1990 *Wis. L. Rev.* 941–1005 (1990), 986–87 (hereafter, Riggs, 1990 *Wis. L. Rev.*). In an era of parliamentary supremacy and, perhaps, sovereignty, it is hardly surprising that American revolutionaries saw parliamentary authority as the principal threat to constitutional—that is, limited—government. Therefore they turned to seventeenth-century English constitutional practice—which included the Magna Carta, its many confirmations, and various medieval charters—as a restraint on arbitrary legislation. American revolutionaries employed the medieval constitution against Parliament just as Coke had used it in Parliament's struggle against the Crown. See Reid, *Constitutional History*, 1:68, 69, 71–72, 236–37; 2:3–4, 5–7, 40.

we will not set forth against him, nor send against him, unless by the lawful judgment of his peers and by the law of the land.[36]

Apparently, the main objective of chapter 39 was to ensure that no freeman could be deprived of life, liberty, or property except by (1) judgment prior to execution of sentence, (2) delivered by one's peers, and (3) according to the laws of England.[37] The last phrase, "by the law of the land," can be read as a restraint on the king's exercise of arbitrary power as well as a guarantee of fair judicial procedure. Beginning with the Magna Carta, therefore, the substantive law imposed limits on the king's power to deprive a freeman life, liberty, and property.

Although Edward III (1327–77) confirmed the Magna Carta on fifteen separate occasions, two confirmations during his reign reenforce the view that chapter 39 is both a substantive restraint on the Crown's arbitrary exercise of power and a guarantee of fair judicial procedure. The first confirmation, in 1351, emphasizes fair procedure—namely, judgment according to the standing law and established rules of judicial procedure.[38] In a second confirmation of 1354 the term "due process" replaces "by the Law of the Land."[39] While some authorities suggest that beginning in 1354 "due process" refers exclusively to procedural guarantees, including trial by jury, it seems likely that the two terms ("due process" and the "law of the land") were used interchangeably between 1331 and 1368. Confirmations of the Magna Carta under Edward III were concerned mainly with judicial procedure. But Parliament's primary objective was to hold the king accountable for the life, liberty, and property of the freeman in the common-law courts

36. Quoted in William S. McKechnie, *Magna Carta: A Commentary on the Great Charter of King John* (Glasgow: James MacLehose & Sons, 1905), 436.

37. *Id.,* 437–41.

38. 25 Edw. 3, st. 5, ch. 4; 1 *Statutes of the Realm* 321. The confirmation of 1351 provides that "none shall be imprisoned nor put out of his Freehold, nor of his Franchises nor free Custom, unless it be by the Law of the Land; It is accorded assented, and stablished, That from henceforth none shall be taken by Petition or Suggestion made to our Lord the King, or to his Council, unless it be by Indictment or Presentment of good and lawful People of the same neighbourhood where such Deed be done, in due Manner, or by Process made by Writ original at the Common Law; nor that none be out of his Franchises, nor of his Freeholds, unless he be duly brought into answer, and forejudged of the same by the Course of the Law; and if any thing be done against the same, it shall be redressed and holden for none."

39. 28 Edw. 3, ch. 3; 1 *Statutes of the Realm* 345. The confirmation of 1354 reads: "That no Man of what Estate or Condition that he be, shall be put out of Land or Tenement, nor taken, nor imprisoned, nor disinherited, nor put to Death, without being brought in Answer by due Process of the Law."

rather than in Council, which was an instrument of royal power. Parliament regarded the common-law courts as an ally in its struggles against the king.[40]

Between the reigns of Edward III and Henry V (1413–22), the Magna Carta was confirmed approximately forty-one times, serving to reenforce its binding character as a rule of law. After the fifteenth century, the Magna Carta does not appear in the statute books until the seventeenth-century parliamentary struggles with the Stuart kings.[41] Sir Edward Coke, the best-known exponent of the Magna Carta, cites it as both a substantive limitation on the Crown and a guarantee of procedural fairness. In his *Institutes of the Laws of England* Coke sometimes employs "the law of the land" to imply a substantive limitation on the Crown's power with regard to property rights. At other times, he uses "due process of law," referring to specific procedural safeguards.[42]

In his analysis of chapter 39 of the Magna Carta, Coke focuses primarily on judicial procedure. He emphasizes that no person can be deprived of life, liberty, or property except according to the standing law, which includes the Magna Carta, common law, and the custom of England.[43] Although Coke equates due process and the law of the land, his reference is to the procedural safeguard

> that no man be taken, imprisoned, or put out of his free-hold with-
> out process of the law; that is, by indictment or presentment of good
> and lawfull men, where such deeds be done in due manner, or by
> writ originall of the common law.[44]

In another context, however, Lord Coke implies that the law of the land incorporates a substantive limitation on the authority of the king, acting either in his legislative capacity or in his executive capacity. "Generally," he comments, "all monopolies are against this great charter [the Magna Carta], because they are against the liberty and the freedome of the subject, and against the law of the land."[45] The fundamental law, including the Magna

40. Riggs, 1990 *Wis. L. Rev.*, 952, 955, 956–57.

41. There is not one reference in 4 *Statutes of the Realm* that covers the period.

42. Lord Edward Coke, *Institutes of the Laws of England*, part 2 (London: E. & R. Brooke, 1797); see esp. ch. 39 (29), 45–57.

43. *Id.*, 45.

44. *Id.*, 50.

45. *Id.*, 47. See also Michael Les Benedict, "Laissez-Faire and Liberty: A Re-evaluation of the Meaning and Origins of Laissez-Faire Constitutionalism," 3 *Law & Hist. Rev.* 293–331 (1985), 315–17, who traces American Whigs' opposition to monopoly franchises to Coke and

Carta, limits the king's power over citizens' liberties. Whether Coke used the two terms interchangeably, as Robert Riggs has claimed,[46] or deliberately misled his contemporaries and generations of legal scholars, as William S. McKechnie stated,[47] Coke's influence was so great that many later American lawyers and commentators viewed due process as incorporating both procedural and substantive limitations on governmental power.[48]

Chapter 39 of the Magna Carta was cited during the seventeenth-century struggles between the king and Parliament as an important source of fundamental rights. During the struggle with Charles I, the Petition of Right (1628) reaffirmed two statutory enactments of the Magna Carta, one adopted under Henry III and the other adopted under Edward III. The first statute (9 Hen. 3) provides "that no Freeman may be taken or imprisoned or be disseised of his Freehold or Liberties or his free Customes or be outlawed or exiled or in any manner destroyed, but by the lawful Judgment of his Peeres or by the Law of the Land."[49] The second statute (28 Edw. 3) states that no man can be denied of life, liberty, or property except "by due pcesse of Lawe."[50] The close juxtaposition of these two recitations, complaints about the military's violation of English law and custom, and charges that the king's Privy Council had imprisoned citizens without judicial process suggest that the Petition of Right incorporates both substantive and procedural guarantees. It is an attempt to restrain Charles I's exercise of arbitrary power over the freeman's fundamental liberties.

If seventeenth-century British constitutional history indicates that due process encompasses both procedural guarantees and substantive restraints on the Crown, American colonial and state histories prior to 1791 reveal a similar broad understanding of due process as a protection against arbitrary government. Colonial charters, statutes, and decisions of the Privy Council

---

the struggle over royal monopolies under James I. In England and the United States, monopolies were viewed as antithetical to free labor and property rights. As young men, both Thomas Cooley and Stephen Field were Jacksonian Democrats who opposed monopolies and special privileges.

46. Riggs, 1990 *Wis. L. Rev.*, 958–60.

47. McKechnie, *Magna Carta*, 447.

48. Edward S. Corwin, "The Doctrine of Due Process of Law Before the Civil War," 24 *Harv. L. Rev.* 366–85, 460–79 (1911), 368 (hereafter Corwin, 24 *Harv. L. Rev.*). "Among those thus misled," Corwin observed, "are the three great commentators on American constitutional law, Kent, Story, and Cooley—willing dupes no doubt, yet dupes none the less." As an advocate of judicial deference to legislatures, during the New Deal Corwin opposed the concept of substantive due process.

49. 3 Car., ch. 1; 5 *Statutes of the Realm* 23.

50. 3 Car., ch. 1; 5 *Statutes of the Realm* 24.

and the Board of Trade imposed substantive restraints on colonial governments.[51] During the period preceding the American Revolution, James Otis and John Adams, among others, argued that the Writs of Assistance and the Stamp Act (1765) were unconstitutional because they violated the Magna Carta and the Petition of Right.[52] Arguing against the constitutionality of the Writs, Otis proclaimed:

> An act against the Constitution is void; an act against natural equity is void; and if an act of Parliament should be made, in the very words of this petition it would be void. . . . Thus reason and the constitution are both against this writ.[53]

Otis rested his argument on natural justice, the seventeenth-century English constitution, and Coke's understanding of the Magna Carta as limitations on arbitrary government.

Sir William Blackstone, among the most influential legal writers of the eighteenth century, employed due process and the law of the land in various contexts, implying both procedural and substantive meaning to the terms.[54] In reference to chapter 39 of the Magna Carta, Blackstone sometimes "identifies 'law of the land' with judicial procedures." At other times, he identifies chapter 39 "with substantive rules of common law or statute" that protect property and personal security.[55] Although he focuses primarily on procedural protections in civil and criminal proceedings, he employs "due process" and "law of the land" as restraints on arbitrary government.

Following the Revolution, various state constitutions, bills of rights, and

51. See Riggs, 1990 *Wis. L. Rev.*, 963–76.

52. Bernard Schwartz also notes that Thomas Hutchinson, lieutenant governor of Massachusetts, claimed that the Stamp Act was "against Magna Carta and the natural rights of Englishmen, and therefore according to Lord Coke null and void." In Virginia, Patrick Henry made a similar claim based on the Magna Carta. Henry's and Cushing's arguments suggest that both men believed that the Magna Carta imposed substantive limits on Parliament's legislative power. See Bernard Schwartz, *The Bill of Rights: A Documentary History*, vol. 1 of 2 (New York: Chelsea House Publishers, 1971), 195–96.

53. Reprinted in Henry Steele Commager, *Documents of American History*, 9th ed., vol. 1 (Englewood Cliffs, N.J.: Prentice-Hall, 1973), 45, 47.

54. Sir William Blackstone, *Commentaries on the Laws of England*, 4th ed., ed. James D. Andrews (Chicago: Callaghan & Co., 1899), ch. 33, 1542–43 (hereafter Blackstone, *Commentaries*). In book 1, chapter 1, Blackstone describes and analyzes the rights of individuals, among which he considers natural and civil liberties. While liberties in a state of nature are absolute, in society they are regulated according to the standing law in order to promote the public good. Blackstone's analysis rests on natural and positive law. *Id.*, bk. 1, ch. 1, 114–17.

55. Riggs, 1990 *Wis. L. Rev.*, 971, 972. See also Blackstone, *Commentaries*, 1542–43.

declarations of rights embraced both substantive and procedural limitations on governmental interference with life, liberty, and property rights. For example, the Virginia Declaration of Rights (1776) contains two provisions protecting life, liberty, and property and iterating specific procedural protections for criminal defendants. While Section One guarantees trial by jury,[56] Section Eight provides: "No man shall be deprived of his liberty, except by the law of the land or the judgment of his peers."[57] As these two sections reveal, the Virginia Declaration rests primarily but not exclusively on English custom, common law, and statutory conceptions of fundamental rights.

Similarly, the Massachusetts Constitution of 1780 contains a separate Bill of Rights that declares that all men

> have certain natural, essential and unalienable rights; among which may be reckoned the right of enjoying and defending their lives and liberties; that of acquiring, possessing, and protecting property; in fine, that of seeking and obtaining their safety and happiness.[58]

Almost identical is Article II of New Hampshire's Bill of Rights (1784), which states: "All men have certain natural, essential, and inherent rights; among which are . . . acquiring, possessing and protecting property—and in a word, of seeking and obtaining happiness."[59] The two documents assert the traditional rights of Englishmen, which American revolutionaries regarded as both natural and inalienable.

On July 13, 1787, during the federal Constitutional Convention, Congress adopted the Northwest Ordinance (1787), which included a law of the land passage.[60] Article Two of the Ordinance provides: "No man shall be deprived of his liberty or property, but by the judgment of his peers or the law of the land."[61] In the event that the territorial government seized an

56. Ben Poore, *The Federal and State Constitutions, Colonial Charters, and Other Organic Laws of the United States*, 2 vols. (Washington, D.C.: GPO, 1877), 1:1908. Section One declares: "That all men are by nature equally free and independent, and have certain inherent rights, of which, when they enter into a state of society, they cannot, by any compact, deprive or divest their posterity; namely, the enjoyment of life and liberty, with the means of acquiring and possessing property, and pursuing and obtaining happiness and safety."

57. *Id.*, 2:1909.

58. *Id.*, 1:957.

59. *Id.*, 2:1280.

60. As Riggs notes, Bernard Schwartz regards the Northwest Ordinance as the first Bill of Rights. See Riggs, 1990 *Wis. L. Rev.*, 976.

61. Quoted in Commager, *Documents*, 1:130–31.

individual's property or required his labor, the Ordinance mandated full compensation. The same article indicates that Congress imposed both procedural and substantive limitations on the Northwest Territory government.[62]

In contrast to the Northwest Ordinance, case law between 1776 and 1791 sheds little light on judicial construction of the due process and law-of-the-land provisions of state constitutions. Both the paucity of cases and the ambiguity of their meaning cast doubt on the framers' understanding of due process as a substantive limitation on legislative power concerning life, liberty, and property rights. Several cases suggest that some constitutionalists understood due process as a "protection of vested property rights against legislative encroachment."[63] During this period, however, judicial review was not an established means of restraining legislative power, even though widely held notions of fundamental rights recommended specific limitations on legislative authority over life, liberty, and property.

Judicial decisions, the Northwest Ordinance, and state constitutions and statutes provide only fragmentary evidence that, by 1791, American constitutionalists understood due process as including limitations on legislative as well as judicial power. Many American constitutionalists rested their arguments on their understanding of the English legal tradition, as confirmed in the Magna Carta and many subsequent documents. Some rested their case on natural-rights theories that recommended general limitations on all governmental power, and specific limitations regarding such core values as life, liberty, and property. Still others employed both natural law and common law to justify restricting governmental power over fundamental rights. Whatever their justification, American constitutionalists understood the need to reconcile fundamental rights of life, liberty, and property with the public welfare, as the Northwest Ordinance acknowledged.

The Bill of Rights

The framing and ratification of the Bill of Rights offer only fragmentary evidence that the Fifth Amendment's due process clause contains judicially enforceable limits on legislative authority regarding life, liberty, and property. Debates in the first Congress and the states' ratifying conventions cast

62. Id.
63. Riggs, 1990 Wis. L. Rev., 984.

little light on the intentions of the framers and ratifiers. However, Congress proposed the Bill of Rights in response to Antifederalist criticism that the Constitution lacked explicit limits on the powers of the national government.[64] Although the Constitution's advocates argued that the national government possessed only delegated powers,[65] in the state ratifying conventions Antifederalist critics attempted to condition ratification on acceptance of specific guarantees of the citizens' rights. The critics failed to achieve their goal of conditional ratification, but their campaign sheds some light on the meaning of the Fifth Amendment's due process clause as a limit on the power of the national government.

Drawing on their states' constitutions and bills of rights, the Antifederalists proposed various due process amendments incorporating procedural and substantive guarantees. In four states (New York, North Carolina, Pennsylvania, and Virginia) the Antifederalists proposed constitutional amendments containing due process or law-of-the-land clauses. Speaking for the dissenting minority in Pennsylvania's convention, Robert Whitehill offered an amendment providing "that no man be deprived of his liberty, except by the law of the land or the judgment of his peers."[66] However, this law-of-the-land provision appears in an amendment that deals with procedural safeguards in the judicial process.[67]

In North Carolina and Virginia, Antifederalists also introduced law-of-the-land amendments. The North Carolina proposal declares:

> That no freeman ought to be taken, imprisoned, or disseized of his freehold, liberties, privileges, or franchises, or outlawed or exiled, or in any manner destroyed, or deprived of his life, liberty, or property, but by the law of the land.[68]

64. Jonathan Elliot, *The Debates in the Several State Conventions on the Adoption of the Federal Constitution* (Philadelphia: J. B. Lippincott Co., 1836). In the following state conventions, delegates expressed fears of a strong national government and demanded a bill of rights: Patrick Henry (Virginia), Matthew Locke and Charles McDowell (North Carolina), Patrick Dollard and James Lincoln (South Carolina), Nathaniel Barrell (Massachusetts), and Tredwell (New York). *Id.*, bk. 1, vol. 2, 159–61, 181–82, 396–406; bk. 1, vol. 3, 445–49, 461–62; bk. 2, vol. 4, 168–70, 210, 336–38, 312–15.

65. See Alexander Hamilton, John Jay, and James Madison, *The Federalist*, ed. Jacob E. Cooke (Middletown, Conn.: Wesleyan University Press, 1961), No. 84 (Hamilton, May 28, 1788), 575–84.

66. Schwartz, *Bill of Rights*, 2:658.

67. In any event, the convention defeated the Antifederalist amendments by a vote of 46–23. *Id.*, 628.

68. *Id.*, 967.

Although the proposed amendment apparently contains a substantive guarantee of life, liberty, and property, similar to the Magna Carta's original
language, it appears in the midst of a series of proposals to ensure procedural fairness in the civil and criminal process. On June 27, 1788, the
Virginia Ratifying Convention proposed a virtually identical law-of-the-land
amendment,[69] which appears between two other amendments providing specific procedural safeguards for liberty and property rights and the rights of
criminal defendants.[70]

The New York convention also proposed that "no Person ought to be
taken imprisoned or disseised of his freehold, or be exiled or deprived of his
Privileges, Franchises, Life, Liberty or Property but by due process of law."[71]
Preceding a series of procedural rights, New York's proposed amendment
appears to be a guarantee of procedural fairness rather than a substantive
restraint on legislative power. Commenting on New York's statutory bill of
rights, which contained similar language, Alexander Hamilton denied that
the term "due process" has a broad, substantive meaning. In fact, he argued, "The words 'due process' have a precise technical import, and are
only applicable to the process and proceedings of the courts of justice; they
can never be referred to an act of legislature."[72] Hamilton denied that the
Magna Carta or Coke's interpretation of its original "law-of-the-land" language comprehend substantive limits on legislative power.

However, New York's proposed bill of rights also contained a hortatory
statement on governmental power vis-à-vis the individual: "That the enjoyment of Life, Liberty and the pursuit of Happiness are essential rights which
every Government ought to respect and preserve."[73] The language of this
proposal expresses a moral duty or obligation to protect core values (life,
liberty, and property) from the arbitrary and capricious exercise of legislative, executive, and judicial power. New York's proposal is a substantive
restraint on the exercise of all governmental power.[74]

In drafting the Bill of Rights, James Madison employed the term "due

69. Charlene B. Bickford and Helen E. Veit, eds., *Documentary History of the First Federal
Congress of the United States of America*, vol. 4 (Baltimore: Johns Hopkins University Press,
1986), 16.

70. *Id.*

71. Schwartz, *Bill of Rights*, 2:912.

72. Speech to the New York State Legislature, February 6, 1787, quoted in Riggs, 1990
Wis. L. Rev., 989.

73. Schwartz, *Bill of Rights*, 2:911.

74. See Douglas Laycock, "Due Process and Separation of Powers: The Effort to Make the
Due Process Clauses Nonjusticiable," 60 *Tex. L. Rev.* 875–95 (1982), 891. But see Frank H.

process," from the New York proposal, rather than Virginia's "law-of-the-land" recommendation. Since his reasons for using the former are unknown, Madison's phraseology does not resolve the question of whether the due process clause of the Fifth Amendment incorporates both substantive and procedural limitations. But Madison also introduced "new language to be interpolated in the Preamble," namely,

> That Government is instituted and ought to be exercised for the benefit of the people; which consists in the enjoyment of life and liberty, with the right of acquiring and using property, and generally pursuing and obtaining happiness and safety.[75]

Although the new language in the Preamble would not have been binding law, as Charles Miller notes, it reveals a commitment to substantive limits on the power of government. However, the House of Representatives failed to adopt Madison's language.

Madison introduced the due process clause on June 8, 1789, as an amendment to Article One, section 9, of the Constitution, which includes a series of substantive limitations on congressional power. The new language would have been inserted between clauses three and four, prohibiting bills of attainder and restricting the imposition of direct head taxes.[76] However tempting it may be to read Madison's original placement of the due process clause as a substantive restriction on Congress, eventually the clause was arranged in a separate bill of rights. On the one hand, Miller argues that the close juxtaposition of the due process clause to the criminal defendant's rights (amendments four through eight) recommends a purely procedural interpretation.[77] On the other hand, Riggs emphasizes its strategic location, following the first four amendments, which contain a series of substantive guarantees—for example, the Fourth Amendment's prohibition of unreasonable searches and seizures. Embedded in the Fifth Amendment, the due process clause follows an enumeration of procedural rights and precedes a substantive limit on congressional power to take property for public use

---

Easterbrook, "Substance and Due Process," 1982 S. Ct. Rev. 85–125 (1982), 98 (hereafter Easterbrook, 1982 S. Ct. Rev.). Easterbrook claims that the due process clause places "little or no legitimate restraint on the contents of legislation." Id.

75. Charles A. Miller, "The Forest of Due Process of Law: The American Constitutional Tradition," in Due Process, ed. J. Roland Pennock and John W. Chapman (New York: New York University Press, 1977), 10.

76. Bickford, Documentary History of the First Congress, 10.

77. Miller, "Forest of Due Process." 10–11.

without just compensation.[78] Given the paucity of debate on the proposed amendments, generally, and virtual congressional silence on the due process clause, in particular, inferring meaning from its placement is like reading tea leaves. Their meaning is in the beholder's eye.[79]

Case Law and Commentaries

While the process of adoption and ratification casts little light, several judicial decisions and legal commentaries reflect late eighteenth- and nineteenth-century thought on fundamental rights compatible with later theories of substantive due process.[80] In *Van Horn's Lessee* v. *Dorrance*, Justice William Paterson articulated his views on fundamental rights, constitutional limitations, and the public welfare.[81] Speaking as a circuit justice, Paterson held that a Pennsylvania statute impairing the obligation of contract violated the U.S. Constitution (Article One, section 10) as well as the state's constitution. Although he acknowledged the British Parliament's supremacy, Paterson argued, in the United States both the federal and the state constitutions impose substantive limitations on legislative power.[82] Asserting the judiciary's power to declare state laws repugnant to the U.S. Constitution null and void, Paterson noted that the Pennsylvania Constitution and Declaration of Rights provide that "the right of acquiring, possessing and protecting property is natural, inherent, and inalienable."[83]

While he rested his argument on constitutional grounds, Justice Paterson turned to social-contract and natural-right thought to support his position:

> Men have a sense of property: property is necessary to their subsistence, and correspondent to their natural wants and desires; its secu-

78. Riggs, 1990 *Wis. L. Rev.*, 997–98.

79. The ratification process is even less informative than the congressional debates on the Bill of Rights. Given the fragmentary nature of the record, the ratification process provides no gloss for the meaning of the Fifth Amendment's due process clause. See Schwartz, *Bill of Rights*, 2:1171.

80. See Lowell J. Howe, "The Meaning of 'Due Process of Law' Prior to the Adoption of the Fourteenth Amendment," 18 *Calif. L. Rev.* 583–610 (1930), 591–93 (hereafter Howe, 18 *Calif. L. Rev.*). Howe argues that due process is the modern embodiment of earlier common-law, natural-right, and social-contract limits on the exercise of governmental power.

81. 2 U.S. (2 Dall.) 304 (C.C. Pa. 1795).

82. *Id.*, 309.

83. *Id.*, 310. Paterson continued, "It is a right not *ex gratia* from the legislature, but *ex debito* from the constitution."

rity was one of the objects that induced them to unite in society. No man could become a member of a community in which he could not enjoy the fruits of his honest labor and industry.[84]

Paterson argued that Pennsylvania's Constitution reflected these social-contract, natural-right principles. His opinion is one of the earliest judicial decisions embodying constitutional limitations, natural-right, and social-contract philosophy as complementary bases for restricting legislative power.

Justice Paterson also recognized the need for individuals to sacrifice their property for the public welfare, but not without just compensation. Only in grave emergencies could the legislature seize property.[85] Implicit in Paterson's reasoning is that only an important public purpose could justify the destruction of property rights. Paterson recognized the need to reconcile individuals' property rights with the public welfare, which he understood as a legislative function, subject to constitutional limitation. While his opinion is significant, *Van Horn's Lessee* does not implicate the Fifth Amendment's due process clause as a restriction on legislative power.

Three years later, in *Calder v. Bull,*[86] the Supreme Court sustained a Connecticut law that in effect set aside a decision of the probate court by permitting a new hearing after the case had been decided.[87] In dictum, Justice Samuel Chase recognized the state legislature's broad power to regulate the transfer of property.[88] Nevertheless, he argued that the social compact limits the exercise of legislative power. The basic purpose of the social compact, Chase remarked, is the protection of personal liberty and private property.[89] As in *Van Horn's Lessee,* the Court recognized limitations on legislative authority but did not decide the case on due process grounds. Thus it is impossible to trace post–Civil War conceptions of substantive due process to these early federal court decisions. At best, the later decisions are compatible with early federal opinions alluding to constitutional limitations and natural justice.

The Supreme Court did not interpret the meaning of the due process

84. *Id.,* 309.
85. *Id.,* 310.
86. 3 U.S. (3 Dall.) 386 (1798).
87. *Id.*
88. *Id.,* 394.
89. *Id.,* 388. Justice Iredell concurred in the Court's decision but rejected Chase's natural-right, social-contract rationales. In a remarkably contemporary criticism, Iredell stressed the abstract and subjective qualities of the concept. Nonetheless, he conceded that the fundamental law of the Constitution restricts legislative policymaking. *Id.,* 398–99.

clause until 1856, in *Murray's Lessee* v. *Hoboken Land & Improvement Co.*[90]
In 1820 Congress enacted a statute authorizing the Treasury Department to
issue distress warrants in order to collect taxes owed to the United States.
After determining that the customs collector for the port of New York owed
$3 million, the Treasury's solicitor issued the distress warrant.[91] Murray, the
customs collector's agent, sued, claiming that the government had deprived
him of his liberty and property without due process of law, since he had not
had a judicial hearing before the writ was enforced. Inasmuch as the statute
permitted collectors to bring suit to recover their property after the warrant
had been executed, Murray claimed, the entire proceeding was judicial
rather than executive in nature. Therefore, the due process clause entitled
him to a predeprivation judicial hearing.[92]

Speaking for a unanimous Court, Justice Benjamin Curtis traced the
meaning of due process from the Magna Carta through Coke's "law-of-the-
land" interpretation. "The words, 'due process of law,'" Curtis states, "were
undoubtedly intended to convey the same meaning as the words, 'by the law
of the land,' in the Magna Carta."[93] Apparently, Curtis believed that the
Fifth Amendment's framers had incorporated Coke's conception in the due
process clause.[94] If so, does the due process clause restrain the power of
Congress to authorize such administrative proceedings?

In answering these questions, Curtis turned to the U.S. Constitution,
American state practice, and British common and statutory law. He noted
that by the 1790s, British law, American state practice, and congressional
statute permitted administrative officers to issue distress warrants in order to
collect public taxes.[95] That is, the law of the land did not prohibit the
administrative proceedings that Congress authorized in the Act of 1820.[96]
Justice Curtis clearly suggests that the due process clause imposes limits on
legislative authority. Curtis asks and answers a central question of the present inquiry:

> But is it [the process authorized] due process of law? The constitu-
> tion contains no description of those processes which it was intended
> to allow or forbid. It does not even declare what principles are to be

90. 59 U.S. (18 How.) 272 (1856).
91. *Id.*, 274–75. See also Easterbrook, 1982 *S. Ct. Rev.*, 100–101.
92. 59 U.S., 273–74, 275.
93. *Id.*, 276.
94. Easterbrook, 1982 *S. Ct. Rev.*, 101.
95. 59 U.S., 277–81.
96. *Id.*, 278.

applied to ascertain whether it be due process. It is manifest that it was not left to the legislative power to enact any process which might be devised. The article is a restraint on the legislative as well as on the executive and judicial powers of the government, and cannot be so construed as to leave congress free to make any process "due process of law," by its mere will.[97]

While holding the statute constitutional, Curtis declares that the due process clause restrains all governmental power—legislative, executive, and judicial.[98] It is a guarantee against the arbitrary and capricious exercise of authority regarding liberty and property rights. However, the Court's holding applies to congressional authority to regulate procedures affecting property interests. *Murray's Lessee* does not answer the broader question—namely, whether the due process clauses permit Congress and the state legislatures to limit liberty and property rights in exercising their respective powers to promote the public welfare.

In the infamous *Dred Scott* decision, Chief Justice Roger B. Taney claimed that the Fifth Amendment limited the national government's authority over "property" in the territories as well as in the states.[99] Recognizing a right of property in persons, Taney "struck down Section 8 of the Missouri Compromise on the basis of the due process provision of the Fifth Amendment."[100] Arguing that the Constitution recognized the right of property in a slave, the chief justice concluded that "no tribunal, acting under the authority of the United States, whether it be legislative, executive, or judicial," has authority to deny citizens their "property rights."[101] Despite Taney's support for the perverse institution of slavery, his opinion provides evidence that, prior to the Civil War, some American jurists viewed the due process clause of the Fifth Amendment as a substantive restriction on the authority of Congress.

Although *Murray's Lessee* and *Dred Scott* are the only pre–Civil War fed-

97. *Id.*, 276.
98. *Id.*
99. Taney (opinion of the Court), *Dred Scott v. Sanford*, 60 U.S. (19 How.) 393 (1857), 449–50. The fatal flaw in Taney's opinion, Harry Jaffa underscores, was the chief justice's belief that "the Negro was not a man but a chattel." Jaffa also claims that Taney, like Rehnquist, ignored the natural-law basis of the Constitution, derived from the Declaration of Independence. See Harry V. Jaffa with Bruce Ledewitz, Robert L. Stone, and George Anastaplo, *Original Intent and the Framers of the Constitution: A Disputed Question* (Washington, D.C.: Regnery Gateway, 1994), 102, 96–104.
100. Strong, *Substantive Due Process*, 39. See also 60 U.S. (19 How.), 449–50.
101. 60 U.S., 451.

eral court decisions defining due process rights, some state courts held that their state's constitutions restricted legislative authority over vested property rights.[102] Between 1843 and 1856 the New York Court of Appeals decided several cases, ruling that New York's due process clause limited the power of the legislature to deprive persons of vested property rights.[103] In *Wynehamer v. New York* the Court of Appeals decided that a law prohibiting the sale of existing stocks of liquor deprived owners of their property without due process of law. Since the act operated retrospectively as well as prospectively, it deprived property owners of their right to acquire, use, enjoy, sell, or otherwise dispose of existing, vested property rights.[104]

In the first of three seriatim opinions, Justice George F. Comstock referred to the Magna Carta, but actually rested his opinion on the New York Constitution's due process clause, which is virtually identical to the Fifth Amendment to the U.S. Constitution. While Comstock denied that due process rights are absolute, he argued that "where rights are acquired by the citizen under the existing law, there is no power in any branch of the government to take them away."[105] If a property right is held contrary to the standing law, courts, rather than the legislature, have authority to deprive citizens of their property in order to promote the public welfare. In effect, the act's total prohibition had deprived New York brewers, distillers, distributors, and bar owners of a vested right, in violation of the state constitution's due process clause.

In defining property rights, Justice Comstock includes the right to ac-

---

102. See, for example, J. Locke, *Trustees of the University of North Carolina v. Foy*, 5 N.C. 57, 62 (1805); 3 Am. Dec. 672, 676; Chancellor Kent's opinion in *Dash v. Van Kleek*, 7 Johns (N.Y.) 477, 502–3 (1811); 5 Am. Dec. 291, 308–9. While the Court of Appeals sustained the statute in question, Kent clearly recognized the limits of legislative power relating to vested property rights. See also *In re Dorsey*, 8 Ala. 295, 359 (1838), and Chief Justice Gibson in *Norman v. Heist*, 5 Watts & Serg. 171, 173 (1843). Although the Pennsylvania Supreme Court found against the plaintiff, Gibson argued that the fundamental law limited the legislature's authority to abolish vested property rights.

103. See Howe, 18 *Calif. L. Rev.*, 600. See also *Taylor v. Porter*, 4 Hill (N.Y.) 140 (1843); 48 Am. Dec. 274. Justice Bronson readily admitted that private interests must yield to public necessity, but he denied that the legislature had authority to divest an individual of his property rights without a trial according to the common law. See also *Westerfelt v. Gregg*, 12 N.Y. (2 Keenan) 202 (1854); 62 Am. Dec. 160. Justices Edwards and Denio agreed that the legislature had exceeded its powers and violated the due process clause of the New York Constitution. Finally, see *Wynehamer v. New York*, 13 N.Y. 378 (1856).

104. *Id.*, 388–89, 397, 398. See also Strong, 15 *Ariz. L. Rev.*, 421. Strong states that *Wynehamer* is the clearest expression of substantive due process regarding tangible property rights prior to the Fourteenth Amendment.

105. 13 N.Y., 393.

quire, use, enjoy, and dispose of property. Since the statute completely destroyed those ancillary rights, requiring the immediate destruction of all existing stocks of liquor, it extinguished the property's principal commercial value, rendering it practically worthless. "This," he emphasized, "is destructive of the notion of property."[106] While expressing deference to the legislature's policymaking authority, Comstock concluded that the act was unconstitutional.

Justice Samuel L. Seldon also conceded the legislature's authority to determine the public welfare, but he asserted the judiciary's authority to impose constitutional limitations on the state legislature.[107] The due process clause, he noted, requires the legislature to afford every citizen a judicial trial before he can be deprived of life, liberty, or property.[108] Unlike Justice Comstock, Seldon also referred to social-contract and natural-right philosophy. Countering the argument that the legislature can authorize the immediate destruction of private property, even in great public emergencies, Justice Seldon contended,

> the legislature does not in these cases authorize the destruction of property; it simply regulates that inherent and inalienable right which exists in every individual to protect his life and his property from immediate destruction. This is a right which individuals do not surrender when they enter into the social state, and which cannot be taken from them.[109]

The state's constitution and the social compact guarantee the inherent right of citizens to defend their liberty and protect their property. Nevertheless, the state can regulate the use and enjoyment of property to promote a well-ordered society. Thus Seldon acknowledged both the private and public elements of property.[110]

106. *Id.*, 397.
107. *Id.*, 428–32, 432–33.
108. *Id.*, 439–40. Like Comstock, Seldon concluded that the statute deprived citizens of their vested property rights by destroying, rather than merely diminishing or regulating, their property rights for a public purpose. Without some compelling state interest posed by immediate and imminent dangers to the public health and safety, the legislature could not destroy property rights or restrict personal liberty. The legislature may be the primary judge of public necessity, but courts reserve the authority to determine whether police-power measures unconstitutionally burden the citizen's fundamental rights.
109. *Id.*, 439.
110. See Kens, 55 *Rev. of Pol.*, 96. As Kens notes regarding liberty of contract, the right may be natural, but it is subject to prospective limitations. Similarly, property is subject to the

Prior to the Civil War some state and federal court decisions suggest that due process embodies substantive guarantees of life, liberty, and property as well as judicial fairness. These opinions also suggest that the Fifth Amendment's due process clause and similar state constitutional provisions limit the exercise of legislative, executive, and judicial power. Due process is a restraint on arbitrary and capricious government. While most of these opinions rest on English common and statutory law and state and federal statutory and constitutional interpretation, some refer to theories of natural justice, natural law, and the social compact. However, these antebellum opinions do not draw a bright line between natural-law reasoning and common-law reasoning, nor do they suggest that the two legal traditions are incompatible, as some recent scholars apparently believe. By the 1850s a small body of judicial opinion supported the theory of substantive due process that evolved further in the 1860s and 1870s.

In addition to judicial opinion, several influential commentators, especially James Kent and Joseph Story, interpreted the meaning of due process of law. In the opening sentence of part 4 of his *Commentaries on American Law*, James Kent declares:

> The rights of persons in private life are either absolute, being such as belong to individuals in a single, unconnected state; or relative, being those which arise from the civil and domestic relations.
>
> The absolute rights of individuals may be resolved into the right of personal security, the right of personal liberty, and the right to acquire and enjoy property. These rights have been justly considered, and frequently declared, by the people of this country, to be natural, inherent, and unalienable.[111]

As Kent notes, these core rights are natural, inherent, and, in a state of nature, absolute. In civil society they are conditional—that is, contingent on legislative considerations of the public welfare.[112]

---

positive law in force at the time. Just as the states can prohibit the making of certain types of contracts, they can also prohibit the use of property in ways that injure the public health and safety.

111. James Kent, *Commentaries on American Law* (Philadelphia: Blackstone Publishing Co., 1889), part 4, vol. 2, lecture 24, 43. Citing both Blackstone's *Commentaries* and Wharton's *Law Lexicon*, Kent defines natural rights as those relating to life and liberty. Inherent rights are rights that individuals possess without having received them from others. Inalienable rights cannot be transferred from one individual to another. *Id.*, n. 2.

112. Kens, 55 *Rev. of Pol.*, 96, argues that antebellum legal thought accepted the view that natural law is modified by societal requirements. Regarding vested property rights, positive law operates prospectively to regulate the uses of property.

At times Kent identifies due process of law with procedural fairness in the civil and criminal process.[113] At other times he refers to guarantees of substantive rights. Quoting from the Declaration of Rights of the Continental Congress (October 1774), he emphasizes

> That the inhabitants of the English colonies in North America, by the immutable laws of nature, the principles of the English constitution, and their several charters or compacts, were entitled to life, liberty, and property.[114]

Referring to New York's Declaration of Rights (1821), he implies that due process has a substantive as well as a procedural component.

According to Kent, these core rights derive from both natural and positive law. Subsequent state constitutions "collect, digest, and declare, in a precise and definite manner," the citizen's civil liberty. Moreover, Kent's declaratory theory posits that American constitutions declare preexisting natural and historical rights rather than create new ones.[115] But he does not preclude either the necessity or the desirability of regulating property or limiting liberty to advance a well-ordered society. American state laws and constitutions regulate the creation, use, enjoyment, and transfer of property as a civil right.

Kent traces the positive-law component of due process from the Magna Carta and other fundamental acts of the British Parliament. These enactments confirm historical guarantees of personal security. Here too Kent refers to due process in procedural and substantive terms. In one passage, he enumerates procedural protections, including a speedy and public trial, an impartial jury, confrontation of witnesses, and assistance of counsel.[116] Several sentences later, he paraphrases the Magna Carta's original law-of-the-land terminology, suggesting that due process has a substantive component. Emphasizing the significance of this component, he claims that Lord Coke's interpretation "is the true sense and exposition of those words."[117] Applying Coke to the American context, Kent cites Justice Thomas Ruffin's opinion

---

113. Referring to the early colonial charters, Kent writes: "The right of trial by jury, and the necessity of due proof preceding conviction, were claimed as undeniable rights; and it was further expressly ordained, that no person should suffer without express law, either in life, limb, liberty, good name, or estate; nor without being first brought to answer by due course and process of law." Kent, *Commentaries*, 44.

114. *Id.*, 48.

115. *Id.*, 49, 52.

116. *Id.*, 55.

117. *Id.*, 56.

in *Hoke* v. *Henderson* (North Carolina) that the law-of-the-land formulation imposes substantive limits on legislative power.[118] Kent understood due process as embodying substantive limits on legislative and judicial power.

In his *Commentaries on the Constitution of the United States*, Justice Joseph Story argued that the national government's basic purpose is to secure liberty.[119] Enunciating this general principle, the Preamble to the Constitution ensures the citizen's political loyalty "by laying the broad foundations of government upon immovable principles of justice."[120] Similarly, Story notes that the grand design of state government is to preserve the blessings of liberty. Within the context of a discussion of state and federal authority, he articulates a compact theory of the Constitution.[121] In exchange for the citizen's patriotism, the government assumes a duty to secure the individual's civil liberty.

Later, in Book III of the *Commentaries*, Justice Story focuses on the meaning of the Fifth Amendment's due process clause. Beginning with the Magna Carta, he equates the law of the land with due process as a series of procedural guarantees in the civil and criminal process.[122] Paraphrasing Coke, Story remarks that due process means "due presentment or indictment, and being brought in to answer thereto by due process of the common law."[123] Although he focuses on the procedural protections of common law, he emphasizes that the Magna Carta's objective was to guard against arbitrary government and preserve the public peace.[124]

In the fourth edition of Story's *Commentaries* (1873), Thomas M. Cooley, who revised the treatise, commented extensively on the meaning of the Fourteenth Amendment's due process clause. As an advocate of constitutional limitations, Cooley stressed the substantive component of due process. After tracing the evolution of the Magna Carta through the seventeenth-century struggles between the English Crown and Parliament, Cooley argues that the more popular the form of government, "the greater, perhaps, may be the danger that excitement and passion will sway the public councils, and arbitrary and unreasonable laws be enacted."[125] While he ac-

118. 15 N.C. 1 (1833); 4 Dev. N.C. Rep. 15.
119. Joseph Story, *Commentaries on the Constitution of the United States* (Boston: Little, Brown & Co., 1873).
120. *Id.*, vol. 1, bk. 3, § 507, 368.
121. *Id.*, §§ 508–16, 368–74.
122. *Id.*, vol. 2, § 1789, 534.
123. *Id.*
124. *Id.*, §§ 1789–90, 534.
125. *Id.*, § 1939, 660.

knowledges that Story's focus is on due process as procedural fairness, Cooley emphasizes the original "law-of-the-land" formulation as a substantive restraint on legislative power. From his examination of American and English jurisprudence and commentary, Cooley concluded that neither courts nor executive officers nor legislatures could deprive individuals of life, liberty, or property, except according to established legal principles.[126] However, neither Story nor Cooley denied that property and liberty are subject to regulations that advance the general welfare.

Despite the persistence of substantive due process, modern jurists tend to shy away from such theories as abstract, subjective, and undemocratic concepts fraught with the dangers of judicial tyranny and confrontation with Congress and the state legislatures. Justice Black and Circuit Judge Easterbrook, for example, reject substantive due process because they claim that it rests on vague theories of natural justice. However, prior to the Civil War, jurists were developing a substantive theory of due process from both positive and higher law. They were evolving concrete legal rights and remedies from American and English legal history, as well as from natural-law and social-contract thought. By the 1850s, legal commentaries and some judicial decisions support the argument that due process imposes substantive restrictions on legislative authority.

According to this view, the purpose of due process is to restrain government from enacting and enforcing arbitrary and capricious laws that burden the core constitutional values of life, liberty, and property. Due process ensures that when courts limit these rights they will do so according to known and accepted procedures. In addition, due process imposes substantive limitations on legislative authority to burden fundamental rights. The due process clauses ensure that when legislatures limit the exercise of such rights they will do so for substantial reasons that advance the public welfare. While legislatures have the initial, primary responsibility for determining the public welfare or the wisdom of policy, the due process clauses afford courts an opportunity to determine whether public laws unnecessarily burden fundamental, constitutionally protected rights without advancing important public purposes.

Even though evolving nineteenth-century jurisprudence endorsed constitutional limitations on all governmental power (legislative, executive, and judicial), did the Fourteenth Amendment's framers embody these views in

126. *Id.*, § 1940, 661; § 1943, 663–64; and § 1945, 664–65. See also Cooley, *Constitutional Limitations*, 339, 351–63.

the due process clause? If the question is answerable, it invites an examination of the framing and language of the Fourteenth Amendment. In addition, contemporaneous legislation between 1866 and 1875 may cast light on the framers' remedial purposes. Some of the amendment's drafters also drafted civil rights and reconstruction measures in the post–Civil War era.[127] Early judicial decisions interpreting the Fourteenth Amendment also may illuminate the meaning of the due process clause. Despite the difficulties inherent in fathoming *the framers' intent*, it is possible and useful to examine the general problems they confronted and their broad remedial intentions when construing the due process clauses today.

127. Inasmuch as Congress drafted much of this legislation as a means to enforce the privileges and immunities, due process, and equal protection clauses, the language and drafting of civil rights and reconstruction legislation may illuminate the meaning and scope of section one, as well as the enforcement powers of Congress under section five of the Fourteenth Amendment.

2

Antecedents of the Fourteenth Amendment's Core Values

By 1866 due process was evolving into substantive as well as procedural limitations on the exercise of governmental power, applicable to the legislative, executive, and judicial branches of government. Some judicial opinions, legal commentaries, and state constitutions supported the view that due process protected individuals against arbitrary, capricious, or unreasonable governmental interference with life, liberty, and property interests.[1] This body of jurisprudence suggests that due process guarantees fairness in the judicial process and restrains the exercise of legislative and executive power vis-à-vis the individual's fundamental rights. Americans sought to promote the security and personal integrity of each person by protecting these civil rights.

However, American jurists and politicians also recognized the need to reconcile the individual's pursuit of happiness with the government's responsibility to promote the general good or collective welfare. In the antebellum period, long before the eras of industrialization, transcontinental expansion (1865–1900), and mature capitalism (1920–39), the states employed the

1. See Riggs, 1990 *Wis. L. Rev.* 941 (1990); Strong, 15 *Ariz. L. Rev.* 419 (1973).

police power to regulate contracts and the use of private property. They justified regulating markets and products, requiring business and professional licenses, and limiting the price of bread, flour, and other necessities as legitimate means of promoting a well-ordered society.[2] Prior to the Civil War, there was less emphasis on the unregulated pursuit of wealth, but in the Gilded Age business and industry sought governmental largesse without intrusion.[3] As early as the 1850s, however, some state courts began to restrain legislative attempts to interfere with vested property rights.[4] Against this background of state regulation, incipient industrialization, and the emerging conflict between economic individualism and public regulation, the Fourteenth Amendment's framers attempted to remedy the unresolved problems of the Civil War and Reconstruction within the context of a state-centered federal system.

In drafting the Fourteenth Amendment, the Thirty-ninth Congress confronted several basic remedial problems as well as a series of tactical and strategic political dilemmas. How could Congress complete the process of emancipation and protect the civil rights of freedmen without fundamentally altering the American federal system?[5] Congressional Republicans also

2. See Novak, 18 *Law & Soc. Inquiry*, 7, 9, 10–15. Novak describes the great variety of regulations and prohibitions that the states adopted to protect the public health, safety, and welfare.

3. Kens, 55 *Rev. of Pol.*, 85, denies that the period from the Revolution to the Civil War was an era of radical individualism and unregulated markets. Like Novak, he cites numerous state regulatory laws to demonstrate that property and contract rights could be limited to promote a well-ordered society. *Id.*, 100–101.

4. *Wynehamer v. New York* (1856), 13 N.Y. (3 Kern) 378. In effect, the New York Court of Appeals denied legislative authority to transfer vested property rights from one person or class to another. However, the Court acknowledged that the legislature could regulate the use of property for a valid public purpose. See Benedict, 3 *Law & Hist. Rev.*, 323, 325.

5. One school of thought argues that the framers of the Fourteenth Amendment did not intend to transform the federal system radically from a state-centered to a nationally centered political system. See Berger, *Government by Judiciary*, 17–18. Also see Harold M. Hyman, *A More Perfect Union: The Impact of the Civil War and Reconstruction on the Constitution* (New York: Alfred A. Knopf, 1973), 298–99, 305, 306; M. E. Bradford, "'Changed Only a Little': The Reconstruction Amendments and the Nomocratic Constitution of 1787," 24 *Wake Forest L. Rev.* 573–98 (1989), 574, 578. Most recently, Earl Maltz claims that the congressional debates and language of the Civil Rights Act of 1866 and the Fourteenth Amendment reveal that Congress intended only a minimum reallocation of power to the national government in order to protect a narrow set of civil rights. Thus the Republicans in Congress did not intend to alter the basic pattern of federalism. See Earl M. Maltz, *Civil Rights, the Constitution, and Congress, 1863–1869* (Lawrence: University Press of Kansas, 1990), 4, 54–55, 58–59, 67–69, 92, 94, 100–101, 118.

Another school of thought claims that the framers did intend a radical transformation of American federalism. See Jacobus ten Broek, *Equal Under Law* (New York: Collier Books, 1965), 159–60, 166–68. See also Michael Kent Curtis, *No State Shall Abridge: The Fourteenth*

sought to wrest control of Reconstruction policy from the White House while avoiding a breach with President Andrew Johnson, a Unionist Democrat from Tennessee who opposed the Radical Republicans' plans to govern the South as a conquered province.[6] As the congressional debates on the Freedman's Bureau bill, the Civil Rights Act, and the Fourteenth Amendment reveal, these political considerations sometimes overshadowed the basic remedial problem of providing equal protection for the core rights of life, liberty, and property.

As the congressional debates also indicate, Republicans shared a political philosophy that justified national protection of civil rights in terms of both higher and positive law.[7] Derived from Jacksonian Democracy, the abolitionist movement, and the states' legal tradition,[8] this multifaceted philosophy included common-law, natural-law, natural-right, and social-contract arguments. Republicans also asserted that "people who live under a republican form of government possess rights arising out of the very nature of the political and social system."[9] The congressional drafters, suggests William Nelson, employed higher-law and republican political rhetoric in appealing to Congress and the American people to secure the fruits of military victory through legal protections of fundamental rights.[10] But this higher-law, republican philosophy "was not, in short, a species of legal doctrine that dictated or even pointed toward certain specific results on any of the questions to which higher law arguments were addressed."[11]

This does not suggest that the drafters of the Fourteenth Amendment and

---

Amendment and the Bill of Rights (Durham, N.C.: Duke University Press, 1986). Curtis argues that the framers intended to incorporate the Bill of Rights in order to afford national protection of the citizen's fundamental rights. If Curtis is correct, the Fourteenth Amendment's framers intended a radical transformation of the federal system.

6. See Horace E. Flack, *The Adoption of the Fourteenth Amendment* (Baltimore: Johns Hopkins University Press, 1908), 12. Johnson's veto of the Freedman's Bureau and civil rights bills created an irreparable breach with congressional Republicans. It became evident that Johnson and the congressional Republicans had different strategic objectives.

7. Curtis, *No State Shall Abridge*, 8, 16, 41, 48–49, 54.

8. See Charles McCurdy, "The Roots of 'Liberty of Contract' Reconsidered: Major Premises in the Law of Employment, 1867–1937," *Supreme Court Yearbook* (1984), 20–33, 27. As McCurdy argues, the Civil Rights and Freedman's Bureau Acts reflected the framers' shared commitment to the free-labor beliefs of Jacksonians and abolitionists. For congressional Republicans, liberty of contract was an essential remedy to bond slavery, which required persons to work at the will of and for the profit of others. In sum, all persons have a property interest in their labor and should be free to sell their labor in the marketplace.

9. William E. Nelson, *The Fourteenth Amendment: From Political Principle to Judicial Doctrine* (Cambridge, Mass.: Harvard University Press, 1988), 24.

10. *Id.,* 8, 10, 21, 24.

11. *Id.,* 23.

civil rights legislation perceived a sharp distinction between natural-law and common-law rights. Often, they employed both legal traditions to justify national protection for the liberty, personal security, and property rights of freedmen. As the debates suggest, they perceived general principles of natural law, natural right, and social contract as compatible with common-law rights and remedies that existed in the American states. The lawyer-draftsmen of the Thirty-ninth Congress drew upon their natural-law beliefs as well as their common-law training in remedying the problems of Reconstruction.

In translating their basic philosophy into specific enforceable rights and legal remedies, the authors of the Fourteenth Amendment turned to the common law, Anglo-American legal tradition, and U.S. constitutional development. The task of translating first principles into specific rights began with the drafting of the Freedman's Bureau bill and the civil rights bill of 1866, which was a dress rehearsal for the adoption of the Fourteenth Amendment. The amendment that emerged from the Thirty-ninth Congress was a broad statement of legal principle rather than a codex of specific, enforceable rights. Congress retained a major role for itself in specifying civil rights and legal remedies, but the courts would have authority to protect life, liberty, and property in the event that the states did not meet their affirmative duty to secure these fundamental rights.[12]

Congressional Antecedents

The Fourteenth Amendment resulted from divergent sources and numerous compromises, but most scholars acknowledge three proximate antecedents: the Thirteenth Amendment (1865), the Freedman's Bureau Extension bill (1866), and the Civil Rights Act (1866). The Freedman's Bureau bill, which President Johnson vetoed, sought to protect the rights of life, liberty, and property for newly emancipated blacks in the states and districts under military rule. By contrast, the Civil Rights Act of 1866 protected the freedman's full and equal enjoyment of the same civil rights against official state discrimination throughout the United States.[13]

12. Id., 38–39.
13. Hyman, A More Perfect Union, 454–59; Flack, Adoption of the Fourteenth Amendment, 40–41; Eric L. McKitrick, Andrew Johnson and Reconstruction (Chicago: University of Chicago Press, 1960), 316–17; Michael L. Benedict, A Compromise of Principle: Congressional

If most scholars agree on the proximate sources of the Fourteenth Amendment, they disagree about the significance of the Freedman's Bureau bill and the Civil Rights Act in construing the privileges or immunities, due process, and equal protection clauses. At one end of the continuum, Raoul Berger argues that the Civil Rights Act is an exclusive codex for determining the specific civil rights that the amendment protects.[14] At the other end of the continuum, Michael Kent Curtis claims that the Civil Rights Act and the Freedman's Bureau bill are merely suggestive, of the rights protected, rather than definitive.[15] According to Curtis, the original Constitution, the Bill of Rights, the Declaration of Independence, and abolitionist, natural-rights thought are germane to defining the broad range of civil rights that the Fourteenth Amendment encompasses.[16] He argues that the amendment protects an irreducible core of substantive rights against infringement by the states, among which is "for blacks the right to acquire and dispose of personal and real property, to testify, and to have their life, liberty, and property protected by the same laws that protected whites."[17]

Whether one accepts Berger's construction of the Fourteenth Amendment or Curtis's, as a minimum, the privileges or immunities clause affords protection to three core constitutional rights: life, liberty, and property. The due process clause of the Fourteenth Amendment imposes on the states limitations similar to those that the Fifth Amendment imposes on the national government concerning these core rights. And, the equal protection clause guarantees equal legal treatment with respect to the individual's fundamental rights. But is the Fourteenth Amendment's due process clause merely a guarantee of established judicial procedure regarding the deprivation of life,

---

Republicans and Reconstruction, 1863–1869 (New York: W. W. Norton & Co., 1974), 146–48. Because the proposed civil rights bill had national implications, it had potentially far-reaching effects on the federal system. See Maltz, *Civil Rights*, 61.

14. Berger distinguishes between civil rights and social and political rights, which the Fourteenth Amendment does not protect. See Berger, *Government by Judiciary*, 20–23, 29, 30–31, 35, 36, 118–20, 133.

15. Curtis, *No State Shall Abridge*, 7–8, 9–11, 16–17, 86–91.

16. *Id.*, 212–20.

17. *Id.*, 54. Referring to section one's protection of life, liberty, and property, Thaddeus Stevens (R-Pa.), a Radical Republican leader, proclaimed that these rights "are all asserted, in some form or other, in our Declaration or organic law." The problem, Stevens noted, was that "the Constitution limits only the action of Congress, and is not a limitation on the States." *Cong. Globe*, 39th Cong., 1st Sess. 2459 (1866). See also *Barron v. Baltimore*, 32 U.S. (7 Pet.) 243 (1833). In *Barron* the Supreme Court decided that the Bill of Rights applied to Congress rather than the states. As some congressional Republicans acknowledged, without an amendment there was no constitutional warrant for the Civil Rights Act of 1866.

liberty, and property interests? Or does the clause impose limitations on the exercise of state legislative power vis-à-vis these core constitutional rights?

Aside from disagreeing about the significance of various sources in interpreting the Fourteenth Amendment, Raoul Berger, Jacobus ten Broek, and Howard Jay Graham dispute the procedural nature of the due process clause versus its substantive nature. Berger argues that due process is exclusively procedural.[18] The remedial objective of the due process clause was to ensure that the states could not deprive individuals of life, liberty, or property rights without going through an established judicial procedure—that is, prior to forfeiture of these rights.[19] He concludes that the framers understood that due process had a fixed, procedural meaning in drafting section one of the amendment.[20]

Jacobus ten Broek asserts a broad substantive view of the due process clause. He acknowledges the procedural interpretation but argues that the words should be read "as if the state were forbidden to deprive persons of life, liberty, or property. This is the familiar substantive connotation which absolutely prohibits the doing of certain things, no matter by what procedure."[21] Ten Broek avers that the framers intended the due process clause (along with the privileges or immunities clause and the equal protection clause) to protect the individual's natural or fundamental rights. Foremost among these are the rights of life, liberty, and property, which are "substan-

18. Berger, *Government by Judiciary*, 194. Quoting approvingly from Alexander Hamilton, Raoul Berger notes: "The words 'due process' have a precise technical import, and are only applicable to the process and proceedings of the courts of justice; they can never be referred to an act of the legislature. No statement to the contrary will be found in any of the constitutional conventions, in the First Congress, nor in the 1866 debates."

19. *Id.*, 195–99. Berger argues that the original meaning of due process "is incompatible with the 'fundamentally fair' procedure structure that the Court has built on the clause." According to this literalist approach, due process is no more than a guarantee that the individual has an "opportunity to answer through service of a writ according to established law" prior to being deprived of life, liberty, or property rights. *Id.*, 198.

20. As Berger notes, the lawyers who framed the due process clause of the Fourteenth Amendment "undoubtedly were familiar with this association of due process with judicial procedure, and a departure from this all but universal connotation must be based on more than bare conjecture; the rule is that it must be proved." *Id.*, 200.

21. Ten Broeck writes: "The clause can be read as a declaration that only in certain circumstances may life, liberty, and property be taken away." Since government has an "inherent duty" to protect these rights, it can deprive them only by following "prescribed procedure." Ten Broek, *Equal Under Law*, 237. However, as he concedes, such a construction requires that the reader drop the conditional clause, "without due process of law." As a minimum, he notes, the due process clause requires the states to afford established judicial procedure before depriving a person of fundamental rights. *Id.*, 238.

tively guaranteed by the due process clause of the Fifth Amendment."[22] While ten Broek refers to due process rights as absolutes, he admits that they are conditional—that is, subject to the states' exercise of their police, tax, and eminent domain powers. In other words, the states can regulate the exercise of fundamental rights only for a valid public purpose.

Similarly, Howard Graham claims that the due process clause imposes substantive limits on legislative authority to interfere with the freedman's life, liberty, and property rights. Representative John Bingham's remedial intent was to secure equal protection for these fundamental rights against state infringement.[23] In this context, Graham observes, the "natural rights usage is here obviously a substantive one."[24] Turning to the protection of corporate property rights, however, Graham denies that the due process clause imposes substantive limits on state legislative power. He rejects the argument that the framers of the Fourteenth Amendment intended to apply its protections to corporations as artificial persons. The privileges or immunities, due process, and equal protection clauses secure the fundamental rights of natural rather than artificial persons.[25]

In determining the scope and character of due process rights there are several caveats. The Fourteenth Amendment's framers focused primarily on sections two through five, dealing with representation, the Civil War debt, disqualification from public office, and congressional enforcement power. Consequently, there is relatively little evidence regarding section one, especially the due process clause.[26] Second, senators and representatives sometimes used terms interchangeably—for example, natural rights, inherent rights, fundamental rights, constitutional rights, and personal rights.[27] As

22. Id.

23. Howard Jay Graham, Everyman's Constitution: Historical Essays on the Fourteenth Amendment, the "Conspiracy Theory," and American Constitutionalism (Madison: Wisconsin Historical Society, 1968), 52. Graham claims that Bingham's substantive understanding of due process is present in his speeches of March 9, 1866, on the civil rights bill, and February 28, 1866.

24. Id.

25. Id., see 35–53, wherein Graham rejects Roscoe Conkling's argument in San Mateo County v. Southern Pacific R.R., 116 U.S. 138 (1882). Conkling, who had been a member of the Joint Committee on Reconstruction, argued that the framers of the Fourteenth Amendment intended its protections for property rights to extend to corporations. Specifically, the aim was to protect foreign (out-of-state) corporations against invidious and discriminatory taxation. Id., 30–31.

26. As Raoul Berger notes, there were only scant "allusions to the [due process] clause in the debates of the 39th Congress." Berger, Government by Judiciary, 201.

27. Richard Kluger observes that the Thirty-ninth Congress shot with a blunderbuss in

William Nelson observes, they used terms rhetorically to persuade a national political audience, rather than in a precise legal sense.[28] Third, they drew fundamental due process rights from both the natural-law tradition and the common-law tradition, with which they were familiar. Fourth, the due process clause is part of a trilogy of rights inextricably linked to but not indistinguishable from the privileges or immunities clause and the equal protection clause. It would therefore be misleading to read these clauses either separately, in vacuo, or as one seamless whole.

Section one of the amendment emerged over time, resulting from a developmental negotiating process. During the process the principal drafters made important linguistic and stylistic changes that affected the substance of this section. The congressional debates on the Freedman's Bureau bill and the civil rights bill elucidate the philosophical and historical antecedents of the due process clause and the civil rights that its framers intended to protect.[29] Since Congress drafted both bills contemporaneously with the Fourteenth Amendment, the debates also elucidate the meaning of the rights that the due process clause encompasses.

The Freedman's Bureau Bill

In January 1866, Senator Lyman Trumbull (R-Ill.),[30] chairman of the Judiciary Committee, reported the Freedman's Bureau extension bill,[31] which provided for equal benefit of civil and criminal law. Trumbull's bill also contained a series of specific substantive guarantees for persons and property. It gave explicit protection to the fundamental rights of free individuals. The

---

drafting the Fourteenth Amendment. The aims and methods of the members were imprecise, and the amendment, he concludes, was an example of sloppy draftsmanship. See Kluger, *Simple Justice* (New York: Alfred A. Knopf, 1976), 654–55.

28. Nelson, *The Fourteenth Amendment*, 36.

29. See Maltz, *Civil Rights*, 55, 78, who argues that Bingham and other moderate Republicans viewed the Civil Rights Act as affording absolute protection only to a limited set of rights against state deprivations.

30. Trumbull, a conservative-moderate Republican, participated in the framing of every major reconstruction and civil rights bill. See Maltz, *Civil Rights*, 28.

31. For the text of the bill, see *Cong. Globe*, 39th Cong., 1st Sess. 318 (1866). See also Hyman, *A More Perfect Union*, 449–53. The bill was an interim, postwar measure designed to establish order, provide legal authority for the military government, and wrest control of Reconstruction policy from President Johnson.

bill recognized that every free person has a right to make and enforce labor contracts. The measure protected the freedman's right to acquire, use, enjoy, and transfer real and personal property.[32] It guaranteed the freedman's right to equal legal protection of property and personal security. Although some of the bill's Radical Republican proponents and Democratic critics claimed that its reach was more extensive, few doubted that section seven provided concrete protection of life, liberty, and property against official deprivation.

As the congressional debates indicate, the bill's proponents and opponents disputed the authority of Congress to pass the legislation. According to the critics, the Thirteenth Amendment ended slavery but did not authorize Congress to enact civil rights legislation. The critics also charged that the Freedman's Bureau bill treated the South as a conquered province, ignoring the states' authority to regulate their own internal affairs under the Tenth Amendment. By establishing a regime to care for the freedman's material needs, the bureau interfered with the states' municipal jurisdictions and exercise of their police powers. Ultimately, the debate focused on the allocation of power in the American federal system. Did the states or the federal government have primary responsibility for protecting citizens' fundamental rights and regulating their civil relations?[33]

There was relatively extensive discussion of the authority of Congress to enact the Freedman's Bureau bill, but only limited debate on the substantive rights that section seven would protect. In the early stages of the House debates, Ignatius Donnelly (R-Minn.) defended the bill as merely enforcing "all the guarantees of the Constitution,"[34] particularly the fundamental rights of life, liberty, and property. Referring to an amendment that John Bingham had introduced, Donnelly asked rhetorically: "Why should this

32. As Herbert Hovenkamp and Earl Maltz observe, these personal rights are essentially economic ones. According to both Maltz and Hovenkamp, by the late 1860s civil rights included (1) equal treatment in state courts and equal access to state agencies and (2) "a set of distinctly *economic* civil rights, namely, the right to make contracts and the right to own property." Herbert Hovenkamp, *Enterprise and American Law, 1836–1937* (Cambridge, Mass.: Harvard University Press, 1991), 94. See also Maltz, *Civil Rights,* 61, who writes: "The economic rights protected are those essential to meaningful participation in a free labor-based economy."

33. As Maltz emphasizes, a primary consideration in framing the Freedman's Bureau bill, the Civil Rights Act, and the Fourteenth Amendment was the impact of these measures on the federal system. As the weight of evidence suggests, the moderate Republicans, who held the balance of power, did not intend a radical transformation of the federal system. See Maltz, *Civil Rights,* 48–49.

34. *Cong. Globe,* 39th Cong., 1st Sess. 586 (February 1, 1866).

not pass? Are the promises of the Constitution mere verbiage? Are its sacred pledges of life, liberty, and property to fall to the ground through lack of power to enforce them?"[35] Answering his own question in an impassioned speech, Donnelly simply assumed that the Constitution granted Congress authority to protect fundamental rights throughout the nation. He observed regretfully, however, "There is no national protection in our land for life, liberty, or property."[36] Given necessity and constitutional authority, Donnelly concluded, there could be no valid argument against the Freedman's Bureau bill. Evidently, Donnelly was unaware of *Barron v. Baltimore* (1833), which precluded enforcement of the Bill of Rights against the states.

The next day, February 2, Representative Michael C. Kerr (D-Ind.) opposed the bill with equal passion, arguing that the Thirteenth Amendment did not authorize Congress to protect "the ordinary civil relations of the negro to the society in which he lives."[37] Although the Thirteenth Amendment had altered the black man's status as a slave, it did not empower Congress to protect his political rights. According to Kerr, the states retained authority to regulate the right of blacks to make contracts. Inasmuch as these civil privileges are unrelated to personal freedom, he claimed, they fall within the states' municipal powers—that is, under the power to promote the public welfare and safety.[38] In other words, Kerr rejected the proponents' argument that freedom of contract is an essential element of personal liberty.

The Senate debated the Freedman's Bureau bill somewhat more extensively than the House of Representatives, but the discussion focused primarily on questions of constitutional authority and the allocation of power between the states and the national government. While some senators rested their arguments on the war powers, others found authority for the legislation in the Thirteenth Amendment. Nevertheless, between late December 1865 and early February 1866, only a few senators examined the basic rights that the bill was designed to protect.

On December 21, Senator Henry Wilson (R-Mass.) defended the bill as an appropriate measure to secure the freedman's liberty. Reacting to the Black Codes that Louisiana and Mississippi had enacted, Wilson noted that the freedman could not sell his labor, "lease land or buy a humble home," or move about freely on the public highways. Without work, unable to find a

35. *Id.*
36. *Id.*
37. *Id.*, 623.
38. *Id.*

home, and subject to vagrancy laws, the freedman would soon be reen-
slaved.[39] In the face of such exigencies, the Thirteenth Amendment granted
Congress power to ensure the freedman's equal, universal, and impartial
liberty.[40] While he included equal access to education and the judicial system, Wilson emphasized personal security, freedom of movement, the right
to make contracts, and protection for real and personal property. Apparently, he believed that these specific and mostly economic rights were fundamental to civil liberty.

A month later, on January 22, Senator Edgar Cowan (R-Pa.),[41] who disagreed with his party on Reconstruction policy, argued that the Freedman's
Bureau bill was unnecessary because the Fifth Amendment's due process
clause already protected blacks from state deprivations. Responding to
Wilson's charge that the southern states had deprived blacks of their freedom, Cowan stated:

> I have only to say that the Constitution of the United States makes
> provision by which the rights of no free man, no man not a slave,
> can be infringed in so far as regards any of the great principles of
> English and American liberty; . . . Under the fifth amendment of
> the Constitution, no man can be deprived of his rights without the
> ordinary process of law.[42]

Cowan clearly believed that the due process clause of the Fifth Amendment
protected unenumerated, fundamental liberties, which he inferred from the
Anglo-American tradition of common and natural law. Like Donnelly, Senator Cowan assumed that federal courts could enforce the Fifth Amendment
against the states.

In a lengthy colloquy that followed, Cowan and Wilson disputed the
scope of rights covered in section seven of the bill. Cowan denied that the
national government had the power to enforce equal political rights—for

39. *Id.*, 111.
40. *Id.*, 111, 112. Wilson stated that Congress had the authority to guarantee that the
freedman "can go where he pleases, work when and for whom he pleases; that he can sue and
be sued; that he can lease and buy and sell and own property, real and personal; that he can
go into the schools and educate himself and his children; that the rights and guarantees of the
good old common law are his, and that he walks the earth, proud and erect in the conscious
dignity of a free man, who knows that his cabin, however humble, is protected by the just and
equal laws of his country." *Id.*, 111.
41. Cowan was a Johnson Conservative who consistently voted against his party's position
on key issues of Reconstruction and civil rights. See Benedict, *A Compromise of Principle*, 351.
42. *Cong. Globe*, 39th Cong., 1st Sess. 340 (1866).

example, the right to vote or run for public office. Nevertheless, he understood equality to encompass the language of the Declaration of Independence. The Declaration, he observed, implies "that each man shall have the right to pursue in his own way life, liberty, and happiness."[43] Even though he rejected national protection of political rights, Cowan conceded that Congress had the authority to protect the fundamental civil rights expressed in the Declaration.

When the Senate resumed consideration of the bill on January 24, James McDougall (D-Calif.) challenged the measure as beyond the national government's constitutional competence. By creating a military regime to enforce the proposed act, Congress would displace the civil power, invade judicial authority to enforce the Constitution, and deprive citizens of their right to judicial process. However, McDougall believed that the Thirteenth Amendment conferred power on Congress to pass legislation protecting the freedman's fundamental rights of life, liberty, and property against burdensome state legislation. He also implied, but did not state explicitly, that the amendment authorized the judiciary to void state and congressional legislation interfering with constitutionally protected liberties. McDougall's views are remarkably similar to the substantive due process philosophy the Supreme Court evolved in the 1880s and 1890s.[44]

Shortly before the Senate concluded debate on the Freedman's Bureau bill, John Sherman (R-Ohio),[45] who had been silent during the discussion, noted the close parallel between section seven and what became the Civil Rights Act, then pending in Congress. The purpose of both measures, he noted, was to define the "incidents of freedom."[46] The Civil Rights Act defined these rights as "the right to sue and be sued, to plead and be impleaded, to acquire and hold property, and other universal incidents of freedom."[47] Sherman did not define these "universal incidents," but acknowledged that both bills guaranteed procedural and substantive rights. They provided for equal access to the judicial process and the right to hold property, free from arbitrary (i.e., class or partial) state regulation.

Although President Johnson vetoed the Freedman's Bureau bill on February 19, 1866, he acknowledged and apparently approved of the bill's funda-

43. Id., 342.

44. Id., 393.

45. Sherman was a conservative-centrist Republican. See Benedict, A *Compromise of Principle*, 352.

46. *Cong. Globe*, 39th Cong., 1st Sess. 744 (1866).

47. Id.

mental objectives. At the beginning of his veto message, the President stated: "I share with Congress the strongest desire to secure to the freedmen the full enjoyment of their freedom and property, and their entire independence and equality in making contracts."[48] Despite his opposition to the measure, Johnson recognized the right to personal security, the enjoyment of property, and freedom to contract one's labor as the essence of civil liberty. The veto message was but another indication of the growing breach between Congress and the President over Reconstruction policy. Although the Senate attempted to override the President's veto on February 20, it failed to do so by the requisite two-thirds vote.[49]

But the congressional attempt to enact a Freedman's Bureau bill was far from over. Over the next five months the House and the Senate struggled to fashion a political compromise. The bill that Congress finally adopted on July 16, over Johnson's veto, authorized the President to "extend military protection and have military jurisdiction over all cases and questions concerning the free enjoyment" of the freedman's rights and immunities. The act acknowledged the core rights of civil liberty, including the right to make labor contracts and to acquire, use, and dispose of real and personal property. It guaranteed the freedman's personal security and freedom of movement. The Act extended the equal protection of law regarding these rights. And, it ensured military protection of the freedman's fundamental rights against burdensome state legislation. Section fourteen of the Freedman's Bureau Act recognized the same core rights as the Civil Rights Act of 1866 and the Fourteenth Amendment.[50]

The Civil Rights Act of 1866

Section one of the proposed Civil Rights Act defined the essence of civil liberty as the right to make contracts, the right to personal security, and

48. *Id.*, 916.

49. The Senate voted to override, 30–18, with 2 absent. *Id.*, 943.

50. Ch. 200, 14 Stat. 173, § 14, 176–77 (1866), provides each freedman "the right to make and enforce contracts, to sue, be parties, and give evidence, to inherit, purchase, lease, sell, hold, and convey real and personal property, and to have full and equal benefit of all laws and proceedings concerning personal liberty, personal security, and the acquisition, enjoyment, and disposition of estate, real and personal, including the constitutional right to bear arms, . . . without respect to race or color, or previous condition of slavery."

protection for real and personal property.[51] Senator Lyman Trumbull, the bill's author, assumed that government has a basic obligation to protect these rights in exchange for citizen loyalty. For the first time, the bill extended equal legal protection of fundamental rights to blacks and guaranteed equal access to the courts in order to protect their civil liberties. In contrast to the Freedman's Bureau bill, the Civil Rights Act employed the federal district and circuit courts to enforce statutorily protected civil rights. In the event that blacks could not secure justice from official discrimination in state courts, the bill also provided for removal of cases to the federal courts.

In addition to defining the citizen's substantive rights, Trumbull's bill had several other interesting features. It employed the federal courts to protect nationally defined civil rights. Despite reservations about the federal judiciary that stemmed from the Supreme Court's *Dred Scott* decision (1857), congressional Republicans distrusted the state courts even more with regard to enforcing the civil rights of freedmen and loyalists against official misconduct and private conspiracies.[52] The bill contemplated federal judicial restraint of arbitrary state legislation and official conduct concerning the specific life, liberty, and property interests defined in section one.[53] The Civil Rights Act of 1866 reflected increasing congressional reliance on the federal courts to protect the fundamental rights of citizens, a trend that would culminate in the Judiciary Act of 1875. Thus the Civil Rights Act foreshadowed only a limited transformation in federalism, from a state-centered system in which state courts enforce their citizens' rights into one in which state and national courts have a statutory duty to enforce a narrow range of fundamental civil rights.[54]

As in the debates on the Freedman's Bureau bill, congressional critics attacked the civil rights measure as constitutionally unwarranted, an invasion of the states' municipal powers, and a radical transformation of the

51. S. 61, 39th Cong., 1st Sess. (January 5, 1866). Section one protected the citizen's right "to make and enforce contracts, to sue, be parties and give evidence, to inherit, purchase, lease, sell, hold, and convey real and personal property, and to full and equal benefit of all laws and proceedings for the security of person and property, and shall be subject to like punishment, pains, and penalties, and to none other, any law, statute, ordinance, regulation, or custom to the contrary notwithstanding." Although there were several amendments to the original bill, there were relatively few changes in the language of section one, which suggests that within the Judiciary Committee there was a consensus on the meaning of "civil rights."

52. *Cong. Globe,* 39th Cong., 1st Sess. 602, 603, remarks of Senator Henry S. Lane (R-Ind.) (February 2, 1866).

53. *Id.,* remarks of Senator Reverdy Johnson (R-Md.), April 5, 1866, 1777.

54. See Maltz, *Civil Rights,* 64–65.

federal system.[55] Without a constitutional amendment, argued Senator Cowan, Congress lacked authority to change the government's federal structure.[56] Predictably, the bill's advocates cited the Thirteenth Amendment as authority to secure the freedman's rights.[57] Questions of constitutional authority dominated the debates, but the members devoted more attention to the scope and origin of the citizen's liberties than they did to debating the Freedman's Bureau bill.

The debates reveal that the members referred liberally to the natural-law or higher-law tradition to justify the proposed legislation. Some appealed to the Declaration of Independence or the immortal Bill of Rights as an expression of inherent rights. Others derived inherent rights from republican principles of government and the nature of the political compact. In translating broad principles into specific, positive legal rights and remedies enforceable in state and federal courts, the bill's proponents relied heavily on English custom and common law as well as on the U.S. Constitution, judicial interpretation, and American state law. The drafters employed a broad variety of legal and philosophical arguments to justify and fashion national protection for civil rights.

Although he opposed the civil rights bill, Senator Cowan indicated that he would support a constitutional amendment securing to "all men of every color and every race and every condition their natural rights, the rights which God has given them, the right to life, the right to liberty, the right to property."[58] Cowan regarded these rights as natural and inherent, but he argued that a constitutional amendment was necessary to extend the national government's protection to blacks and Asians.[59]

Responding to Cowan's remarks, Jacob Howard, a member of the Joint Committee on Reconstruction,[60] asserted that the Thirteenth Amendment granted Congress power to confer all the incidents of freedom on the former slaves. Among the liberties essential to every free person, Howard emphasized, are the right to acquire property, the right to personal security, and

---

55. *Cong. Globe*, 39th Cong., 1st Sess., remarks of Senators Peter G. Van Winkle (Unionist-W.Va.), 497, 498 (January 30, 1866); Edgar Cowan (R-Pa.), 499, 500; and Johnson, 504, 505, 1778 (April 5, 1866).

56. *Id.*, February 2, 1866, 603, 604.

57. *Id.*, remarks of Senator Jacob M. Howard (R-Mich.), January 30, 1866, 503.

58. *Id.*, colloquy between Cowan and Trumbull (January 30, 1866), 500.

59. *Id.*

60. Howard was a Radical-Centrist Republican who occasionally supported black suffrage. Prior to Senator Fessenden's illness, Howard played only a minor role in the Joint Committee's deliberations on the Fourteenth Amendment. Benedict, *A Compromise of Principle*, 353.

the right to make and enforce contracts. With regard to the exercise of these basic civil rights, the proposed act promised legal equality. While Howard alluded to a broad range of civil rights, he articulated specifically the rights of life, liberty, and property.[61]

In the context of a debate on the definition of citizenship, Senator Trumbull claimed that the civil rights bill articulated the basic philosophy of the Declaration of Independence. He characterized the bill's essential purpose as securing equal protection for the inalienable rights of life, liberty, and property. Distinguishing civil rights from political rights, Trumbull proclaimed: "[The bill] declares that all persons in the United States shall be entitled to the same civil rights, the right to the fruit of their own labor, the right to make contracts, the right to buy and sell, and enjoy liberty and happiness."[62] From Trumbull's perspective, the civil rights bill had a substantive and a procedural component. It gave positive, legal definition to fundamental rights and ensured the citizens of each state access to the federal courts for the protection of life, liberty, and property.[63]

Following President Johnson's veto message, Trumbull once again explained his views on the civil rights that the proposed legislation protected. "To be a citizen of the United States," he stated, "carries with it some rights."[64] In defining the nature of the citizen's civil rights, he said, "They are those inherent, fundamental rights which belong to free citizens or free men in all countries, such as the rights enumerated in this bill."[65] Foremost among these is the right to freedom of movement and the national government's corresponding obligation to protect the physical security of its citizens throughout the United States.

Senator Trumbull rested his argument for the national protection of civil rights on both natural and common law. Relying on Blackstone and Kent, he argued that equal protection of civil rights is the basis for the political commonwealth. Quoting from Kent's *Commentaries*, Trumbull emphasized the absolute and inherent nature of the right to personal security, personal liberty, and the right to acquire and enjoy property.[66] These rights, which belong to all citizens, he stressed, are inalienable. "Allegiance and protection," concluded Trumbull, "are reciprocal rights."[67]

61. *Cong. Globe*, 39th Cong., 1st Sess. 503, 504 (1866).
62. *Id.*, 599.
63. *Id.*, 600.
64. *Id.*, 1757.
65. *Id.*
66. *Id.*
67. *Id.*

Reporting the bill to the House, James F. Wilson (R-Iowa), chairman of the Judiciary Committee,[68] described it as articulating the citizen's right to equal protection for personal security, personal liberty, and the right to acquire and enjoy property.[69] In his opening statement, Wilson appealed to natural-rights theory as a justification for the measure. Referring to the definition of civil rights in *Bouvier's Law Dictionary*, he stated: "Civil rights are the natural rights of man; and these are the rights which this bill proposes to protect every citizen in the enjoyment of throughout the entire dominion of the Republic."[70] While relying on natural law, Wilson turned to the U.S. Constitution and judicial precedent to describe the specific civil rights that he viewed as fundamental. He denied that he was proclaiming a new or revolutionary concept—the proposed bill merely affirmed existing constitutional law. He claimed that the measure rested on the privileges and immunities clause of Article Four, *Corfield v. Coryell*, and the Thirteenth Amendment.[71] Like several other members, Wilson ignored the fact that the privileges and immunities clause of Article Four applied exclusively to interstate travelers.

After defending the authority of Congress to secure the freedman's civil rights, Wilson attempted to define the "great fundamental rights" that the proposed act was designed to protect. Referring to Blackstone and Kent, he drew upon and attempted to harmonize English and American legal principles.[72] Wilson emphasized the absolute nature of these personal rights of life, liberty, and property. Although he characterized these personal rights as "the inalienable possession of both Englishmen and Americans," he also argued that the Constitution's general and specific terms encompassed the basic civil rights embodied in section one of the proposed bill.

Wilson's remarks suggest at least three possible but not mutually exclusive sources for the citizen's civil rights. First, life, liberty, and property rights are antecedent to the Constitution, resting on natural law as well as British and American legal history. Second, there is ample authority in the Constitution's specific limitations on state power—for example, the Thirteenth Amendment and the privileges and immunities clause of Article Four. Third, even if the Constitution had not mentioned these rights specifically,

68. As chairman of the House Judiciary Committee, Wilson played an instrumental role in drafting the Civil Rights Act. Wilson's views on civil rights generally were centrist rather than radical.

69. *Cong. Globe*, 39th Cong., 1st Sess. 1117 (1866).

70. *Id.*

71. *Id.*, 1117–18.

72. *Id.*, 1118.

they are implied by its general terms and its fundamental principles of republican government. Wilson's third concept is similar to contemporary theories of unenumerated fundamental rights, which exist in the recesses of various constitutional provisions—for example, the Ninth and Fourteenth Amendments.[73]

Throughout the debate, Representative Wilson wavered between his role as politician and draftsman. He began and ended his remarks by appealing to basic principles that would unite congressional Republicans and mobilize popular support for Reconstruction. In his final summation, for example, Wilson returned to the broadest possible justification for the civil rights bill, resting his case on natural-right and social-contract theory:

> Before our Constitution was formed the great fundamental rights which I have mentioned, belonged to every person who became a member of our great national family. No one surrendered a jot or tittle of these rights by consenting to the formation of the Government. The entire machinery of government as organized by the Constitution was designed, among other things, to secure a more perfect enjoyment of these rights.[74]

He also anchored civil rights in a broad interpretation of the Constitution. Concluding his remarks, Wilson asserted that Congress had adequate constitutional authority to accomplish the great purposes or essential functions of republican government. The national government had the power and political obligation to protect the citizen's civil rights against burdensome state legislation. According to Wilson's expansive reading, the "necessary and proper" clause gave Congress the same constitutional authority to protect unenumerated fundamental rights as it did to carry out specifically delegated powers.[75] Wilson either ignored or brushed aside the limitations

73. See, for example, Douglas, J. (opinion of the Court), *Griswold v. Connecticut*, 381 U.S. 479 (1965). Citing the First, Third, Fourth, Fifth, and Ninth Amendments, Douglas argued that "these specific guarantees in the Bill of Rights have penumbras, formed by emanations from those guarantees that help give them life and substance. Various guarantees create zones of privacy." *Id.*, 484. In a concurring opinion, Justice Harlan argued that the Fourteenth Amendment encompasses "basic values 'implicit in the concept of ordered liberty.'" *Id.*, 500. The due process clause of the Fourteenth Amendment, Harlan implied, is a source for an unenumerated fundamental right to privacy that encompasses a married couple's decision to use contraceptives.

74. *Cong. Globe*, 39th Cong., 1st Sess. 1119 (1866).

75. *Id.*

imposed by the Tenth Amendment as well as by *Barron v. Baltimore* and *Dred Scott*.[76]

Another Republican, M. Russell Thayer (R-Pa.),[77] focused on the bill's remedial purposes. Following the Civil War, he noted, the former rebel states had adopted laws (the Black Codes) depriving the freedmen of their constitutionally protected "fundamental rights of citizenship"[78]—that is, the right to own real property and to make and enforce contracts. Section one of the bill removed these burdens by guaranteeing "equal benefit of all laws and proceedings for the security of person and property."[79] Thayer asked rhetorically, what "kind of freedom" prohibits individuals from moving from one place to another, deprives them of the right to make and enforce contracts, or denies them "the liberty to engage in the ordinary pursuits of civilized life[?]."[80] The bill would protect the fundamental rights of citizenship by giving these rights specific definition in positive law.

As the debates continued, the battle lines became clear. The bill's proponents argued that the national government had the power to protect a core of fundamental rights against deprivations by the states. The proposed legislation provided concrete definition of the citizen's fundamental rights. Although the Constitution did not enumerate these rights, they were rooted in the common law, principles of republican government, and conceptions of natural law and the social contract, upon which limited, constitutional government rested.

In addition to sharp divisions between Democrats and Republicans, within the Republican Party there were significant differences of opinion among moderates, conservatives, and radicals. Some moderates like William Lawrence (R-Ohio) found support for fundamental rights in the Declaration of Independence, the Preamble to the Constitution, and various constitutional provisions, such as the privileges and immunities clause (Article Four) and the Fifth and Thirteenth Amendments.[81] Other moderates ap-

---

76. *Id.*, 1120. In response to Wilson's speech, Representative Andrew J. Rogers (D-N.J.) denied that Congress had authority to protect life, liberty, and property rights against burdensome state actions without a constitutional amendment. Given Rogers's voting record, however, his remarks seem disingenuous.

77. Thayer was a centrist Republican. Benedict, *A Compromise of Principle*, 350.

78. *Cong. Globe*, 39th Cong., 1st Sess. 1151 (March 2, 1866).

79. *Id.*

80. *Id.*, 1152.

81. Representative Lawrence argued that the proposed Civil Rights Act merely declared the preexisting rights of a free people. Life, liberty, and property rights, he observed, had come down through the ages, from the Magna Carta, from British common and statutory law, and from the Declaration of Independence. Furthermore, Lawrence argued that these rights are

pealed to general principles of the political contract—that is, to the reciprocal duties between governors and the governed. In exchange for citizen loyalty, government has an obligation to protect the individual's fundamental
rights throughout the United States.

Some radicals like William Windom (R-Minn.) stressed the inalienable,
preconstitutional basis of the citizen's rights. Other radicals, such as John
Broomall (R-Pa.)[82] and Samuel Shellabarger (R-Ohio),[83] emphasized the
government's basic duty to protect fundamental liberties. According to
Broomall, the Preamble establishes a basic obligation to protect every person within the jurisdiction of the federal government, at home and abroad.[84]
Furthermore, the Constitution's "general welfare," "necessary and proper,"
and "privileges and immunities" clauses confer ample power to carry out the
government's constitutional obligations to its citizens. Beyond these constitutional arguments, Broomall anchored his case in the nature of the political contract. If government is not capable of protecting the individual's
fundamental rights, there is no basis for the citizen's political obligation.[85]

Responding to John Bingham's call for a constitutional amendment, Representative Shellabarger reiterated that citizens and government have a reciprocal duty to each other. While the national government is obliged to
protect the citizen's civil rights, the citizen has a duty to render service and
allegiance to the nation.[86] The civil rights bill, Shellabarger claimed, simply
specified the "rights of person and property" to which individuals are entitled.[87] As the debate drew to a close, James Wilson endorsed Shellabarger's
position, claiming that the national government had the constitutional authority to protect the citizen's rights, whenever the states deny life, liberty,
or property without due process of law. Like Shellabarger, Wilson argued
that government has a duty to protect these rights in exchange for the
citizen's allegiance.[88] Unless the national government affords such protec-

---

absolute. Finally, he recognized that a state could deny these rights in several ways, either by
enacting laws that interfered with the individual's exercise of rights, or by failing to protect a
person's life, liberty, or property interests. *Id.*, 1833.

82. As a Radical Republican, Broomall voted consistently for black suffrage during the
Thirty-ninth Congress. Benedict, *A Compromise of Principle*, 351.

83. Although Shellabarger was a Radical Republican, he did not vote consistently for black
suffrage. *Id.*, 350.

84. *Cong. Globe*, 39th Cong., 1st Sess. 1263 (1866).

85. *Id.*

86. *Id.*, 1293.

87. *Id.*

88. *Id.*, 1294.

tion, he concluded, "the Republic becomes an oppressor, exacting a discharge of duty by the citizen, in the absence of the power to return a protective compensation."[89]

Although Representative Bingham supported the bill's objectives, he argued that the states had the sole responsibility to enforce the Bill of Rights. Protection for life, liberty, and property rights, Bingham continued, "is of the reserved powers of the States, to be enforced by State tribunals and by State officials acting under the solemn obligation of an oath imposed upon them by the Constitution of the United States."[90] Without a constitutional amendment, as Bingham now realized, the national government lacked the power to displace the states' civil and criminal codes regarding racial discrimination. The civil rights bill breached the power that the Tenth Amendment reserved to the states, and Congress could not alter the federal plan of government by simple legislation.

During the floor debates the opposition sang a common refrain: there was no constitutional warrant for the civil rights bill. The bill would destroy the states' sovereignty, absorb their police and municipal powers, and subject their respective judiciaries to criminal penalties for enforcing otherwise valid state laws. At most, the Thirteenth Amendment granted Congress power to protect the freedman's right to contract his labor. However, the amendment did not confer authority on the national government to place the freedman on an equal footing with regard to civil rights.

Advancing beyond the now familiar refrain, Representative Michael C. Kerr (D-Ind.) denied that there is a common core of national rights or privileges and immunities. Since all citizenship derives from an individual's state citizenship, the national government has no constitutional authority to define the citizen's privileges and immunities. The privileges and immunities clause (Article Four) only requires that the states treat their own citizens and interstate travelers similarly. But the states are free to determine the substantive rights to which their own citizens and interstate travelers, alike, are entitled.[91] Thus Kerr rejected the view that the national government had constitutional authority to define and enforce a common core of fundamental rights vis-à-vis the states.

The congressional debates on the Civil Rights Act indicate that the bill's proponents and some of its opponents believed that "civil rights" encom-

89. Id.
90. Id., 1291.
91. Id., 1268, 1270.

passed fundamental life, liberty, and property rights. The bill defined and attempted to accord national judicial protection for the individual's physical security, personal liberty, and real and personal property. By providing for removal of cases from state to federal courts, the act contemplated a limited rather than a radical transformation of American federalism. It afforded the states an opportunity to protect the individual's fundamental rights but left the federal courthouse door open in the event that the states failed to discharge their responsibilities.

Although the bill's first section did not refer explicitly to "privileges and immunities," "equal protection," and "due process" as legally enforceable rights, all three elements of the Fourteenth Amendment are recognizable in the Civil Rights Act. The specific "civil rights" that the act protects are among the privileges and immunities of national citizenship. The guarantee of equal treatment in the civil and criminal process, and the prohibition on class legislation, ensure equal enjoyment of fundamental rights. And the act's provision for access to the federal courts is a promise of fundamental fairness in the judicial process. However, it remains unclear whether the authors of the Civil Rights Act also viewed due process as a limitation on the states' legislative power regarding constitutionally protected life, liberty, and property interests.

While the members of both houses disputed the constitutional authority of Congress to enact the Freedman's Bureau Act and the Civil Rights Act, they acknowledged that these two statutes would afford national protection to the individual's fundamental rights to personal security and personal liberty and to acquire, use, and dispose of property. Congressional Republicans appealed to Anglo-American law and principles of republican government to justify national protection of fundamental rights. The debates also echo with references to natural law, natural right, and the social contract. Republicans referred to the Declaration's bold articulation of seventeenth- and eighteenth-century natural-rights philosophy, which suggests that government's first duty is to protect the individual's property, liberty, and security. As a general charter of government, they argued, the Constitution fulfilled the philosophical promise of the Declaration of Independence. One of the Constitution's basic purposes, as expressed in the Preamble, is to safeguard fundamental rights against the arbitrary exercise of governmental power.[92]

According to some of the radicals, social-contract theory also supported

92. Here, as elsewhere, the term "arbitrary" is used to denote partial or class legislation that is unrelated to a public purpose—namely, an objective that is within the constitutional competence of the state or national government.

the argument that citizens and governments have reciprocal rights and duties. While governments have a duty to protect the citizen's basic rights, citizens owe allegiance to their nation. But a government that fails to protect its citizens' civil rights does not deserve their allegiance. Protection of fundamental life, liberty, and property rights is the basis for political obligation and stability. "Given the pervasiveness of ideas about the rights of citizens in a republic," writes William Nelson, "it was natural" that the members of Congress referred to republican principles during the debates on the Freedman's Bureau and civil rights bills.[93]

The legislative drafters of the Thirty-ninth Congress grounded the Freedman's Bureau and Civil Rights Acts in higher law, principles of republican government, and Anglo-American legal history. English custom and common law, U.S. constitutional development, and state legal practice provided an important but often ignored framework for translating first principles into legal rights. Legal history, as interpreted by commentators and judges, was a significant basis for the specific rights and remedies in both statutes. These two laws, in turn, were a frame of reference for the Fourteenth Amendment, but there is little evidence that they are an exclusive codex for determining the meaning of the privileges or immunities, due process, and equal protection clauses. While Congress drafted all three contemporaneously, the Fourteenth Amendment developed as a broad statement of legal principle rather than an explicit legal code.

If congressional Republicans disputed the outer limits of fundamental or civil rights, they expressed a consensus about the core of these rights. They defined fundamental rights largely but not exclusively in economic terms. In a republican society, free and equal individuals have a fundamental right to make economic choices for themselves, subject to regulations that serve a valid public purpose. Both the Freedman's Bureau Act and the Civil Rights Act stress equal protection for the right to make contracts and to have one's property and personal security safeguarded. The two statutes extended national protection to these rights.

The congressional debates on the two bills were a prelude to the floor debates on the Fourteenth Amendment, which the Joint Committee on Reconstruction reported to Congress on April 25. By that time Democrats and Republicans of all hues had articulated their views on the nature and origin of the fundamental rights of each citizen, respective duties of the state and national governments to protect those rights, and the structure of

93. Nelson, *The Fourteenth Amendment*, 70.

the federal union. With Andrew Johnson's veto of the Civil Rights Act, the breach between Congress and the President had become transparent. On March 27, 1866, the Senate received the veto message, and within the next two weeks both houses overrode the President's veto.[94] The stage was now set for consideration of the joint committee's resolution proposing a constitutional amendment.

94. On April 6 the Senate voted 33–15, and on April 9 the House vote was 122–41 to override the veto.

3

Framing the
Fourteenth Amendment

During the Thirty-ninth Congress a consensus emerged among Republicans that civil or fundamental rights encompass protection for life, liberty, and property. Although some radicals also attempted to include the franchise and the entire Bill of Rights, they lacked a congressional majority. As Herbert Hovenkamp and Earl Maltz stress, the Civil Rights Act of 1866 defined the citizen's fundamental rights as the right to make and enforce contracts; the right to acquire, use, enjoy, and dispose of real and personal property; and the right to equal protection for property and personal security.[1] It liberated freedmen from bond slavery by protecting their equal right to make economic choices for themselves.

The Civil Rights Act did not contain such terms as "privileges or immunities," "due process," and "equal protection of the law," but it did address those concepts in specific terms. In contrast to the language of the civil rights bill, the Fourteenth Amendment is a statement of broad legal principles. Section one imposes a general duty on the states to protect the individual's life, liberty, and property rights. Section five confers power on Con-

---

1. Hovenkamp, *Enterprise and American Law,* 94; Maltz, *Civil Rights,* 62.

gress to remedy the states' arbitrary deprivation of a limited set of fundamental rights.[2]

Although Congress retained remedial power, the due process, equal protection, and privileges or immunities clauses are self-enforcing provisions. In
the event that the states did not meet their responsibility, the federal courts
could intervene in cases within their jurisdiction to protect constitutional
life, liberty, and property rights against official deprivation. Even if Congress failed to enact remedial legislation, as William Nelson suggests, the
federal courts could exercise their power of judicial review to enforce the
guarantees of section one.[3] However, between 1866 and 1875 Congress
adopted a series of civil rights acts that created federal and state court jurisdiction and remedies to enforce specific civil rights. With the Fourteenth
Amendment, Congress and the federal courts began the long process of
translating widely held republican beliefs into legal principles, rules of constitutional interpretation, and specific legal rights, duties, and remedies.[4]

The privileges or immunities clause does not define the specific rights
that are encompassed, but even the narrowest definition would include protection for personal liberty, personal security, and real and personal property
against burdensome state action.[5] At a minimum, the equal protection
clause prohibits state actors from burdening fundamental rights on the basis
of an individual's race. However, is the due process clause merely a guarantee that no state can deprive a person of life, liberty, or property except by
established judicial procedure, as Raoul Berger argues?[6] Or is it a restriction
on the exercise of legislative policymaking authority concerning these fundamental rights, as Howard Jay Graham suggests?[7]

2. See Maltz, *Civil Rights*, 102, who writes: "The strong preponderance of the evidence
indicates that when compared to the privileges and immunities clause, the due process and
equal protection clauses were intended to guarantee a smaller group of rights to a larger class
of individuals and that Congress would have only a limited power to enforce these guarantees."
3. Nelson, *The Fourteenth Amendment*, 55–58.
4. See *id.*, 148–49. As Nelson argues, during the next thirty years the Supreme Court
elaborated the meaning of section one in more specific and coherent terms than congressional
Republicans had during the framing of the amendment and subsequent civil rights legislation.
5. 6 F.Cas. 546 (C.C. E.D. Pa. 1823) (No. 3230), 551.
6. Berger, *Government by Judiciary*, 197–200.
7. Graham, *Everyman's Constitution*, 52. See also Maltz, *Civil Rights*, 99, who argues that
the mid-nineteenth century understanding of substantive due process "applied only to denials
of the fundamental vested rights of life, liberty, and property," as distinguished from other
rights or benefits defined in state law. But see Hovenkamp, *Enterprise and American Law*, 171–
75, who argues that substantive due process stemmed from the Supreme Court's creative
jurisprudence after 1885.

The Substance of Due Process

Raoul Berger appears to make a persuasive case for a procedural interpretation of due process. First, he argues that the lawyers who drafted the Fourteenth Amendment universally associated "due process with judicial procedure."[8] Second, Berger claims that Coke, Blackstone, Kent, and Story defined due process exclusively in procedural terms. "In the interval between 1789 and 1866," Berger writes, "the procedural nature of due process received the imprimatur of Kent and Story, who relied on Coke."[9] Third, he argues that in 1866 virtually all state constitutions included either law-of-the-land or due process requirements in provisions "dealing exclusively with the conduct of criminal trials, with the privileges of the accused," or with deprivations "of life, or *personal* liberty, or property for a crime."[10] Fourth, Berger claims that John Bingham, a principal drafter of section one, understood due process in purely procedural terms.[11] If Berger's analysis is correct there is little warrant for either Howard Graham's or Justice Stephen J. Field's substantive interpretation of the due process clause as a limitation on legislative policymaking.

Berger's argument suffers from several flaws. First, he dismisses the substantive component of the Magna Carta's "law-of-the-land" formulation. He argues: "Whether due process and 'law of the land' were identical in English law need not detain us; for present purposes it may suffice that both related to *judicial procedures* preliminary to the prescribed forfeitures" of life, liberty,

8. Berger, *Government by Judiciary*, 200. Although due process is a term of art lifted from British common and statutory law, Berger discounts its substantive evolution from the thirteenth through the eighteenth century, when the authors of the Fifth Amendment employed it as a restraint on congressional power.

9. *Id.*, 199.

10. *Id.*, 200. Here, Berger is quoting from Charles E. Shattuck, "The True Meaning of the Term 'Liberty' in Those Clauses in the Federal and State Constitutions Which Protect 'Life, Liberty and Property,'" 4 *Harv. L. Rev.* 365–92 (1890–91), 369 (hereafter Shattuck, 4 *Harv. L. Rev.*). However, Shattuck recognizes that most of these constitutions also included substantive restrictions on the states' authority to burden life, liberty, or property interests. Furthermore, Shattuck's principal concern is defining the scope of liberty and property interests that due process encompasses.

11. Berger's reference is to an exchange between Bingham and Rogers on February 28. *Cong. Globe*, 39th Cong., 1st Sess. 1089 (1866). Berger's reliance on Bingham's construction of due process seems odd since he refers to the Ohio Republican in the most disparaging terms. "Bingham," writes Berger, "was a muddled thinker, given to the florid, windy rhetoric of a stump orator, liberally interspersed with invocations to the Deity, not to the careful articulation of a lawyer who addresses himself to great issues." Berger, *Government by Judiciary*, 145. Berger also characterizes Bingham as "an imprecise thinker who exhibited little more understanding of the Bill of Rights than Graham credits the abolitionists with." *Id.*, 231.

or property rights.[12] The statute that Berger cites (28 Edw. 3 [1352])[13] is a guarantee that individuals will be summoned only after a common-law court has issued the appropriate writ. Parliament's objective in enacting the statute was to hold the king accountable in the common-law courts rather than in his own Council, when proceeding against a freeman's life, liberty, or property rights. Parliament's confirmation of the Magna Carta (28 Edw. 3) imposed substantive limits on the king's power to deprive freemen of their fundamental rights by holding royal agents accountable to common-law judges who were parliamentary allies in the struggle against the Crown.

Second, Berger ignores the substantive component in Coke's, Blackstone's, Kent's, and Story's commentaries. Although Coke emphasized judicial procedure in his analysis of chapter 39 of the Magna Carta, he also acknowledged that the "law of the land" imposes substantive limits on the Crown, acting in its legislative and executive capacities. Coke, for example, opposed monopolies as a restraint on the individual's liberty and as a violation of the law of the land.[14] Blackstone also used the term "law of the land" in both a procedural and a substantive sense. Referring to the Magna Carta (chapter 39), Blackstone identified the law of the land with established judicial procedure and with substantive rules of common and statutory law protecting property and personal security.[15]

The antimonopoly component of Coke's substantive interpretation was attractive to congressional Republicans who shared a Jacksonian faith in equality of economic opportunity. In a republican society, they believed, individuals should be free to care for themselves and their families. Monopoly, like bond slavery, prevented individuals from contracting their labor, from pursuing all lawful callings and professions, and from acquiring property. Slavery, monopoly, exclusive franchises, and special privileges interfered with the fundamental, equal right of all persons to be free, independent, and happy.[16]

As the congressional debates suggest, Republicans viewed civil rights largely, but not exclusively in economic terms,[17] as the equal right of all persons to make economic decisions for themselves. While they opposed class legislation, the framers understood that the states could put limits on liberty and property to promote the public welfare. The Fourteenth Amend-

12. Id., 195.
13. Id., 197.
14. Coke, Institutes of the Laws of England, part 2, 47.
15. Blackstone, Commentaries, 1542–43.
16. Nelson, The Fourteenth Amendment, 64, 67–68.
17. See Hovenkamp, "The Political Economy of Substantive Due Process," 40 Stan. L. Rev. 379–447 (1988), 395 (hereafter Hovenkamp, 40 Stan. L. Rev.).

ment would not interfere with the states' valid exercise of the police power, but it would prevent the states from putting limits on economic liberty and property rights for the purpose of giving an advantage to one class or group at the expense of another.

The two most influential American commentators to whom Berger refers, Kent and Story, also acknowledged substantive restraints on the arbitrary exercise of governmental power. Chancellor Kent identified due process of law with a guarantee of substantive rights, as well as with procedural fairness in the civil and criminal process.[18] While Kent argued that life, liberty, and property rights are inherent, he recognized that they are conditional—that is, subject to legislative considerations of the public welfare. In cases of conflict, judges have a responsibility to reconcile the states' exercise of their police powers with the individual's claim of fundamental right. Justice Story focused on the procedural component of due process, but he too noted that the Magna Carta's broad objective was to prevent arbitrary government and preserve civic peace.[19]

Third, Berger focuses on the law-of-the-land and due process clauses in sections of state constitutions dealing with the defendant's rights and post-conviction forfeiture of life, liberty, and property interests. However, he ignores other provisions that protect liberty, property, and personal security against arbitrary government. He also overlooks early state constitutions, bills of rights, and federal statutes that contain substantive as well as procedural protections for life, liberty, and property rights. The Virginia Declaration of Rights (1776), the New Hampshire Bill of Rights (1784), and the Northwest Ordinance (1787) provided for procedural protections in the judicial process and substantive limitations on the exercise of legislative power.[20]

Turning to state constitutions extant in 1866, Berger observes correctly that a majority of those constitutions had law-of-the-land or due process clauses in sections that dealt with forfeiture of the defendant's life, liberty, or property rights. These constitutions prohibited the states from depriving individuals of fundamental rights except according to established judicial procedure.[21] However, thirty-two state constitutions also contained general provisions regarding the protection of life, liberty, and property rights

18. Kent, *Commentaries*, 48, 49, 52.
19. Story, *Commentaries*, 368–74, 547
20. See Adams, *The First American Constitutions*, 193–94.
21. Approximately twenty-two state constitutions contained such procedural safeguards. See, for example, Pennsylvania Constitution, Art. IX, Sec. 9; Poore, *Federal and State Constitutions*, 2:1564.

against arbitrary governmental deprivation. Article One of the New Jersey Constitution (1844) was characteristic of these provisions:

> All men are by nature free and independent, and have certain natural and unalienable rights, among which are those of enjoying and defending life and liberty, acquiring, possessing, and protecting property, and of pursuing and obtaining safety and happiness.[22]

These hortatory provisions reflect a belief in civil equality and substantive limits on governmental power, which the framers of the Fourteenth Amendment articulated in the Thirty-ninth Congress.

In addition to the state constitutions, in 1861 Congress established a government for the Territory of Colorado. Section six of the territorial statute conferred general legislative authority on the legislature but imposed restrictions on the taxing power. Following these restrictions, in the same section, Congress prohibited the territorial legislature from enacting any law "impairing the rights of private property."[23] Thus Congress imposed a substantive limitation on the legislature's authority to deprive a person of vested property rights.

Despite Berger's claim that the lawyers who framed the Fourteenth Amendment had a purely procedural understanding of due process, the historical evidence suggests otherwise. Undoubtedly, the lawyers of the Thirty-ninth Congress were familiar with due process as a guarantee that courts could not deprive individuals of life, liberty, or property except by following established procedure. But this hardly proves that they viewed due process exclusively in procedural terms. Coke's, Blackstone's, Kent's, and Story's substantive interpretations suggested that due process also could be used to prohibit arbitrary legislation concerning fundamental rights.[24]

Finally, Berger argues that a brief exchange between Representatives John Bingham (R-Ohio) and Andrew Rogers (D-N.J.) "left no room for specula-

22. *Id.*, 1314.
23. Ch. 59, 12 Stat. 172, § 6, 174 (1861).
24. The evidence also is at odds with Hovenkamp's claim that the history of the Fourteenth Amendment "was all but irrelevant" in the evolution of substantive due process or that the doctrine was the product of "loose constructionism." See Hovenkamp, *Enterprise and American Law,* 171–74. However, it is accurate to say that courts derived or inferred liberty of contract from the due process clauses. This book's central thesis is that the inference was both warranted and consistent with American jurisprudence at the time of the Fourteenth Amendment's framing and ratification.

tion as to what he [Bingham] meant by 'due process.'"[25] During Bingham's explanation of H.R. 63, an early draft of his constitutional amendment, Rogers asked, "I only wish to know what you mean by 'due process of law.'" Bingham replied, "The courts have settled that long ago, and the gentleman can go and read their decisions."[26] Does Bingham's reply indicate that due process has a fixed, exclusively procedural meaning, as Berger insists, or was it simply a curt response to a fatuous question?[27] Rogers's question was an obvious attempt to discredit the proposed constitutional amendment.

Berger to the contrary, Bingham's remarks demonstrate that he viewed the early draft of the amendment (H.R. 63) as a substantive restraint on state legislative authority. If legislators or other state officers violated their oath to protect the individual's fundamental rights, the proposed amendment would authorize Congress to secure these rights against burdensome state legislation. As Bingham described the proposed amendment, if the states' legislators "conspire together to enact laws refusing equal protection of life, liberty, or property, the Congress is thereby vested with power to hold them to answer before the bar of the national courts for the violation of their oaths and of the rights of their fellow men."[28] The passage suggests that Bingham interpreted the proposed amendment as a substantive restraint on all state officers regarding the citizen's life, liberty, and property rights. If there was some doubt about Bingham's intent, a few moments later he remarked:

> But, sir, there never was even colorable excuse, much less apology, for any man North or South claiming that any State Legislature or State court, or State Executive, has any right to deny protection to

25. February 28, 1866. Berger, *Government by Judiciary*, 203. Berger later states, in reference to Bingham's reply to Rogers, that he never revealed his intention of embodying substantive due process in section one of the Fourteenth Amendment. *Id.*, 232. Again, referring to the exchange with Rogers, Berger writes: "Bingham himself stated that 'due process' was used in its customary decisional, that is, procedural, sense." *Id.*, 241.

26. *Cong. Globe*, 39th Cong., 1st Sess. 1089 (February 28, 1866).

27. Why should Berger attribute such significance to Rogers's question, when he also describes the New Jersey Democrat as a "bitter opponent of the several Reconstruction measures," who "charged that section 1 'consolidates everything into one imperial despotism,' and 'annihilates' States' Rights." *Id.*, 189. Furthermore, Berger identifies Rogers as one of a group of "Democratic worthies" who gave section one of the civil rights bill and the proposed amendment a "revolutionary reading." Among other things, Rogers claimed that the civil rights bill would promote miscegenation and public school desegregation. *Id.*, 158, 159–60, 161. Generally, Rogers's comments were intended to discredit the bill (H.R. 61) and the joint resolution (H.R. 63).

28. *Cong. Globe*, 39th Cong., 1st Sess. 1090 (1866).

any free citizen of the United States within their limits in the rights of life, liberty, and property.[29]

During the debates on the civil rights bill, Bingham offered both a substantive and a procedural explanation of due process. Although he doubted that Congress had the authority to protect citizens' civil liberty without a constitutional amendment, Bingham acknowledged explicitly that the due process clause of the Fifth Amendment had a substantive component.[30] "If the bill of rights, as has been solemnly ruled by the Supreme Court of the United States," Bingham stated, "does not limit the powers of the States and prohibit such gross injustice by States, it does limit the power of Congress and prohibit any such legislation by Congress" depriving life, liberty, or property without due process of law.[31] As the law of the land, the Constitution places substantive restraints on the power of Congress to burden or to deny equal protection for fundamental rights.[32]

The congressional debates and the proceedings of the Joint Committee on Reconstruction indicate that Bingham's purpose remained constant, but his methodology evolved over time. His early draft (H.R. 63) granted Congress direct, prophylactic power to enforce individual rights, while the later omnibus proposal (H.R. 127) provided limited, remedial authority to correct the states' deprivations. Although he was prepared to compromise on language and methodology, Bingham had a fixed purpose—namely, to require the states to afford protection for every person's fundamental rights.[33] Thus the final compromise draft opened the federal courthouse door should the states ignore their constitutional duty.

Bingham may have been ambiguous about the scope of fundamental rights, but, along with many of his Republican cohorts, he believed that the core rights embraced security for life, liberty, and property. Rather than being muddled, as Raoul Berger claims, Bingham and other moderate Republicans were searching for an acceptable formula around which the party could coalesce. They stated the case for an amendment in rhetoric that would unify the Republicans in Congress and mobilize a national electorate.

29. Id.

30. Id., 1291 (March 9, 1866).

31. Id., 1292.

32. Although section one was debated behind closed doors, as William Nelson observes, one plausible interpretation is that the Joint Committee "intended to incorporate a concept of substantive due process into the Fourteenth Amendment." Nelson, The Fourteenth Amendment, 57.

33. See Maltz, Civil Rights, 53.

Republican politicians were attempting to consolidate the victory of Appomattox in the halls of Congress.

Bingham's Early Draft

On January 12, 1866, John Bingham introduced a constitutional amendment providing that "Congress shall have power to make all laws necessary and proper to secure to all persons in every state within this Union equal protection in their rights of life, liberty, and property."[34] Bingham's constitutional amendment, which eventually became the core of section one, provided for a broad, positive grant of congressional power to enforce the equal protection of every person's life, liberty, and property rights throughout the United States. Unlike section two of the Thirteenth Amendment, which granted Congress power to enforce its provisions by appropriate legislation, his original proposal conferred all power necessary and proper. Opponents later criticized Bingham's choice of language, saying that John Marshall had given the "necessary and proper" clause (Article One, section eight, paragraph eighteen) a broad construction in *McCulloch v. Maryland*.[35] Several critics argued that Bingham's original draft would promote centralized government by authorizing Congress to adopt a national civil and criminal code for the states. Representative Bingham's early, positive draft would have greatly enlarged congressional authority to protect fundamental rights against state deprivations, whether legislative, executive, or judicial in origin.

Inasmuch as the proposal contained no state-action requirement, it would also have permitted Congress to enforce fundamental rights against private deprivations. The amendment's original language implied a major revolution in American federalism. It made Congress the principal arbiter of national-state relations concerning the citizen's fundamental liberties. Under the pro-

34. Benjamin Kendrick, *The Journal of the Joint Committee of Fifteen on Reconstruction, 39th Congress, 1865–1867; Columbia University Studies in History, Economics and Public Law,* vol. 62 (New York: Columbia University Press, 1914), 46. Bingham moved that his amendment be referred to a subcommittee of five chaired by Senator William Pitt Fessenden (R-Maine) and Representative Thaddeus Stevens. Fessenden was a conservative-centrist Republican. See Benedict, *A Compromise of Principle,* 352. The subcommittee also included Senator Jacob Howard (R-Mich.), who managed the floor debates on the Fourteenth Amendment during Fessenden's illness, and Representatives Conkling (R-N.Y.) and Bingham. Kendrick, *Journal,* 47.

35. 17 U.S. (4 Wheat.) 316 (1819), 420–21.

posed amendment, Congress could have intervened in the states' municipal or domestic jurisdictions, enacting direct legislation to secure the individual's life, liberty, and property interests. In the early phases of the floor debates, the protagonists clearly understood the far-reaching implications of Bingham's proposal.

On January 20 the subcommittee of five reported two alternative amendments ("A" and "B"), along with John Bingham's resolution ("C"), to the Joint Committee on Reconstruction.[36] The third resolution ("C"), an expanded version of Bingham's original proposal, included the equal protection of both civil rights and political rights.

> Congress shall have power to make all laws which shall be necessary and proper to secure all persons in every state full protection in the enjoyment of life, liberty and property; and to all citizens of the United States in any State the same immunities and also equal political rights and privileges.[37]

The resolution also protected citizens against unequal punishments or penalties in the civil and criminal process. Amendment C would have granted Congress wide-ranging prophylactic power to protect a common core of civil and political rights against public and private abuse.

On January 27 Bingham offered a revised version of his amendment, which stated:

> Congress shall have power to make all laws which shall be necessary and proper to secure all persons in every state full protection in the enjoyment of life, liberty and property; and to all citizens of the United States in any State the same immunities and also equal political rights and privileges.[38]

In addition to securing full protection of life, liberty, and property throughout the United States, the revised draft still promised equal protection for political rights and immunity from unequal civil and criminal laws. The

36. Amendments "A" and "B" dealt with representation but also included clauses guaranteeing the citizen's civil rights. Kendrick, *Journal*, 50. In addition to ensuring equality of civil rights, Amendment "A" would have guaranteed such political rights as the franchise. Amendment "B," which Thaddeus Stevens supported, provided for the proportional reduction of a state's representation in the House in relation to its deprivation of voting rights on the basis of race, creed, or color. *Id.*, 51.

37. *Id.*, 56.

38. *Id.*

amendment's language gave Congress broad prophylactic power to protect the individual's civil and political rights against public and private deprivations.

After several weeks of maneuvering, Representative Bingham introduced a substitute, which stated:

> The Congress shall have power to make all laws which shall be necessary and proper to secure to the citizens of each state all privileges and immunities of citizens in the several states (Art. 4, Sec. 2); and to all persons in the several States equal protection in the rights of life, liberty and property (5th Amendment).[39]

He had deleted any reference to political rights but retained a positive grant of congressional power to protect the citizen's fundamental rights, similar to the Civil Rights Act. The draft resolution now contained the germ of the Fourteenth Amendment's equal protection and privileges or immunities clauses.

While the language concerning citizens' privileges and immunities was ambiguous, the floor debates indicate that Bingham believed there was a core of fundamental rights—rights of life, liberty, and property—for which his proposal would afford constitutional protection. However, the resolution's language is amenable to a more limited interpretation. With its reference to Article Four, section two, the resolution can be read as affording little more than equal protection for whatever basic privileges the states create as a matter of public policy. But such a reading is inconsistent with Bingham's basic objective.

Introducing his constitutional amendment in the House,[40] John Bingham explained the remedial objectives of H.R. 63. Since he doubted the constitutionality of the civil rights bill, he believed that an amendment was necessary to protect the citizen's fundamental liberties against state deprivations. Although he believed that the states had a moral obligation to protect life, liberty, and property rights, this amendment would impose a legally binding and enforceable duty on state legislative, executive, and judicial officers.[41] If the states had maintained their fidelity to the Constitution, "to

39. *Id.*, 61. Apparently, Bingham either fused or confused due process and equal protection.
40. *Cong. Globe*, 39th Cong., 1st Sess. 1033–34 (February 26, 1866).
41. *Id.*, 1034. See also Maltz, *Civil Rights*, 94.

this immortal Bill of Rights embodied in the Constitution," such an amendment would be superfluous. But the officials of eleven states had utterly disregarded their oath (Article Six, section three) to enforce the Constitution as the supreme law of the land.[42]

Following Bingham's lead, most of the proponents focused primarily on the need for a constitutional amendment. They also claimed that the amendment merely restated other constitutional provisions concerning congressional power to enforce the citizen's basic rights. The proposed amendment, William Higby (R-Calif.) concluded, merely gave force to the Fifth Amendment and the interstate privileges and immunities clause of Article Four.[43] Higby simply ignored *Barron* v. *Baltimore,* which denied that the Fifth Amendment was applicable to the states.[44]

The resolution's opponents portrayed it as a radical departure from the original federal plan of government. Robert Hale (R-N.Y.)[45] claimed that the proposed amendment would interfere in the states' domestic jurisdictions.[46] Hale criticized the amendment as "a grant of the right to legislate for the protection of life, liberty, and property, simply qualified with the condition that it shall be equal legislation."[47] Neither Article One of the Constitution nor the Fifth Amendment authorized Congress to enact primary legislation to safeguard life, liberty, and property rights. The Fifth Amendment, Hale noted, is a judicially enforceable restraint on arbitrary congressional legislation concerning these rights, rather than a restriction on the states. The proposed amendment would intrude on the states' valid exercise of the police power under the Tenth Amendment.

In his concluding remarks Bingham once again attempted to clarify the amendment's essential purposes. First, the resolution granted Congress power to ensure the equal protection of life, liberty, and property against state deprivation. Second, the proposed amendment afforded protection to "the privileges and immunities of citizens in the several states."[48] Bingham was ambiguous about the precise meaning of the term "privileges and immunities," but at several points in the debate he indicated that the term guaranteed equal protection for the fundamental rights of life, liberty, and prop-

42. *Cong. Globe,* 39th Cong., 1st Sess. 1034 (1866).

43. *Id.,* 1054. See also Maltz, *Civil Rights,* 101, who argues that section one apparently restated preexisting rights.

44. 32 U.S. (17 Pet.) 243 (1833).

45. Hale was a conservative Johnson Unionist. Benedict, *A Compromise of Principle,* 349.

46. *Cong. Globe,* 39th Cong., 1st Sess. 1063 (1866).

47. *Id.,* 1064.

48. *Id.,* 1089.

erty in all the states.[49] His remarks imply that the amendment would not interfere with the states' exercise of their police, tax, eminent domain, or other powers for valid public purposes.

The Search for a Compromise

Between December 1865 and March 1866 there were numerous efforts to draft measures on reconstruction, representation, the franchise, and the protection of civil rights.[50] Among these was an omnibus proposal that Robert Dale Owens presented to Oliver Morton, Thaddeus Stevens, and William Pitt Fessenden.[51] Owens's proposal, which Stevens introduced in the Joint Committee, provided in part:

> Section 1. No discrimination shall be made by any state, nor by the United States as to the civil rights of persons because of race, color, or previous condition of servitude.
>
> Sec. 5. Congress shall have power to enforce by appropriate legislation, the provisions of this article.[52]

The Stevens-Owens plan contained several important changes in language that implied changes in remedial intent. Section one was now phrased in the negative, prohibiting the states and the national government from discriminating on the basis of race. It was a self-enforcing provision that the courts could apply to state deprivations of civil rights. Section five authorized Congress to adopt appropriate legislation to enforce the amendment's provisions. Under section five, Congress could define specific statutory rights and provide executive and judicial remedies for violations. Evidently, these changes reflected growing criticism that Bingham's earlier drafts had conferred too much power on Congress vis-à-vis the states.

49. Id., 1089–90.
50. See Eric L. McKitrick, *Andrew Johnson and Reconstruction* (Chicago: University of Chicago Press, 1960), 336.
51. Id., 345. Owens's plan provided for (1) equal civil rights, (2) impartial or universal suffrage in every state, (3) reduction of representation in proportion to the denial of the right to vote on the basis of race, (4) repudiation of both the Confederate war debt and compensation for the emancipation of the former slaves, and (5) congressional authority to enforce the amendment through appropriate legislation. Id., 346. For a brief, but thorough analysis of Owens's plan, see Maltz, *Civil Rights*, 79–81.
52. Kendrick, *Journal* (April 21, 1866), 83–84.

Taken together, sections one and five imply that the power of Congress is remedial rather than prophylactic. The enforcement section's language was now similar to the Thirteenth Amendment rather than to the "necessary and proper" clause of Article One. In juxtaposition, the two sections suggest that the enforcement power of Congress is limited to correcting past deprivations. If the states deprive individuals of equal protection for their civil rights, Congress could adopt remedial legislation. If Congress failed to exercise its remedial authority under section five, the federal courts could exercise their power of judicial review to protect the individual's fundamental rights.[53]

After Stevens submitted the resolution to the Joint Committee, Bingham moved to amend section one by adding the following language: "nor shall any state deny to any person within its jurisdiction the equal protection of the laws, nor take private property for public use without just compensation."[54] Although the committee rejected Bingham's language,[55] he returned to the substance of his proposal later in the meeting. Bingham introduced a substitute for section five, which read:

> No state shall make or enforce any law which shall abridge the privileges or immunities of citizens of the United States; nor shall any state deprive any person of life, liberty or property without due process of law, nor deny to any person within its jurisdiction the equal protection of the laws.[56]

After several days of discussion, the committee adopted Bingham's substitute.[57] The language of the draft resolution was now virtually identical to section one of the Fourteenth Amendment. As Joseph James notes, Bingham's proposal was a self-enforcing limitation on state power to interfere with the individual's fundamental rights, rather than a broad grant of prophylactic authority to Congress to protect these rights.[58]

The records of the Joint Committee and the House of Representatives are

53. See Nelson, *The Fourteenth Amendment*, 55–58.

54. Kendrick, *Journal*, 85. In subsequent drafts Bingham dropped the reference to the Fifth Amendment's "takings" and "just compensation" clauses.

55. The committee rejected Bingham's amendment by a vote of 5–7. The first section was then adopted 10–2, with Bingham voting for Stevens's draft language. *Id.*

56. *Id.*, 87.

57. *Id.* (April 25, 1866), 98.

58. James, *Framing of the Fourteenth Amendment*, 106. Despite Bingham's expansive language, at this point in the committee's deliberations he was still unclear about which rights were fundamental.

ambiguous, but they indicate that John Bingham sought to protect the fundamental rights of life, liberty, and property by expanding federal power vis-à-vis the states. Bingham's various changes in language probably reflected his recent reading of John Marshall's opinion in *Barron*, limiting the applicability of the Bill of Rights to Congress. One of his objectives was to overcome *Barron*, making the Constitution's protection of fundamental rights applicable to the states.[59] Another objective was to place the individual's fundamental rights beyond the whims of future congressional majorities. Under the proposed amendment, aggrieved individuals could turn to the judiciary to enforce their civil rights against burdensome state action. After several attempts, near failure, considerable compromise, and Andrew Johnson's veto of the Civil Rights Act, the Joint Committee on Reconstruction reported H.R. 127 to Congress.

The Debate and Adoption

The House and Senate debated the resolution sporadically between April 30 and June 8. But the record does not illuminate the framers' remedial intent regarding the definition of fundamental rights, since the members spent little time debating the meaning of section one. The proponents claimed that the amendment merely enforced the Constitution's existing provisions against state deprivation. Its opponents portrayed the joint resolution as a radical transformation of the federal system, authorizing the national government to invade the states' reserved powers. However, both sides agreed that without a constitutional amendment the national government lacked the power to protect the individual's fundamental rights.[60]

Opening the House debate on May 8, Representative Stevens made one of the few statements relevant to section one. For Stevens, section one guaranteed the individual's inherent right to be secure in his person and property against the arbitrary exercise of governmental power. It provided legally enforceable protection for life, liberty, and property against burdensome state conduct.

All of the rights asserted in the due process and equal protection clauses,

59. *Id.*, 104–6.
60. *Cong. Globe*, 39th Cong., 1st Sess., statement of Representative Thomas D. Eliot (R-Mass.), May 9, 1866, 2511; statement of Representative Henry J. Raymond (R-N.Y.), May 9, 1866, 2512–13. For a good summary of the arguments pro and con, see Nelson, *The Fourteenth Amendment*, 104–11, 114–16.

Stevens noted, are "in some form or other, in our Declaration or organic law."[61] In a vague reference to *Barron*, he observed that the amendment merely conferred authority on Congress to enforce the Constitution against the states.[62] The Fourteenth Amendment represented a national commitment to require the states to enforce a limited set of fundamental rights.

Like Stevens, Representative Henry Raymond (R-N.Y.)[63] supported the resolution because it would remove any doubt about congressional authority to enact the Civil Rights Act.[64] Responding to Raymond's comments on the act, Representative Wilson, chairman of the House Judiciary Committee, noted the parallel objectives of the two measures. "The first section of that bill," he observed, "embodies its essential and vital principle."[65] The civil rights bill's first section "was simply a declaration that all persons without distinction of race or color should enjoy in all of the States and Territories civil rights and immunities."[66] During the debates on the Civil Rights Act, Wilson had defined civil rights as the fundamental rights of personal security, personal liberty, and real and personal property.[67]

61. *Cong. Globe*, 39th Cong., 1st Sess. 2459 (1866).

62. "This amendment," Stevens emphasized, "supplies that defect, and allows Congress to correct the unjust legislation of the States, so far that the law which operates upon one man shall operate equally upon all." *Id.*

63. Raymond was a conservative Johnson Unionist. Benedict, *A Compromise of Principle*, 349.

64. *Cong. Globe*, 39th Cong., 1st Sess. 2502 (1866).

65. *Id.*, 2505.

66. *Id.*

67. *Id.*, 1118. Wilson's and Raymond's colloquy does not prove that the rights protected under section one of the act and the constitutional amendment were identical. The debate leaves open whether section one of the Fourteenth Amendment encompasses a broader set of rights than the Civil Rights Act protected. In either event, Wilson and Raymond discussed these issues in the context of congressional authority to enforce the civil rights of freedmen through criminal prosecution in the absence of a constitutional amendment. Raymond argued that the act unconstitutionally restricted state legislative authority in areas reserved to the states under the Tenth Amendment. *Id.*, 2512–13.

Representative Rogers (D-N.J.) made the clearest statement identifying section one of the act and of the amendment as identical twins. Referring to the joint resolution, Rogers said that it was "no more nor less than an attempt to embody in the Constitution of the United States that outrageous and miserable civil rights bill which passed both Houses of Congress and was vetoed by the President of the United States upon the ground that it was a direct attempt to consolidate the power of the States and to take away from them the elementary principles which lie at their foundation." *Id.*, 2338. Rogers claimed that both would permit the national government to regulate virtually all civil relations, including marriage, the franchise, contracts, and jury service. Concluding the parade of horribles, Rogers predicted that the amendment would revolutionize the American political system. *Id.* Given Rogers's hostility to both the bill and the joint resolution, one should not assign great weight to his statement. He was either confused or mendacious in viewing civil rights as identical to social and political rights.

In the closing hours of the debate, several members addressed the Four-teenth Amendment's essential purposes. John Farnsworth (R-Ill.)[68] regarded the intent as self-evident; no man could "fail to see and appreciate" the amendment's great remedial purpose.[69] Farnsworth stressed that section one afforded the equal protection of the law, which he viewed as indispensable to enjoying "the equal rights of 'life, liberty, and the pursuit of happiness.'"[70]

Appealing to his colleagues' republican beliefs, John Bingham justified the amendment in terms of the political compact. The objective of the first section, he began, is "to protect by national law the privileges and immu-nities of all citizens of the Republic and the inborn [inherent] rights of every person within its jurisdiction whenever the same shall be abridged or denied by the unconstitutional acts of any State."[71] While Bingham remained elu-sive about the fundamental rights that section one protected, he addressed the Speaker:

> Sir, the words of the Constitution that "the citizens of each State shall be entitled to all privileges and immunities of citizens in the several States" include, among other privileges, the right to bear true allegiance to the Constitution and the laws of the United States, and to be protected in life, liberty, and property. Next, sir, to the allegiance which we all owe to God our Creator, is the allegiance which we owe to our common country.[72]

Once again, Bingham stressed the reciprocal relationship in a republican society between the government's duty to protect fundamental rights and the citizen's political obligation or allegiance to the nation. As a politician, he appealed to the basic principles of government that united Republican representatives and voters in the aftermath of the war.

Introducing the proposed amendment in the Senate, Jacob Howard ex-plained the intent of section one by referring to the privileges and immu-nities clause of Article Four.[73] He claimed that the original intent of the clause was "to put the citizens of the several States on an equality with each

68. Farnsworth was a Radical Republican who occasionally voted for black suffrage. Bene-dict, *A Compromise of Principle,* 350.

69. *Cong. Globe,* 39th Cong., 1st Sess. 2539 (May 10, 1866).

70. *Id.*

71. *Id.,* May 10, 1866 (evening session), 2542.

72. *Id.*

73. May 23, 1866. Howard was standing in for the ailing William Fessenden, chairman of the Joint Committee on Reconstruction.

other as to all fundamental rights."[74] He defined the privileges and immunities of citizenship according to Justice Washington's circuit opinion in *Corfield* v. *Coryell*, which emphasized the states' obligation to afford equal protection for life, liberty, and property rights.[75] In addition to these privileges and immunities, Senator Howard enumerated the personal rights guaranteed by the first eight amendments to the Constitution. Clearly, he regarded all of these rights, privileges, and immunities as the fundamental rights of national citizenship. But Howard's expansive position reflected the views of Radical Republicans rather than those of the centrist-conservative Republicans who dominated the Senate during the Thirty-ninth Congress.[76]

Aside from Senator Howard's remarks, the Senate record reveals little discussion of section one. During the final stage of the debate, only two senators made significant statements relevant to the first section. Luke Poland (R-Vt.) defended the proposed constitutional amendment as merely securing the citizen's existing privileges and immunities against state deprivation. However, he also proclaimed that the resolution embodied the basic principles of justice articulated in the Declaration of Independence.[77] Apparently, Poland believed that section one addressed a broad range of fundamental rights, but his vague statement obscures rather than clarifies the scope of the privileges or immunities, due process, and equal protection clauses.

Following Poland's statement, Senator Stewart also commented on the resolution's essential purposes: "It declares that all men are entitled to life, liberty, and property, and imposes upon the Government the duty of discharging these solemn obligations."[78] Stewart viewed the amendment as containing substantive guarantees for these fundamental rights. The Senate droned on for three days, but following Stewart's brief statement the resolution's opponents spent most of their time attacking its legitimacy, necessity, and potential effects on the federal system. The final days of the debate cast no light on the scope of section one or on congressional and judicial power to enforce the amendment's provisions.

Although it is impossible to divine the framers' intent with certainty, several conclusions seem plausible. As Maltz observes, the framers did not attempt

---

74. *Id.*, 2765.

75. 6 F.Cas. (No. 3230) 546 (C.C. E.D. Pa. 1823), 551–52. First among Washington's partial enumeration of privileges and immunities were "the enjoyment of life and liberty, with the right to acquire and possess property of every kind, and to pursue and obtain happiness and safety." *Id.*

76. Benedict, *A Compromise of Principle*, 28.

77. *Cong. Globe*, 39th Cong., 1st Sess. 2961 (June 5, 1866).

78. *Id.*, 2964.

to radically transform American federalism into a centralized national political system. Instead, they imposed an affirmative constitutional duty on the states to afford equal protection for liberty, property, and personal security. The early drafts of John Bingham's resolution granted Congress direct authority to protect these rights throughout the states. But Congress rejected Bingham's approach, either because it conferred too much power on the national government or because it left the definition of fundamental rights to the whims of future legislative majorities. The final compromise resolution conferred limited remedial power on Congress to correct the states' deprivation of fundamental rights. Nevertheless, the amendment imposed an affirmative duty on the states to protect the individual's life, liberty, and property, which the judiciary could safeguard against burdensome official conduct.[79]

However, neither the language nor the history of the Fourteenth Amendment defines the substantive rights that the due process clause encompasses. While Howard Jay Graham argues that some framers viewed due process as a limitation on legislative policymaking, Raoul Berger insists that they had a fixed, procedural understanding of due process. According to Berger, by 1866 due process prohibited courts from depriving a person of life, liberty, or property rights, except by established judicial procedure. But Berger dismisses or ignores a body of jurisprudence and political theory suggesting that due process prohibits legislatures from depriving anyone of constitutionally protected life, liberty, or property rights except for substantial reasons of the public welfare.

Although the Fourteenth Amendment's framers did not explicitly embody natural-right, natural-law, or social-contract theory in the due process clause, there is ample evidence that these beliefs shaped their thinking about civil or fundamental rights. Referring to life, liberty, and property as natural rights, some framers argued that these rights are inherent and inalienable. Turning to social-contract theories of government, they claimed that government has an obligation to protect liberty, property, and personal security in exchange for allegiance from its citizens. Equal protection of fundamental rights, several framers concluded, is essential to the perpetuation of the republican society and political institutions that the Constitution established. As a legal construct, substantive due process is compatible with the underlying political philosophy of individual rights, limited government, and constitutionalism that many Republicans in Congress held.

Congressional Republicans expressed Jacksonian and Abolitionist com-

---

79. Maltz, *Civil Rights*, ch. 6, 79–92. See also Nelson, *The Fourteenth Amendment*, 58.

mitments to a civil society in which all persons have equal opportunity in their personal lives. In a free republic everyone is entitled to physical security, personal liberty, and protection for property.[80] Republican senators and representatives defined civil or fundamental rights primarily in economic terms. In contrast to the bond slave, free persons have a right to contract their labor, to acquire, use, and dispose of property, and to make their own economic decisions. The Fourteenth Amendment prohibited the states from burdening these rights unless they could demonstrate a valid public purpose.[81]

Following the adoption of the Fourteenth Amendment and between 1867 and 1875, Congress enacted a series of reconstruction and civil rights legislation that elaborated the remedial objectives of the Fourteenth Amendment's framers. In these statutes, Congress translated section one of the amendment into specific rights and duties enforceable in state and federal courts. Since some members of the Thirty-ninth Congress also participated in drafting Reconstruction and civil rights legislation in the postwar period, these later acts provide additional evidence for interpreting the due process clause as a substantive limitation on the states' exercise of their police, tax, and eminent domain powers. Reconstruction era judiciary and civil rights acts also furnish evidence that Congress expected the federal courts to play an expanded role in protecting national constitutional rights against state deprivation.

80. See Nelson, *The Fourteenth Amendment*, 60, 64–65, 72, 74.
81. *Id.*, 82–83.

4

Congressional Protection of Fundamental Rights in the Reconstruction Era

During the Reconstruction Era, Congress expanded the power of the national government to protect life, liberty, and property rights against public and private deprivation. Employing its enforcement powers under the Thirteenth, Fourteenth, and Fifteenth Amendments, Congress adopted a series of civil rights acts that extended judicial and executive protection to all persons against state interference with, or failure to protect, fundamental rights.[1] While the civil rights acts authorized the federal courts to protect the statutory rights that Congress conferred, the Circuit Court Jurisdiction Act (the Removal Act) of March 3, 1875, greatly expanded national court jurisdiction over virtually all cases raising federal constitutional and statutory questions.[2] By providing access to a federal forum, the Removal Act

1. The Enforcement Act of 1870, Ch. 114, 16 Stat. 140 (1870), which reenacted the Civil Rights Act of 1866; the Enforcement (Ku Klux Klan) Act of 1871, Ch. 22, 17 Stat. 13 (1871), codified at 42 U.S.C. § 1983, which established civil liability for state deprivations of federally protected rights; and the Civil Rights Act of 1875, Ch. 114, 18 Stat. 335 (1875), which provided for equal access to transportation and places of public accommodation (hereafter referred to as the Public Accommodations Act).

2. Circuit Court Jurisdiction Act of March 3, 1875, Ch. 137, 18 Stat. 470 (1875). In controversies exceeding a value of five hundred dollars, Congress authorized the removal of

facilitated national judicial protection of civil rights against state indifference and interference.

Between 1866 and 1875 Reconstruction Era Congresses turned to the task of translating the Fourteenth Amendment's general principles into specific legal rights, duties, and remedies. As the debates suggest, Congress confronted both official attempts to reenslave the freedman and private violence against southern blacks and loyalist whites. In this context of intimidation and violence, Republicans in Congress focused on physical security and freedom of movement. Without physical security, freedmen could not enjoy the other fundamental rights protected by the due process clause. Without freedom of movement, they could not participate equally in the nation's economic life. As the legislative drafters realized, security for persons and property, as well as freedom of movement, are prerequisites for equality of opportunity—that is, the equal right to pursue the common callings, to acquire wealth, and to achieve personal independence.[3]

The proponents of civil rights legislation believed that the Fourteenth Amendment authorized Congress to enforce fundamental rights against infringement by the states. In justifying the substantive rights that the amendment included, they relied on the common law, judicial decisions, legal commentary, natural justice, and republican political principles. Both the natural-law and positive-law traditions provided a foundation for substantive restraints on the exercise of governmental power. In contrast to the Fourteenth Amendment's framers, however, later Reconstruction Era congresses focused on specific rights and remedies rather than general legal principles. As the debates on the Public Accommodations Act of 1875 underscore, proponents and opponents alike debated the common-law duties of the states to protect equal access to public transportation and places of public accommodation. Indeed, Republicans argued that the Fourteenth Amendment embodied common-law rights that included protection for physical security and freedom of movement.

Republicans and Democrats continued to disagree about congressional authority to displace the states as the primary guardians of constitutional rights. Some Republicans and most Democrats opposed the expansion of

---

cases from state to federal courts. In the event that a circuit court dismissed or remanded a petition to the state courts, Congress granted the Supreme Court appellate jurisdiction to review the decision.

3. See Hovenkamp, 40 *Stan. L. Rev.*, 395. Hovenkamp argues that the framers of the Fourteenth Amendment and the Civil Rights Act of 1866 conceived of civil rights largely in economic terms.

federal judicial and executive power into areas that the Tenth Amendment reserved to the states. They denied that the Fourteenth Amendment empowered Congress to enact primary legislation protecting life, liberty, and property against private violence and conspiracies as well as official indifference, complicity, or inability to protect freedmen and loyal whites. At most, the Fourteenth Amendment authorized Congress to remedy state interference with the individual's right to equal protection and due process of law. Despite these conflicts, Reconstruction Era Congresses expanded the national government's power to protect fundamental rights.[4]

Although the members of Congress disputed whether the states or the federal government should be the primary guardian of fundamental rights, a consensus emerged about the core rights included in the Fourteenth Amendment. The framing of the Enforcement Act of 1871 (the Ku Klux Klan Act) and the Public Accommodations Act of 1875 (the Civil Rights Act of 1875) reflects both the emerging consensus on fundamental rights and the continuing conflict over the power of the national government. In the debates on these two acts, many senators and representatives argued that fundamental rights encompass the protection of specific life, liberty, and property interests against burdensome governmental conduct. The legislative drafters of the Enforcement and Public Accommodations Acts assumed that section one of the Fourteenth Amendment placed substantive limitations on the states' authority to interfere with the right to physical security, to personal liberty, and to acquire, use, enjoy, and dispose of property. They believed that the Fourteenth Amendment imposed an affirmative duty on the states to protect these fundamental, civil rights, which Congress could authorize the courts and the executive to enforce when the states failed to discharge their constitutional obligations.[5]

4. The consensus of scholarly opinion is that Congress expanded the power of the federal courts to protect constitutional rights but did not intend to alter the basic pattern of American federalism. See Phillip S. Paludan, *A Covenant with Death: The Constitution, Law, and Equality in the Civil War Era* (Urbana: University of Illinois Press, 1975), 47, 49, 52–53, 54–55. See also Hyman, *A More Perfect Union*, 467–68, 473–74. Hyman argues that the framers of the Fourteenth Amendment left the states free to define the content of liberty, but he concedes the expansion of federal judicial power. See also Note, "Section 1983 and Federalism," 90 *Harv. L. Rev.* 1133–61 (1977), 1142, 1144–45, 1146, 1152–53 (hereafter Note, 90 *Harv. L. Rev.*). More recently, see Maltz, *Civil Rights*, 102–3, which argues that Congress expanded the Fourteenth Amendment's protection beyond the intentions of its framers by prohibiting private conduct that violates due process and equal-protection rights.

5. Although the debates on the Enforcement Act of 1871 and the Public Accommodations Act of 1875 are not dispositive of the Fourteenth Amendment's meaning or the intentions of its framers, they offer a relatively contemporaneous congressional understanding of the amend-

The Enforcement Act of 1871

The legislative history of the Enforcement Act suggests that the Forty-second Congress had a broad conception of its authority to enforce constitutionally protected life, liberty, and property rights. Section one of the act established civil liability for

> any person who, under color of any law, statute, ordinance, regulation, custom, or usage of any State, shall subject, or cause to be subjected, any person within the jurisdiction of the United States to the deprivation of any rights, privileges, or immunities secured by the Constitution of the United States.[6]

In section two Congress conferred jurisdiction on the courts to enforce the act's criminal penalties for conspiracies against the lives and property of individuals who attempted to exercise other federally protected rights.[7] As the legislative record indicates, Congress was concerned with the failure of the states and their agents to protect constitutional rights as well as active deprivation of such rights by states.[8]

---

ment. Inasmuch as some of the members of the Thirty-ninth Congress also served in the Fortieth through the Forty-third Congress, their views should be given some weight in construing the amendment's meaning. With the passage of time and the pressures of public life, however, their memories probably faded. Furthermore, only about fifty members who served in the Thirty-ninth Congress also served in the Forty-second Congress, which adopted the Enforcement Act of 1871. At the time the Forty-third Congress enacted the Public Accommodations Act, there were only thirty-seven senators and representatives who had been in the Thirty-ninth Congress. And by 1875 many of the amendment's key framers had passed from the congressional scene. See, however, Maltz, *Civil Rights*, 104, who argues that the congressional debates of the 1870s are not a reliable guide to the intentions of the drafters of the Fourteenth Amendment. Maltz concedes that much of the debate between 1870 and 1875 may have been law-office history crafted to support or oppose federal intervention under section five of the Fourteenth Amendment.

6. Ch. 22, 17 Stat. 13 (1871).

7. *Id.*, 13–14.

8. On the Enforcement Act, see Curtis, *No State Shall Abridge*, 157–62. See also Robert J. Kaczorowski, "The Enforcement Provisions of the Civil Rights Act of 1866: A Legislative History in Light of *Runyon v. McCrory*," 98 *Yale L.J.* 565–95 (1989), 566, 567, 570 (hereafter 98 *Yale L.J.*); Note 90 *Harv. L. Rev.*, 1153, 1154–55; and Marshall S. Shapo, "Constitutional Tort: *Monroe v. Pape*, and the Frontiers Beyond," 60 *Nw. U. L. Rev.* 277–329 (1965), 278–82 (hereafter Shapo, 60 *Nw. U. L. Rev.*). While Kaczorowski and the authors of the *Harvard Law Review* note take a broad view of the act's reach, Shapo argues that the legislative record could support either a narrow reading or a broad reading. Most recently, see Maltz, *Civil Rights*, 102–3, which suggests that, in confronting the southern states' deprivations of rights, Congress went beyond the intentions of the framers of the Fourteenth Amendment.

Similarly, section three of the act empowered the President to employ military force to suppress violence, insurrection, and conspiracies that deprived "any portion or class of the people of such State of any of the rights, privileges, or immunities, or protection, named in and secured by this act."[9] In the event that state officials were unable, failed, or refused to protect individuals in the equal enjoyment of their constitutional and statutory rights, the act authorized the President to employ state militias and the U.S. Army to suppress such conspiracies.[10] In empowering the President, Congress contemplated the failure (or inaction) of the states to safeguard the right to equal protection for life and property.

The Enforcement Act represented an important expansion of federal authority vis-à-vis the states to protect the rights embodied in the Fourteenth and Fifteenth Amendments. The act explicitly recognized that the states had failed to safeguard constitutional rights, and it provided various remedies for state deprivations, including the use of military force, suspension of the writ of habeas corpus, and federal civil and criminal liability.[11] Given the historical context and the remedial intent of Congress, what specific rights does the act encompass?[12] While the statutory language indicates the general intentions of the framers, the congressional debates elucidate the specific rights, remedies, and federal enforcement powers that the act created.

Drafting the Ku Klux Klan Act

As the debates indicate, the bill's proponents and opponents addressed several major issues: the empirical necessity for civil rights legislation, the constitutional authority for the bill, and the legal rights and remedies that H.R. 320 (the Enforcement Act) would confer. First, did conditions in the South justify federal intrusion into the states' municipal jurisdictions? Second, did the Fourteenth Amendment authorize Congress to adopt remedial and/or primary legislation for the protection of life and property? Third, could

9. Ch. 22, 17 Stat. 13, 14.

10. *Id.*

11. *Id.*, § 3, 14; § 4, 14–15; and § 2, 13–14.

12. For a discussion of the scope and legislative history of the Act, see n. 7, supra. See also Edward Keynes, "42 U.S.C. § 1983 and State Inaction," in *Action and Agency*, ed. Roberta Kevelson (New York: Peter Lang, 1991), 157–81.

Congress reach private conduct as well as state action? Fourth, which rights, privileges, and immunities could Congress protect against burdensome state conduct? Inasmuch as the proponents of H.R. 320 were attempting to strike at private conspiracies that implicated county and municipal law enforcement officials, the debate focused primarily on the failure, indifference, and reticence of the states to protect life and property rather than legislation or other affirmative actions burdening federally protected rights.

Since there was virtual consensus on section one, the debates do not clarify the specific substantive rights protected, so it is necessary to refer to the language and consideration of the other sections in order to determine the intentions of the Congress. Section three, which concerns insurrection, domestic violence, and unlawful combinations and conspiracies, addresses the failure of state authorities to protect constitutional rights.[13] Although Congress rejected an amendment that would have made municipal corporations liable for private riotous conduct, both the language of the proposed amendment and the tenor of the debate suggest that the members of the House and, to a lesser degree, the Senate sought to remedy the failure of public agents to protect life, liberty, and property rights.[14]

Official Misconduct

When the House of Representatives took up H.R. 320, Samuel Shellabarger (R-Ohio), the bill's floor manager, immediately addressed the scope of the rights and judicial remedies that section one incorporated. Shellabarger stressed that the bill enforced the same rights of property and physical security as the Civil Rights Act of 1866.[15] Other representatives who supported

13. Ch. 22, 17 Stat. 13, § 3, 14. In the event that "the constituted authorities of such State shall either be unable to protect; or shall, from any cause, fail in or refuse protection of the people in such rights, such facts shall be deemed a denial by such State of the equal protection of the laws to which they are entitled under the Constitution of the United States."

14. Note, "Damage Remedies Against Municipalities for Constitutional Violations," 89 *Harv. L. Rev.* 922–60 (1976), 939, 945–46, 947–49. The note's authors correctly distinguish between municipal liability for a state actor's conduct, which the framers intended, and municipal liability for private, riotous conduct, which they did not intend. In other words, section 1983 makes municipal taxpayers responsible for official conduct that deprives individuals of their constitutional rights.

15. *Cong. Globe,* 42d Cong., 1st Sess. 317 (March 28, 1871). Shellabarger attempted to reassure the bill's opponents that the privileges and immunities covered were as Justice Washington defined in *Corfield.* See Arnon D. Siegel, "Section 1983 Remedies for the Violation of Supremacy Clause Rights," 97 *Yale L.J.* 1827–46 (1988). Shellabarger may have given a narrow definition of the privileges and immunities of citizenship, but he did not doubt that

the bill observed that it merely enforced the Fourteenth Amendment. Representative George Hoar (R-Mass.), for example, stated that Congress had authority under the amendment to protect life, liberty, and property rights against burdensome state actions.[16] Some Republicans, such as James Monroe (R-Ohio) and David Lowe (R-Kans.),[17] argued that if government could not protect the citizen's right to life and liberty it had failed to perform its fundamental responsibility to "secure to all . . . their natural and inalienable rights."[18]

During the House debates only a few other representatives addressed the substantive rights covered in section one of the bill. John Hawley (R-Ill.) and Joseph Rainey (R-S.C.) emphasized that the first section included only such constitutional rights as life, liberty, and property.[19] Although given to hyperbole, Ben Butler (R-Mass.) saw the protection of these fundamental rights against burdensome state action as essential to republican government.[20] Justifying the bill's substantive scope, Henry Dawes (R-Mass.) argued that the privileges and immunities of citizenship embraced the rights to life, liberty, and the pursuit of happiness. The proposed measure simply offered individuals access to the federal courts and provided civil and criminal remedies for violations of the constitutional right to life and liberty.[21]

In the Senate, section one received even less attention than it had in the House of Representatives. Senator George Edmunds (R-Vt.), the Republican floor manager, remarked that the President could employ military power (under section three) if unlawful conspiracies or insurrections had in fact

---

section five of the Fourteenth Amendment granted Congress affirmative power to afford equal protection for these fundamental rights. See also Flack, *Adoption of the Fourteenth Amendment*, 228.

16. *Cong. Globe*, 42d Cong., 1st Sess. 334 (March 29, 1871). According to Flack, Hoar believed that Congress had power to reach both state action and private conduct. Flack, *Adoption of the Fourteenth Amendment*, 229.

17. As Monroe emphasized, "in interpreting the constitution of any great, free country there is a fair presumption that it contains sufficient grants of power to the legislative body to secure the great primal objects for which constitutions and Governments exist." *Cong. Globe*, 42d Cong., 1st Sess. 370 (March 31, 1871).

18. *Id.* (March 31), 374.

19. *Id.* (April 1), 380, 395.

20. *Id.* (April 4), 448. As Butler commented, "[i]f the General Government has not the constitutional power to protect the lives, liberty, and property of its citizens upon its own soil when such protection is needed, then it ought to have such power; it should reside somewhere in the Government. For without the power to protect the lives of its citizens, a republican government is a failure, and if such be constitutional law, to be a citizen of the United States is to be the most unprotected of all mankind."

21. *Id.* (April 5), 475, 476.

prevented a state's authorities from enforcing state and federal law and had denied to "portions and classes of the people of a State of their constitutional rights of life, liberty, and property, and the protection of the laws."[22] Although section three refers to conspiracies, insurrections, and domestic violence, the debate provides a gloss for the rights that section one includes. In his introductory remarks, Senator Edmunds observed that section one of H.R. 320 carried out "the principles of the civil rights bill [of 1866], which have since become a part of the Constitution."[23] According to Edmunds, section one merely provided civil remedies for state actions that deprive individuals of due process and equal protection for liberty, property, and personal security.[24] As his remarks demonstrate, the principal objective was to transform general guarantees into enforceable rights by providing legal remedies.

Like most moderate Republicans, Edmunds argued that the Fourteenth Amendment simply overcame the limitations of Barron v. Baltimore and prohibited the states "from depriving a man of life, liberty, or property without due process of law."[25] The proposed legislation merely enforced the amendment's promise of due process and equal protection against state interference with these fundamental rights.[26] By contrast, some Radical Republicans, such as Charles Sumner (R-Mass.), implied that the Fourteenth Amendment embodied the basic principles of the Declaration of Independence,[27] but Sumner failed to specify which principles he meant. Presumably, he meant the Declaration's inalienable rights of life, liberty, and the pursuit of happiness, but the record is silent.

Opponents of the measure, including Lyman Trumbull and Garrett Davis (D-Ky.), attacked the bill as a usurpation of state authority to protect the citizen's rights. Trumbull denied that the national government had constitutional authority to protect "rights of person and property." Because the Fourteenth Amendment had not extended "the rights and privileges of citizenship one iota," Trumbull noted, there was no authority for legislation creating new substantive rights.[28] But he conceded that the national govern-

22. Id. (April 11), 567.
23. Id., 568. See U.S. Constitution Amend XIV and the Civil Rights Act of 1870, Ch. 114, 16 Stat. 140, which reenacted the Civil Rights Act of 1866.
24. Cong. Globe, 42d Cong., 1st Sess. 568 (1871).
25. Id. (April 14), 693.
26. Matthew Carpenter (R-Wis.), who shared Edmunds's views, later represented the State of Louisiana before the U.S. Supreme Court in The Slaughterhouse Cases. Id. (April 11), 577.
27. Id. (April 13, 1871), 651.
28. Id. (April 11, 1871), 575. Senator Trumbull's statement should be given considerable

ment had the power to prevent the states from depriving persons of life, liberty, and property without due process of law.[29] During the same debate, Senator Davis expressed similar views, adding that the purpose of the Fourteenth Amendment (section one) was to "abolish discriminations" regarding fundamental rights.[30] Both senators acknowledged that the amendment imposed substantive limits on state power.

Apparently, the radicals were less persuasive in the Senate than in the House of Representatives. Senators who favored the bill took a more limited view of the rights that section one protected than their cohorts in the House. Nevertheless, senatorial proponents of H.R. 320 assumed that Congress had authority under section five of the Fourteenth Amendment to secure the individual's physical security, personal liberty, and real and personal property against burdensome state conduct. The opponents delivered a jeremiad, claiming that the bill would confer unwarranted substantive rights, transform the American federal system radically, and convert the states into provinces of a centralized empire. Responding to the criticism, advocates defended the bill as an enforcement measure that created no new rights or liabilities. In sum, the House and Senate debates demonstrate that deep divisions concerning the federal government's power to safeguard fundamental rights persisted.

Official Inaction and Private Misconduct

Despite these divisions, proponents shared the belief that Congress had authority to protect all persons against the failure of the states to enforce civil rights. The Forty-second Congress attempted to secure the rights of freedmen and loyalist whites who had been subjected to private violence while state, county, and municipal authorities refused or were unable to suppress the Ku Klux Klan and other conspiracies. At least sixteen members of Congress specifically addressed the issue of state inaction and one, Ben Butler, stated expressly that the Fourteenth Amendment imposes an affirmative duty on the states to enforce the right to due process and equal protection.

Examining the bill as a whole, Representative Lionel Sheldon (R-La.) found it unthinkable that Congress lacked the power to enact remedial legis-

---

weight because he chaired the Judiciary Committee during the Thirty-ninth Congress. Trumbull was the principal author of the Civil Rights Act of 1866.

29. Id., 576, 577, 578, 579.

30. Id. (April 13), 648.

lation in the event that the states fail to protect life, liberty, or property. He observed:

> Shall it be said that the citizen may be wrongfully deprived of his life, liberty, and property in his own country and at his own homestead, and the national arm cannot be extended to him because there is a State government whose duty it is to afford him redress, but refuses or neglects to discharge that duty?[31]

Both James Monroe[32] and David Lowe (R-Kans.) also argued that the Fourteenth Amendment would have no "practical operation and effect"[33] if Congress could not secure fundamental rights in the face of state inaction.

In a lengthy philippic, Ben Butler (R-Mass.) claimed that Congress had an affirmative duty to protect fundamental rights in the event that a state failed or neglected to do so. Butler asked rhetorically:

> Is it one of the rights of a State not to protect its citizens in the enjoyment of life, liberty, and property, and thereby deny him the equal protection of the laws, so that, when the General Government attempts to do for the protection of the citizen what the State has failed to do, it is to be held an interference with the rights of the State?[34]

As the House debates indicate, the proponents believed that the Fourteenth Amendment authorized Congress and the federal judiciary to protect both procedural and substantive due process rights against official indifference to private misconduct. While the members disagreed about the scope of the amendment, they understood that the due process clause imposed substantive limits on state government.

Unlike the House debates, Senate consideration of H.R. 320 does not further illuminate its authors' original understanding. Only two advocates, Senators Edmunds (the floor manager) and John Pool (Whig-N.C.), expressed their views on the states' failure to enforce due process rights. Pool

31. *Id.* (March 31), 368.
32. *Id.*, 370. Monroe asked rhetorically: "In case life and liberty are insecure in any State, and that State virtually denies the necessary protection, are we still to be told that even now the Constitution does not confer upon Congress sufficient power to provide for this emergency?"
33. *Id.*, 375. See also Flack, *Adoption of the Fourteenth Amendment*, 237.
34. *Cong. Globe*, 42d Cong., 1st Sess. 448 (April 4, 1871).

averred that the states have an obligation to enforce the right to personal liberty and security,[35] and he had no doubt about congressional power to remedy the states' failure as well as their active deprivation of due process rights.

Later in the debate, Edmunds asserted that in the eight hundred years since the Magna Carta, government had an obligation to protect the citizen's rights and liberties. He argued that this governmental duty is affirmative rather than "a mere denial of the right of a State to interfere with life, liberty, and property, and to prevent due redress."[36] Obviously referring to the Fourteenth Amendment, Senator Edmunds concluded that the national government had the power to protect citizens should local officials tolerate or knowingly wink at deprivations of fundamental rights.[37]

The congressional debates suggest that the right to physical security and the right to acquire, enjoy, and dispose of property are so fundamental that they deserve statutory protection against inaction as well as against state action. The framers recognized that in the face of private conspiracies and open rebellion, state and local officials might be unable or unwilling to afford protection for civil rights. Thus they provided for the exercise of federal executive, military, and judicial power under those conditions to secure both life and property. While some members of Congress expressed a broad view of fundamental rights, most of the proponents who expressed their opinions believed that Congress had the authority to protect the physical security, personal liberty, and property of individuals.

The consensus that emerged in the Forty-second Congress was similar to the moderate approach that prevailed in drafting the Civil Rights Act of 1866 and the Fourteenth Amendment. As a minimum, section one of the Fourteenth Amendment encompasses protection for the basic rights that Justice Washington enumerated in *Corfield v. Coryell*, foremost among which is protection for life, liberty, and property. Section one of the Civil Rights Act of 1866 enumerated these rights in specific terms. Reenacted in 1870, the 1866 act defined the essence of civil liberty and afforded statutory protection against burdensome state legislation and other actions.

35. *Id.* (April 12), 608. Pool commented: "The protection of the laws can hardly be denied except by failure to execute them. . . . Rights conferred by laws are worthless unless the laws be executed. The right to personal liberty or personal security can be protected only by the execution of the laws upon those who violate such rights. A failure to punish the offender is not only to deny to the person injured the protection of the laws, but to deprive him, in effect, of the rights themselves."

36. *Id.* (April 14), 697.

37. *Id.*, 697, 698.

The Enforcement Act of 1871 extended protection for fundamental rights into a twilight zone in which state actors, typically county and municipal law enforcement officers, failed or refused to exercise their authority to secure the individual's constitutional rights although they were aware of private deprivations of life and property. In exercising its enforcement powers, Congress employed civil and criminal penalties to encourage state actors to perform their affirmative constitutional duties to protect life, liberty, and property rights. As a deterrent to official complicity, the Ku Klux Klan Act gave state and local officials an opportunity to enforce the law, while increasing the likelihood of federal judicial and military intervention.

In addition to casting light on the core rights that the Fourteenth Amendment protects, the House and Senate debates on H.R. 320 yield four important propositions concerning the state-action doctrine. First, the proponents believed that the framers of the Fourteenth Amendment contemplated both state action and inaction depriving individuals of their constitutional rights; second, that the states and the national government have an affirmative duty or obligation to protect the citizen's constitutional rights; third, that when the states fail to act Congress has adequate authority under section five of the Fourteenth Amendment to enforce these rights; and fourth, that H.R. 320 was intended to remedy the states' failure to protect all persons in the enjoyment of their constitutional rights. The authors of the Enforcement Act assumed that the Fourteenth Amendment imposes both constitutional limitations and affirmative duties on state actors—legislative, executive, and judicial—to secure fundamental rights. Although the framers of the Enforcement Act did not intend to alter the federal system radically, they greatly expanded federal jurisdiction and provided judicial remedies to secure life, liberty, and property rights.

The Public Accommodations Act of 1875

If the Enforcement Act represented an expansion of federal power, the opponents of the Public Accommodations Act of 1875 assailed the measure as an invasion of state authority, an attempt to impose social equality between the races, and an intolerable interference with freedom of association. However, both the proponents and the opponents conceded that fundamental rights or the privileges and immunities of citizenship encompassed protection of life, liberty, and property. First introduced in 1871 by Senator

Charles Sumner, a longtime champion of the freedmen's rights, the bill provided for equal access to public schools, churches, cemeteries, and state and federal juries, as well as to public transportation and places of public accommodation.[38]

During the five years that Congress considered Sumner's public accommodations bill, the measure faced formidable opposition. As finally adopted in 1875, the act provided more limited protection than the original bill. The Public Accommodations Act stated:

> All persons within the jurisdiction of the United States shall be entitled to the full and equal enjoyment of the accommodations, advantages, facilities, and privileges of inns, public conveyances on land and water, theaters, and other places of public amusement; subject only to the conditions and limitations established by law, and applicable alike to citizens of every race and color, regardless of any previous condition of servitude.[39]

Congress granted the federal courts exclusive jurisdiction to hear criminal complaints arising under the act, with a right of appeal to the Supreme Court. The act also conferred concurrent state and federal jurisdiction over civil penalties.[40] The Public Accommodations Act created specific rights and remedies that its framers drew largely, but not exclusively, from the states' common law.

Although the Forty-first Congress took no action, Charles Sumner reintroduced the measure (as S. 99) in 1871. He articulated the bill's remedial purpose by commenting on the experience of his black colleague Hiram Revels (R-Miss.), who could not "travel to his home as you can without being insulted on account of his color."[41] "How can the Republican party turn to their colored fellow-citizens for their votes," Sumner asked, "when they leave them to be insulted, as they are now, whenever they travel upon

38. *Cong. Globe*, 41st Cong., 2d Sess. 3434 (1870). Although the text of S. 916 is not reprinted, Sumner summarized the bill's contents. On the Public Accommodations Act, see also Flack, *Adoption of the Fourteenth Amendment*; Robert J. Harris, *The Quest for Equality: The Constitution, Congress, and the Supreme Court* (Baton Rouge: Louisiana State University Press, 1960); and Hyman, *A More Perfect Union*.

39. Ch. 114, 18 Stat. 335, 336 (1875).

40. *Id.*, 336, 337. Section two authorized aggrieved individuals to bring suit either in a state court or a federal court. Once having elected a course of action, the moving party was barred from proceeding to another jurisdiction.

41. *Cong. Globe*, 42d Cong., 1st Sess. 21 (1871).

a railway or enter a hotel?"[42] Sumner advanced a broad conception of liberty and equality, to which freedom of movement or locomotion was essential.

If the concept of liberty has an irreducible meaning, Sumner emphasized, it encompasses freedom of movement. Drawing on Blackstone, he observed:

> Next to personal security, the law of England regards, asserts, and preserves, the personal liberty of individuals. This personal liberty consists in the power of locomotion, of changing situation, or moving one's person to whatsoever place one's own inclination may direct, without imprisonment or restraint, unless by due course of law.[43]

Equal access to means of public transportation and places of public accommodation is indispensable to freedom of movement.[44] As an active member of the Congress that adopted the Civil Rights Act of 1866, Charles Sumner was aware of the conceptions of liberty that animated the earlier debates. However, Sumner did not explicitly link constitutional liberty, freedom of locomotion, and equal access to public transportation and places of public accommodation during his struggle to pass the Public Accommodations Act.

During the long battle to enact a bill, the proponents generally argued that the Fourteenth Amendment comprehended equal access to public transportation and places of public accommodation either as a fundamental civil right or as a privilege and immunity of citizenship, sometimes using those terms interchangeably. Rather than creating new substantive rights and liabilities, the proponents observed, they were simply attempting to protect individual liberty in the face of the states' inability or refusal to enforce their own common-law responsibilities. The proponents denied that they were attempting to adopt primary legislation interfering with state authority to regulate their citizens' private conduct. The proposed public accommodations bill, the proponents insisted, was a remedial measure de-

42. Id.
43. Blackstone, *Commentaries*, bk. 1, ch. 1, 123.
44. In the context of a discussion of trespass, Blackstone notes that the law of trespass does not usually apply to inns, which are places of public accommodation. Blackstone's statement rests on the theory that an inn or a public house is a business affected with a public interest and that access to such places of public accommodation is essential to freedom of movement around the country, given the rudimentary nature of transportation in England at the time. *Id.*, bk. 3, ch. 12, 1009–10.

signed to overcome the states' failure to protect rights that both the Fourteenth Amendment and the Civil Rights Act of 1866 contemplated.

During the debates in the Forty-third Congress, Representative William Lawrence (R-Ohio) argued that the states had a common-law duty to ensure equal access to common carriers.[45] According to Lawrence, the Fourteenth Amendment anticipated the failure of public officials to secure equal protection for civil rights. "There are sins of omission as well as commission," he observed.[46] The states have an obligation to protect all of the privileges and immunities of citizenship, he emphasized, including the equal benefit of law. Among these is the common-law duty of common carriers to "carry all orderly and well-conditioned persons."[47] Quoting from Story, Representative Lawrence noted:

> The first and most general obligation on their [the common carriers'] part is, to carry passengers whenever they offer themselves and are ready to pay for their transportation. . . . [T]hey are no more at liberty to refuse a passenger, if they have sufficient room and accommodation, than an inn-keeper is to refuse suitable room and accommodation to a guest.[48]

The failure to enforce this common-law duty constituted a breach of equal protection for the liberty of locomotion. Thus Lawrence concluded that the proposed public accommodations bill was an appropriate remedy for an evil that Congress had contemplated in adopting the Fourteenth Amendment and the Civil Rights Act of 1866.[49]

In the early stages of the legislative struggle, opponents assailed the bill as an interference with individual liberty. During the Forty-second Congress, Senator Allen Thurman (D-Ohio) and Representatives James Blair (R-Mo.) and Henry McHenry (D-Ky.) attacked various versions of the public accommodations bill as a threat to freedom of association and conscience. The "true idea of civil liberty," Thurman argued, is freedom from government restraint. Only an important governmental purpose such as protection of the public peace and safety could justify interfering with individ-

45. Debates on H.R. 796, 43d Cong., 1st Sess. (1874), 2 *Cong. Rec.* 412 (1874). Lawrence had served during the Thirty-ninth Congress, which drafted the Fourteenth Amendment, the Freedman's Bureau Extension Act, and the Civil Rights Act of 1866.

46. *Id.*

47. *Id.*

48. *Id.* See Story, *Commentaries,* § 591.

49. 2 *Cong. Rec.* 413 (1874).

uals' "liberty to choose their own associates in places of public amusement, in the church, or in the school."[50]

Following the Supreme Court's decision in The Slaughterhouse Cases in April 1873,[51] opponents of the proposed legislation shifted their tactics somewhat, emphasizing that the bill intruded on the reserved powers of the states. Referring to Slaughterhouse specifically, Representative John T. Harris (D-Va.) claimed that the rights encompassed in the public accommodations bill were neither civil rights nor privileges and immunities of national citizenship. The Fourteenth Amendment, Harris observed, leaves the states free "to manage their internal policy as to them shall seem best, only guaranteeing to each citizen of the United States the same protection of life, liberty, and property guaranteed to its [each state's] own citizens."[52] Since the southern states had not passed laws abridging the privileges and immunities of U.S. citizens, the proposed legislation sought to regulate private conduct, which, he stressed, is beyond the competence of Congress under the Fourteenth Amendment.[53] Although he conceded that the privileges or immunities clause embodied the fundamental rights of life, liberty, and property,[54] Harris simply ignored the failure of the states to enforce the

50. Cong. Globe, 42d Cong., 2d Sess. 27 (1872). Thurman's analysis could be applied to subsequent Jim Crow laws that prevented individuals from freely associating with one another on the basis of race. See also the statements of Representatives Blair, id., A 144, and McHenry, id., A 219.

51. In Slaughterhouse, 83 U.S. (16 Wall.) (1873), the Supreme Court held that the privilege of operating a slaughterhouse is a privilege of state rather than national citizenship. Sustaining the Louisiana statute in question, Justice Miller noted that the purpose of the Fourteenth Amendment was to confer citizenship on the Negro and to give definition to the privileges and immunities of national citizenship. In defining these privileges and immunities, Miller relied on Justice Washington's opinion in Corfield v. Coryell. Slaughterhouse is particularly significant because it was the Supreme Court's first interpretation of the Fourteenth Amendment.

52. 2 Cong. Rec. 376 (1874).

53. Harris's criticism anticipated the Supreme Court's narrow construction of "state action" in The Civil Rights Cases, 109 U.S. 3 (1883), by almost a decade. In these five cases the United States brought actions under the Public Accommodations Act of 1875 against four private parties and a railroad company for denying blacks equal access to facilities covered under the act. In declaring the act unconstitutional, as applied, the Court held that section five of the Fourteenth Amendment could not authorize Congress to prohibit private discrimination. Congress has only remedial power to redress state legislation or action in violation of the Fourteenth Amendment. Thus the Supreme Court narrowed the scope of congressional authority to redress the states' failure to enforce their own statutory and common-law duties.

54. 2 Cong. Rec. 376 (1874). Once again referring to Slaughterhouse, Harris remarked: "The amendment to the Constitution guarantees to the colored race, as to all others, the privileges and immunities of a citizen of the United States. The majority and minority of the court both concur in definition of these terms—that they mean 'the fundamental rights of life, liberty, and property.'"

common-law duty of common carriers and places of public accommodation to provide equal access to all persons.

In defining the privileges and immunities of citizenship, Harris relied on Justice Samuel F. Miller's *Slaughterhouse* opinion,[55] which embodied Justice Washington's definition of the term in *Corfield*. Quoting from *Corfield*, Miller acknowledged that among the fundamental privileges and immunities of national citizenship is the right to governmental protection for life and property. However, Washington also ranked liberty on the same plane with life and property as fundamental rights.[56] As he recognized, the essential purpose of the privileges and immunities clause (Article Four, section two) was to protect freedom of movement from state to state by ensuring that travelers would receive the same treatment as a state's citizens with regard to protection of fundamental rights of life, liberty, and property.[57] Repre-

55. 83 U.S. (16 Wall.).

56. Commenting on the fundamental principles underlying the privileges and immunities clause of Article Four, Washington wrote: "They may, however, be all comprehended under the following general heads: Protection by the government; the enjoyment of *life and liberty*, with the right to acquire and possess property of every kind, and to pursue happiness and safety; subject nevertheless to such restraints as the government may justly prescribe for the general good of the whole." 6 F.Cas. 546 (C.C. E.D. Pa. 1823) (No. 3230), 551–52 (emphasis added). In *Slaughterhouse*, Miller misquotes Washington's opinion, omitting two important phrases. First, he omitted "the enjoyment of life and liberty"; second, he deleted "justly." *Slaughterhouse*, 83 U.S., 76. On the possible explanations for Miller's two pregnant omissions, see Robert C. Palmer, "The Parameters of Constitutional Reconstruction: *Slaughter-House, Cruikshank*, and the Fourteenth Amendment," 1984 *U. Ill. L. Rev.* (1984) 739–770, 753–56.

The omissions were significant, because both terms served to qualify the states' authority to restrict liberty. The term "justly" can be read as a reasonableness or rational-relation requirement—that is, state regulations of constitutionally protected life, liberty, and property rights must be reasonable or rationally related to the states' exercise of their police, tax, and eminent domain powers. Miller's omission is also significant because he indicates that the Court relied on Washington's definition of privileges and immunities in such recent decisions as *Ward v. Maryland*, 79 U.S. (12 Wall.) 418 (1871); *Paul v. Virginia*, 75 U.S. (8 Wall.) 168 (1869); and *Crandall v. Nevada*, 73 U.S. (6 Wall.) 35 (1868). 83 U.S. (16 Wall.), 76–79. Thus Justice Washington's opinion became dispositive of the law of the land in these cases.

It is interesting that Justice Field (dissenting) quoted Washington's circuit opinion accurately, including the terms Miller had omitted. He noted that Senator Trumbull had relied on Washington's conception of privileges and immunities in the debates on the Civil Rights Act of 1866. However, Field did not point out Miller's omissions or their implications for the majority's decision.

57. Dissenting, Justice Field argued that the Fourteenth Amendment placed a core of rights under national protection. The creation of a monopoly, which was not reasonably related to a legitimate public-health objective, represented an unacceptable interference with the right of free people to pursue their lawful callings. For Field, the Fourteenth Amendment protected every individual's right to pursue an occupation, acquire and dispose of property, and to make lawful contracts regarding labor and property. See Field (dissenting), 83 U.S. (16 Wall.), 87–88, 88–89, 90–92. During the next seventeen years, Field eventually secured a majority for

sentative Harris refused to acknowledge that Senator Sumner sought to protect the same fundamental right of all persons to travel freely throughout the United States.

Although the protagonists disputed the authority of Congress to enact primary legislation, they shared the belief that life, liberty, and property are fundamental rights that deserve governmental protection. During the Forty-third Congress, Senator Frederick T. Frelinghuysen (R-N.J.), an advocate of the bill (H.R. 796), argued that the primary remedial objective was to protect the privileges and immunities of national citizenship. Citing *Corfield*, Frelinghuysen noted that among these privileges is the right to equal protection for life, liberty, and property.[58] Supporting Frelinghuysen's position, Senator Timothy Howe (R-Wis.) observed that the right to travel is a basic privilege or immunity of national citizenship. Howe also claimed that the Fourteenth Amendment authorized Congress to secure equal protection for such fundamental rights against state interference. Emphasizing the higher-law philosophy of the Declaration of Independence, he concluded that the essential purpose of government is to secure equal protection for the inalienable rights of life, liberty, and the pursuit of happiness.[59]

Senator Thomas Norwood (D-Ga.), one of the bill's opponents, conceded that citizens of the United States have a right "to life, liberty, and property until deprived thereof by due process of law,"[60] but he argued that the states are the primary custodians of those fundamental rights. He attacked the bill as a Republican attempt to manipulate the enforcement power of Congress under the Fourteenth Amendment. Norwood concluded that the measure would vitiate the legislative power of the states, reduce their executives to a shadow, abolish their civil and criminal codes, and transfer civil and criminal cases from state to federal courts, leaving state judges with little more than their robes.[61]

The House debates mirror the divisions that existed in the Senate. Republican representatives claimed that H.R. 796 afforded equal protection for the privileges and immunities of national citizenship, while their Democratic colleagues characterized the bill as primary legislation interfering with

---

his position. For a further analysis of Field's position, see Chapter 5. See also Carl Brent Swisher, *Stephen J. Field: Craftsman of the Law* (Hamden, Conn.: Archon Books, 1963).

58. 2 *Cong. Rec.* 3451, 43d Cong., 1st Sess. (1874).

59. *Id.*, 4147, 4148–49, 4151.

60. *Id.*, A 243.

61. *Id.* Echoing Norwood's position, Senator James Kelly (D-Or.) recognized that the privileges and immunities of citizenship encompass protection for life, liberty, and property, but denied that Congress had authority to enact primary legislation to protect these rights. The proposed bill, he concluded, invaded the reserved power of the states. *Id.*, 4164.

the states' exercise of their domestic powers. Representative Robert Elliott (R-S.C.), for example, denied that Justice Miller's *Slaughterhouse* opinion prohibited the bill, since the remedial objective was to ensure equal protection for civil rights. As Elliott noted, Miller had conceded that the Fourteenth Amendment's basic purpose was to secure equal protection for life, liberty, and property against class legislation. Representative Elliott denied that the public accommodations bill added any new substantive rights to the Fourteenth Amendment.[62]

Leading the attack on the public accommodations bill, Representative Harris admitted that fundamental rights include protection for life, liberty, and property, but he denied that the legislation implicated such rights or that the southern states had denied any of the privileges or immunities of national citizenship.[63] Echoing Harris's statement, Roger Mills (D-Texas) confessed that the privileges and immunities clause (Article Four, section two) and the Fourteenth Amendment afforded protection for life, liberty, and property against state interference. In defining the meaning of fundamental rights or privileges and immunities, Representative Mills turned to Justice Story's and Chancellor Kent's *Commentaries* and to Justice Washington's opinion in *Corfield*. As he observed,

> the privileges and immunities mentioned in the fourteenth amendment are only such as conferred by the Constitution itself as the supreme law over all; that they are fundamental, such as lie beneath the very foundation of the Government; that they are fixed and absolute. . . . These privileges are, among others, the right to the enjoyment of life, liberty, property, and the pursuit of happiness.[64]

Since the real objective was social equality, according to Mills, the bill was beyond the remedial powers of Congress.[65]

62. *Id.*, 410. Following Elliott's speech on January 5, 1874, the next day (January 6), Representative Lawrence delivered his speech asserting that the states had a responsibility to enforce the common-law duties of railroads and places of public accommodation to provide equal access without regard to race or color. Referring specifically to Elliott's remarks, Lawrence asserted that the proposed bill was appropriate legislation (under section five) to enforce one of the civil rights that the Fourteenth Amendment protected. Adopting the measure, he concluded, "is simple justice." *Id.*, 412, 414. Several other representatives, including Josiah Walls (R-Fla.), William Stowell (R-Va.), and Ben Butler (R-Mass.), urged passage of the bill as an appropriate means to ensure equal protection for life, liberty, and property. *Id.*, 416, 426–27, 455, 455–56.

63. *Id.*, 376.

64. *Id.*, 384.

65. *Id.* Throughout the debates in the Forty-third Congress, 1st session (from December

Throughout the Forty-third Congress the terms of debate changed little. Republicans continued to claim authority for the bill under the privileges and immunities clause, while Democrats opposed the legislation as a regulation of private conduct and an invasion of the states' reserved power. However, some Democrats conceded that the Fourteenth Amendment granted Congress power to enact remedial legislation protecting life, liberty, and property rights against burdensome state action. After five years, on March 1, 1875, Senator Sumner's bill became the law of the land, which the Supreme Court nullified eight years later in *The Civil Rights Cases* (1883).

Despite the Supreme Court's narrow construction of the Fourteenth Amendment in such decisions as *The Slaughterhouse Cases* (1873) and *The Civil Rights Cases* (1883), during the 1870s Congress interpreted its powers to enforce the amendment liberally. In the Civil Rights Act of 1870, the Ku Klux Klan Act of 1871, and the Public Accommodations Act of 1875, Congress extended federal judicial and executive power to protect life, liberty, and property interests throughout the United States. Although the Democrats and some Republicans opposed extending the power of the national government, a congressional majority adopted legislation that anticipated the states' failure as well as their interference with equal protection for the individual's physical security, personal liberty, and property interests. The civil rights acts targeted all state actors—legislators, executives, judges, and local law enforcement officials—who deprived individuals of these fundamental rights through legislation, judicial decision, and administrative policy, indifference, and collusion.

In addition to relying on natural law and social-contract theory, the drafters of the Public Accommodations Act believed that the Fourteenth Amendment embodied a common-law understanding of fundamental rights in the Constitution. Under the amendment the states had a common-law and statutory-law duty to afford equal protection for constitutional life, liberty, and property rights. And those who drafted the legislation argued that section five of the Fourteenth Amendment afforded Congress sufficient remedial authority to protect fundamental common-law rights in the event that the states failed to meet their affirmative duties.

Slaughterhouse to the contrary and with few exceptions, congressional Re-

---

1873 through June 1874), the Democratic chorus sang this common refrain. See, for example, the statements of Representatives Milton Durham (D-Ky.), 405–6; William Herndon (D-Texas), 419–21; John Atkins (D-Tenn.), 453–55; Milton Southard (D-Ohio), A 1–A 3; John M. Glover (D-Mo.), A 4–A 5; and William Read (D-Ky.), A 342–A 343.

publicans believed that the privileges or immunities, due process, and equal protection clauses prohibited the states from exercising their police, tax, and eminent domain powers arbitrarily vis-à-vis fundamental rights. Although the authors of civil rights legislation acknowledged a legitimate state authority to promote the public health, safety, welfare, and morals, they believed that the Fourteenth Amendment limited the states' reserved power under the Tenth Amendment. Therefore, in the Removal Act of 1875 and various civil rights acts, Congress authorized the federal courts to exercise their jurisdiction and powers of judicial review as custodians of the individual's constitutional rights. Insofar as the drafters recognized that the Eleventh Amendment immunized the states against suit in federal courts, they authorized civil and criminal actions against state agents who abuse official power.[66]

In *Slaughterhouse* Justice Miller denied that the privileges and immunities of national citizenship embrace the liberty to engage in the common callings or professions. During the Reconstruction Era, however, some senators and representatives articulated a constitutional order of free and autonomous individuals who have a fundamental right to define and pursue their own interests, acquire property, support themselves and their families, develop their professions, and fulfill their personal ambitions, consistent with the public welfare. Dissenting in *Slaughterhouse*, Justice Stephen J. Field reflected this philosophy of individual freedom. For Field, liberty to contract one's labor or services was but a means to ensure every person's fundamental right to develop his full human potential. In the United States, free government, concluded Field, is one "under which the inalienable right of every citizen to pursue his happiness is unrestrained, except by just, equal, and impartial laws."[67] While Field could not persuade a majority of his brethren to adopt this conception of liberty in 1873, eventually his views triumphed in the 1890s. Frustrated by the Court's emasculation of the privi-

66. The Supreme Court has construed the Eleventh Amendment to prohibit a state's citizens as well as the citizens of other states from suing a state government in federal court without its permission. See *Hans* v. *Louisiana*, 134 U.S. 1 (1890). However, the Court also has held that a state's agents may be liable for actions taken under color of law that violate an individual's constitutional rights. Since a state can act only through its agents, the distinction is judicial legerdemain, an evasion of the Eleventh Amendment's doctrine of sovereign immunity.

67. 83 U.S. (16 Wall.), 111. Quoting from Sharswood's edition of Blackstone's *Commentaries*, Field observed: "'Civil liberty,' the great end of all human society and government, is that state in which each individual has the power to pursue his own happiness according to his own views of his interest, and the dictates of his conscience, unrestrained, except by equal, just and impartial laws." *Id.*, n. 1. See Swisher, *Field*, 416–20.

leges or immunities clause, Stephen Field, Joseph Bradley,[68] and other justices turned to the due process clauses of the Fifth and Fourteenth Amendments as sources of substantive restraint on the police power.

68. Also dissenting in *Slaughterhouse*, Bradley, with Chief Justice Chase and Justice
Swayne, foresaw the possibilities that the due process clause offered for the protection of life,
liberty, and property interests. He argued that the due process clause has a substantive component that limits the states' exercise of power vis-à-vis fundamental rights. Bradley turned to
the pre–Civil War political and constitutional theory of natural right, natural law, and social
contract as well as the common law in defining substantive limitations. He also anticipated
the problems that Blackstone's absolutist views of life, liberty, and property rights would pose
for the legitimate exercise of the states' police powers. Like Justice Washington, he recognized
the need to accommodate competing liberty and property interests in a complex social order.
83 U.S. (16 Wall.), 111–19.

5

The Supreme Court, the Public Interest, and Economic Liberty, 1873–1921

In the thirty-five years following the Civil War, the United States became a transcontinental nation linked by railroad and telegraph. Between 1865 and 1900 the public corporation emerged as the dominant form of industrial capitalism. A new wave of immigrants landed in Boston, New York, Philadelphia, Chicago, and other cities. Looking for economic opportunity, the new immigrants, largely from southern and eastern Europe, became the backbone of America's industrial labor force. The nation's cities began to grow like Topsy, formerly serene residential neighborhoods cheek to jowl with noisy and dirty industrial quarters.

Confronted with the problems of urbanization, industrialization, economic integration, and concentrations of wealth, the states and the federal government employed their respective powers to accommodate the new industrial order. The states attempted to ameliorate the effects of the machine age, market distortions, rapid urban growth, and the arrival of millions of immigrants by enacting worker compensation laws, wages-and-hours regulations, mine-safety statutes, public-health inspection laws, consumer-protection statutes, and railway and public-utility rates and regulations, among other measures. Cities adopted zoning codes, erected public works, and created new municipal services attempting to accommodate urban growth. Bowing to pressure for reform, Congress adopted the Interstate Commerce Commission Act (1887) and the Sherman Antitrust Act (1890), although it is not clear whether any major changes were expected. These reforms may have advanced the public welfare, but they often gave particular groups an advantage and placed new restrictions on property and economic liberty.

During the Gilded Age a struggle developed between economic individualism and governmental regulation of business, industry, and agriculture. As Congress and the state legislatures flexed their regulatory muscles, the Supreme Court took an increasingly dim view of attempts to interfere with economic liberty. Although the Waite Court (1874–88) usually was deferential to the states' exercise of their police, tax, and eminent domain powers, Justices Stephen J. Field and Joseph Bradley questioned public interference with vested property rights and the individual's liberty to make labor contracts. As early as 1873, Field and Bradley began to articulate principles of substantive due process that would become an important judicial vehicle for promoting both economic growth and liberty. By the late 1890s some members of the Fuller Court (1888–1910) used Field's laissez-faire constitutional principles to justify maximum economic liberty and minimum government interference in the marketplace.[1] Field's views, however, should not be confused with later Social Darwinism, which was employed to justify greed, corruption, and concentrations of economic power that undermined liberty, equality, and market freedom.

Reacting to the Waite Court's deference to legislative policies concerning the public health, safety, welfare, and morals, between 1873 and 1888 Justice Field forged a coalition that criticized the majority's construction of the police power of the states. He argued that the Fifth and Fourteenth Amend-

---

1. As recent scholarship suggests, post–Civil War jurists and legal scholars such as Stephen J. Field, Joseph Bradley, Thomas F. Cooley, Francis Wharton, John Norton Pomeroy, Christopher G. Tiedeman, John Appleton, and Joel Parker believed that the Fourteenth Amendment embodied substantive restraints on the states' police power. These jurists and scholars derived their views from the classical economic, common-law, and natural-law theories prevalent at the time the amendment was framed. From their perspective, the Fourteenth Amendment protected the individual's liberty against arbitrary conduct by the state. See, for example, Benedict, 3 *Law & Hist. Rev.* 293–331. See also Herbert Hovenkamp, "The Political Economy of Substantive Due Process," 40 *Stan. L. Rev.* 379–447 (1988) (hereafter Hovenkamp, 40 *Stan. L. Rev.*), and Thomas R. Haggard, "Work, Government, and the Constitution: Determining the Proper Allocation of Rights and Powers," in *Liberty, Property, and the Future of Constitutional Development*, ed. Ellen F. Paul and Howard Dickman (Albany: SUNY Press, 1990).

ments embodied unenumerated rights derived from the Anglo-American common-law and natural-law traditions, which imposed constitutional limitations on Congress and the state legislatures. Sometimes concurring, at other times dissenting, Stephen Field crafted the legal concepts of constitutional limitations and the police power that triumphed during his tenure on the Supreme Court.[2] Field and Bradley conceded that the states could limit economic liberty and property rights for valid public purposes. But they could not use the tax and police powers to adopt class legislation, favoring a particular group, unless the law also advanced the public health, safety, welfare, or morals.[3] As a Jacksonian Democrat, Stephen Field opposed monopolies, exclusive franchises, and special privileges because they were forms of class legislation that perverted public authority and blocked economic opportunity, without advancing the general welfare.[4]

Like Thomas Cooley and John Appleton, Field denied that the state had constitutional authority to redistribute property among private parties. He described such legislation as unreasonable (i.e., partial) because it did not serve a public purpose within the bounds of the police power or the taxing power. As his opinions demonstrate, Justice Field believed that the due process clause imposed substantive limits on the exercise of the police power

2. Strong, 15 Ariz. L. Rev., 424–25. See also Hyman and Wiecek, Equal Justice Under Law, 336, 349, 350, 353–55. During and after the Civil War, legal theory began to advance the Court's role as a restraint on erring legislative majorities. As Hovenkamp notes, Field's jurisprudence coincided with the publication of Francis Wharton's Commentaries on Law (1864), Thomas M. Cooley's Constitutional Limitations (1868), John Norton Pomeroy's Introduction to the Constitutional Law of the United States (1886), and Christopher G. Tiedeman's Treatise on the Limitations of Police Power in the United States (1886). See Hovenkamp, 40 Stan. L. Rev., 396–97.

3. See Note, "Resurrecting Economic Rights: The Doctrine of Economic Due Process Reconsidered," 103 Harv. L. Rev. 1363–83 (1990), 1369–70. The author argues that economic liberty and property rights were among the most important natural rights that the framers of the Fourteenth Amendment and the Civil Rights Act of 1866 sought to protect. As Hovenkamp notes, most of the rights that the Civil Rights Act of 1866 protected were economic in nature. See Hovenkamp, 40 Stan. L. Rev., 395–96. See also James W. Ely Jr., The Guardian of Every Other Right: A Constitutional History of Property Rights (New York: Oxford University Press, 1992), 3–4. Throughout U.S. history, Ely observes, property rights and economic liberty have been essential elements of American constitutionalism. In the Lockean tradition, American constitutionalists regarded the protection of property as government's essential function. The Fourteenth Amendment created new possibilities for oversight of state legislation affecting property and economic liberty. Id., 82.

4. Nelson, The Fourteenth Amendment, 156–58. Field advanced a moderate view of the Fourteenth Amendment that reconciled liberty and property rights with local self-government and the public welfare. Id., 164.

that were designed to keep the public and private spheres separate. He sought to preserve the state as a neutral umpire in the economic realm. A neutral state could neither favor particular interests nor be exploited by them to the detriment of the public welfare.[5]

The Rise and Evolution of Substantive Due Process

The *Slaughterhouse Cases*[6] epitomize the differences between Samuel Miller's and Stephen Field's conceptions of the police power. Miller characterized the Louisiana monopoly statute, which granted an exclusive franchise to the Crescent City Live-Stock Landing & Slaughterhouse Company to slaughter all livestock in the City of New Orleans, as a reasonable police measure.[7] Field viewed the law as class legislation that favored the monopoly's economic interests to the detriment of small, independent butchers. In fact, the statute was both a police measure and a forced transfer of property.[8]

By construing the police power broadly and the Thirteenth and Fourteenth Amendments narrowly, Miller sustained the legislature's discretionary authority to determine the public welfare. Absent a clear constitutional breach, legislatures rather than the courts, he argued, must decide the wisdom or utility of policy.[9] Because utility (i.e., the calculation of the greatest

5. See Howard Gillman, *The Constitution Besieged: The Rise and Demise of Lochner Era Police Power Jurisprudence* (Durham, N.C.: Duke University Press, 1993), 55–58, 61–63, 66–67. See also Hovenkamp, 40 *Stan. L. Rev.*, 380, 387–89, and Strong, *Substantive Due Process*, 79–80, 91–92.

6. 83 U.S. (16 Wall.) 36 (1873).

7. *Id.*, 59–61. The Act to Protect the Health of the City of New Orleans, etc., provided that all slaughtering was to be done in a central slaughterhouse south of New Orleans. For a fee, butchers could slaughter livestock at the facility. The act regulated the maximum fees that the company could charge. Representing the butchers, John Campbell argued that the right to pursue a lawful calling, to use one's faculties and enjoy the fruits of one's labor, is a fundamental right of national citizenship. Therefore, monopoly is opposed to the principle of liberty insofar as it prevents individuals from pursuing previously lawful callings and using their property for lawful purposes. *Id.*, 45–57. Representing Louisiana, T. J. Durant and Matthew Carpenter claimed that neither the Thirteenth nor the Fourteenth Amendment prohibited the state from granting an exclusive charter.

8. Benedict, 3 *Law & Hist. Rev.*, 328.

9. *Id.*, 74–77. Because the creation of a monopoly to promote the public health is not a form of servitude, the act did not violate the Thirteenth Amendment. Furthermore, Miller argued, the privilege of conducting a trade is not a privilege and immunity of national citizenship. It is a privilege of state citizenship, which must yield to considerations of the public welfare. The act was a legitimate exercise of the state's police power, which is an open-ended

good for the greatest number) is the measure of policymaking in a democracy, popularly accountable legislators should make judgments about the collective welfare. However, when utility conflicts with constitutional limitations, should policy yield to principle or vice versa? Justice Miller answered the question: "Unless, therefore, it can be maintained that the exclusive privilege granted by this charter to the corporation, is beyond the power of the legislature of Louisiana, there can be no just exception to the validity of the statute."[10]

Dissenting, Stephen Field defended economic liberty against monopoly and privilege disguised as the collective welfare. Looking behind the legislature's ostensible purpose, he denied that the statute was a legitimate exercise of the police power. For the most part, the law was a mercantilist regulation that transferred wealth and economic opportunity from one group to another. Only two provisions, noted Field, advanced the public health and safety. The first required the landing and slaughtering of all livestock south of New Orleans. The second required that all livestock be inspected before being slaughtered. In all other respects, the act was a grant of an exclusive privilege, repugnant to individual liberty, as embodied in the Constitution, in common law, and in the Declaration of Independence.[11] Moreover, the statute was a perversion of the police power since it furthered a particular interest rather than the public welfare.

With his dissent in *Slaughterhouse*, Field began to articulate a theory of constitutional limitations and unenumerated fundamental rights that characterized his major contribution to American public law.[12] In the absence of

---

grant incapable of precise definition. *Id.*, 62. For an analysis of Miller's view, see Kendrick, *Journal*, 22–23, 24, 24–26. See also Paludan, *Covenant with Death*, 269, 270–71. But see Herbert Hovenkamp, *Enterprise and American Law, 1836–1937* (Cambridge, Mass.: Harvard University Press, 1991). *Slaughterhouse* was in part a mercantilist decision that restricted economic opportunity and transferred wealth from one group to another. *Id.*, 4.

10. 83 U.S. (16 Wall.), 65. Although Miller conceded that the wisdom of granting a monopoly could be questioned, he denied that the act destroyed either a vested property right or a liberty interest. *Id.*, 61–62.

11. As Field wrote, "under the pretense of prescribing a police regulation the state cannot be permitted to encroach upon any of the just rights of the citizen, which the Constitution intended to secure against abridgement." *Id.*, 87. But see Hovenkamp, *Enterprise and American Law*, 116–22, who quarrels with the interpretation that the monopoly statute was merely special interest legislation.

12. Edward S. Corwin describes Field as the principal architect of judicial protection of individual liberties. Edward S. Corwin, "The Supreme Court and the Fourteenth Amendment," 7 *Mich. L. Rev.* 643–72 (1909), 652, 652–53, 653–54, 655 (hereafter Corwin, 7 *Mich. L. Rev.*). Robert Cushman and Howard Graham also recognized Field's influence on the evolution of substantive due process. Howard J. Graham, "Justice Field and the Fourteenth

a public purpose, the state cannot prohibit individuals from pursuing a previously lawful common calling. The state's denial of the right to engage in a lawful business or profession was a form of servitude, which the Thirteenth Amendment prohibited. Monopolies deny the privilege of all free persons to enjoy the fruits of their labor, which is a right secured by the Fourteenth Amendment and the Civil Rights Act of 1866. According to Field, the amendment protected a core of fundamental rights, of persons and property, from arbitrary and unreasonable state action—that is, from laws that are partial and are not clearly related to a public purpose.[13]

Referring to Justice Washington's opinion in *Corfield* v. *Coryell* (1823), Field asserted that the enjoyment of life, liberty, and property, subject only to just considerations of the public welfare, was among the privileges and immunities of national citizenship. Distinguishing the fundamental rights of citizens in a free society from the special privileges that the states may confer on their citizens, Field asserted that the Fourteenth Amendment placed these common rights under national protection. Although the right to engage in a lawful calling was not enumerated in the Fourteenth Amendment or in the Civil Rights Act, Field argued that the framers understood this right to be among the unenumerated privileges of national citizenship.[14]

Liberty to pursue a lawful calling was constitutionally protected and indispensable to the prosperity of a good society. Quoting from Adam Smith's *Wealth of Nations*, Field observed that the individual's labor is the "foundation of all other property."[15] Moreover, an individual's right to labor and support a family is "sacred and inviolable." Unless an individual injures his or her neighbor, the state should not interfere with the worker's "just liberty." By engaging in lawful callings, individuals define and advance their personal happiness as well as promote the society's wealth and good order. The equal right to pursue all lawful callings, Justice Field concluded, "is the fundamental idea on which our institutions rest, and unless adhered to in the legislation of the country our government will be a republic only in

---

Amendment," 52 *Yale L.J.* 851–89 (1943), 856–57, 888. See also Robert E. Cushman, "The Social and Economic Interpretation of the Fourteenth Amendment," 20 *Mich. L. Rev.* 737–64 (1922), 741–44 (hereafter Cushman, 20 *Mich. L. Rev.*).

13. 83 U.S. (16 Wall.), 87–89, 90–93, 96–97.

14. *Id.*, 97–98, 100–103. According to Field, the amendment's framers understood and accepted the English legal concept that the right to engage in a lawful occupation is a fundamental right—namely, the right to maintain one's self and family. Furthermore, both the common law of England and the civil code of Louisiana condemned monopolies as a deprivation of liberty. *Id.*, 104, 105.

15. *Id.*, 110 n. 1. See Hovenkamp, 40 *Stan. L. Rev.*, 407.

name."[16] According to Field, the Fourteenth Amendment advanced both individual liberty and the general welfare by imposing substantive limits on the police power of the states.

Justice Joseph P. Bradley concurred in Field's dissent but rested his argument on the due process clause. Like Field, Bradley denied that the monopoly statute was related to a public purpose. The law merely enriched one class of individuals at the expense of another. It conferred an exclusive privilege that interfered arbitrarily with the butchers' right to choose a previously lawful calling.[17] Although the due process clause did not explicitly mention the right to pursue common occupations and professions, Bradley regarded this right as both absolute and indispensable to liberty and to property interests.[18] Without any rationale directly related to the public welfare, the law arbitrarily transferred the butchers' constitutionally protected property rights to "a few scheming individuals."[19]

Despite Bradley's concurrence, his absolutist interpretation of fundamental rights would have been far more intrusive on the police power than Field's moderate interpretation of the Fourteenth Amendment. Field suggested a possible accommodation between constitutional limitations and republican determinations of the public welfare in a federal system. As politically accountable institutions, the state legislatures must initially decide questions of utility or the collective welfare. However, legislative policies are subject to judicially enforceable constitutional limitations. In determining whether legislation offends the privileges or immunities and due process clauses, the Supreme Court should give weight to legislative fact-finding and policymaking. But if a statute is devoid of any public purpose, the Court can impose constitutional limitations on the misuse of the police power. When deciding whether a statute is reasonable, the justices can review the legislative record to discover whether there is a clear relationship between the means (in this case, an exclusive grant) and the constitutionally permissible ends (i.e., protecting the public health).

16. 83 U.S. (16 Wall.), 110 n. 1.

17. Id., 119–20.

18. Id., 116. As Ely argues, Bradley's views on property and economic opportunity anticipated the concept of economic due process. See Ely, The Guardian of Every Other Right, 86. Both Bradley and Field believed that property and economic liberty were indispensable to the protection of all other rights. Without security for property and economic opportunity, individuals could not be free, independent, or happy. As John Locke and the classical economists argued, the protection of property was government's primary responsibility. See Hovenkamp, Enterprise and American Law, 68, 71, 74–75.

19. 83 U.S. (16 Wall.), 120.

By treating rights as conditional, Justice Field charted a moderate course between constitutional limitations and republican government.[20] He might be criticized for failing to realize that his views could be used to justify the rapacious or predatory pursuit of wealth during the Gilded Age, but he did not justify either unregulated economic liberty or the use and enjoyment of property to the detriment of the common welfare. His argument for substantive limitations on regulatory power is hardly a call to substitute the law of the survival of the fittest for laws that promote a well-ordered society.

In the years following *Slaughterhouse*, the Waite Court confronted numerous conflicts between the states' exercise of their tax, police, and eminent domain powers and due process claims of vested property rights or economic liberty. These cases involved the power of the states (1) to regulate or prohibit business activity, (2) to determine railroad and public utility rates and conditions of service, and (3) to alter or revoke corporate charters and public-utility franchises. During this period, Justices Field, Bradley, Noah Swayne, and later John M. Harlan attempted to convince their brethren that the due process clauses of the Fifth and Fourteenth Amendments imposed substantive limitations on congressional and state legislative power. Field, in particular, insisted that legislation must serve a public purpose, not the interests of a special class or group.

Following *Slaughterhouse*, the justices sustained the exercise of state police power in several important cases involving vested property rights. In *Bartmeyer* v. *Iowa*[21] the Court validated an Iowa statute prohibiting the sale of liquor. Speaking for the majority, Justice Samuel Miller argued that the law did not abridge a privilege or immunity of national citizenship.[22] Concurring in the decision, Bradley conceded that the prohibition statute was a legitimate police regulation and not an unconstitutional deprivation of property. Unlike *Slaughterhouse*, he concluded, the state merely had prohibited the sale of goods deemed injurious to the public's health and morals. Also concurring, Field contrasted the Iowa statute with the Louisiana monopoly law, which he continued to characterize as unrelated to the protection of the public's health. Since the Iowa prohibition statute was directly related to

20. See Nelson, *The Fourteenth Amendment*, 158–60, 161, 164.

21. 85 U.S. (18 Wall.) 129 (1873). For a discussion of the relationship between the pre–Civil War doctrine of vested property rights and the evolution of economic due process, see Ely, *The Guardian of Every Other Right*, 79–80. See also Benedict, 3 *Law & Hist. Rev.*, 323.

22. 85 U.S. (18 Wall.), 132–33. Adhering to *Wynehamer* v. *New York*, he averred that only a total deprivation of a vested property right would violate the due process clause. Inasmuch as Bartemeyer was not in possession of the liquor at the time the law was enacted, he had not been deprived of a vested property right.

protecting the public morals, Bradley and Field justified the law as a reason-able restraint on the use of property and comparable to the abatement of a public nuisance.[23]

Eleven years later, in *Butchers' Union Co.* v. *Crescent City Co.*, the Su-preme Court again confronted the Louisiana monopoly statute.[24] Speaking for the majority, Miller asserted that no legislature could bargain away, by contract, future legislative authority to enact police measures to promote the public health and morals.[25] Although Field concurred, he observed that the states could not use the police power in derogation of constitutional and natural rights. He also attacked the original monopoly statute as infringing the common-law right to engage in a legitimate trade, a civil liberty pro-tected by the Fourteenth Amendment.[26]

Monopolies, Field emphasized, discourage labor and industry; they pre-vent free people from earning an honest livelihood. Monopoly interferes with "certain inherent rights [that] lie at the foundation of all action."[27] Among these inalienable rights

> is the right of men to pursue their happiness, by which is meant the right to pursue any lawful business or vocation, in any manner not inconsistent with the equal rights of others, which may increase their prosperity or develop their faculties, so as to give them their highest enjoyment.[28]

In addition to infringing a fundamental civil liberty, the monopoly statute was a perversion of the police power, because it merely transferred wealth from one group to another without serving a public purpose.

While Bradley concurred, along with Justices Harlan and William Woods, he acknowledged the states' power to grant public-utility franchises

23. *Id.*, 136, 137, 138.

24. 111 U.S. 746 (1884), 748. This time, however, the Crescent City Company challenged Articles 248 and 258 of the Louisiana Constitution of 1879, which abolished all monopoly charters except for railroad companies. The company claimed that the Louisiana constitution and subsequent municipal ordinances impaired an exclusive grant, which a previous legislature had made.

25. See also Chief Justice Waite's opinion for the Court in *Stone* v. *Mississippi*, 101 U.S. 814 (1880).

26. *Id.*, 755–57. Field embraced both natural law and common law to justify the right to pursue the common callings and engage in freedom of trade.

27. 111 U.S., 756. While Field opposed monopolies in areas previously free, he admitted that the state could regulate the market through exclusive franchises for bridges, ferries, and other public services. Hovenkamp, *Enterprise and American Law*, 113.

28. 111 U.S., 757.

and licenses. He argued, however, that common professions or avocations must be "open to all alike who will prepare themselves with the requisite qualifications, or give the requisite security for preserving public order."[29] Unlike ordinary occupations, the states could restrict the performance of services that government itself might provide. As a requirement for granting an exclusive franchise, the states could establish rates and determine the conditions of service of railroads and public utilities. But they could not use the police power to the advantage of one individual or group over another.

In the so-called Chinese laundry cases, Justice Field continued to elaborate his theory of constitutional limitations, unenumerated fundamental rights, and the police power. Sustaining a San Francisco ordinance that limited the operating hours of laundries, in *Soon Hing* v. *Crowley*[30] Field observed that the liberty to conduct a profession can be regulated by just and impartial laws.[31] He acknowledged that the states could limit the hours of labor, define a day's work, prescribe a shop's closing times, and set Sunday aside as a common day of rest.[32] Refusing to examine legislative motives for enacting the ordinance, Field articulated the rule that facially valid police measures are entitled to great respect, if not presumptive validity.[33] However, speaking for the majority in *Yick Wo* v. *Hopkins*, Stanley Matthews found that the San Francisco ordinance permitted local authorities to make arbitrary and discriminatory (i.e., class) distinctions based on race.[34] The

29. *Id.*, 763. Bradley argued that the legislature had the authority to grant such exclusive franchises "as that of constructing and operating public works, railroads, ferries, &c.," which required public permission. *Id.*

30. 113 U.S. 703 (1885). See also *Barbier* v. *Connolly*, 113 U.S. 27 (1884). The Court sustained the municipal ordinance in both cases.

31. 113 U.S., 709.

32. *Id.*, 710. These regulations could be justified as means to prevent the moral and physical debasement of individuals. As Field wrote, the states' high courts had recognized such regulations as falling within the ambit of the police power since they were enacted for the general welfare.

33. *Id.*, 710–11. He recognized the difficulty of fathoming individual legislators' motives as well as the body's collective motivation. It was futile, he concluded, to penetrate into the "hearts of men," and ascertain their true motives. *Id.*, 711. As Carl Swisher noted, Field's attitude toward the Chinese had changed considerably since the early 1880s. Initially opposed to class legislation directed against the Chinese, by 1885 Field's "decisions were . . . much more frequently against the Chinese." Swisher, *Field*, 226.

34. 118 U.S. 356 (1886), 366–68. While the Court voided the statute, Matthews adhered to the principle that judges should defer to legislative determinations of the public welfare unless legislation clearly offends the Fourteenth Amendment.

ordinance was facially valid but administered in an invidiously discriminatory manner. As applied, the law was a form of class legislation that burdened a distinct racial group without serving a valid public purpose.[35]

During the last three years of Morrison Waite's tenure as Chief Justice,
the Supreme Court sustained as reasonable police measures a Louisiana
quarantine law,[36] a Kansas[37] and an Iowa[38] statute prohibiting the manufac-
ture and sale of alcoholic beverages, and a Pennsylvania consumer-protection law prohibiting the sale of oleomargarine. And although it sustained
the Kansas prohibition law in *Mugler* v. *Kansas*,[39] Justice Harlan clearly articulated the principles of judicial inquiry that would later be crystallized as
substantive due process. Harlan emphasized the legislature's primary responsibility to determine the public welfare, but he asserted the Supreme Court's
authority to decide "whether the legislature has transcended the limits" of
the police power.[40]

In evaluating regulatory policy, Harlan asserted, legislation is entitled to a
presumption of validity. Nevertheless, courts must decide whether regulations of property have a reasonable relation to the legislature's stated objectives. Does the regulation clearly serve a public purpose, or is it merely class
legislation that favors a particular interest? He acknowledged that all property is subject to considerations of the public health and safety but stressed

35. *Id.*, 373–74. See also Gillman, *The Constitution Besieged*, 72–73. As Gillman argues,
special burdens must be justified by general benefits. The state cannot exercise the police and
tax powers merely for partisan or factional advantage.

36. *Morgan v. Louisiana*, 118 U.S. 455 (1886).

37. *Mugler v. Kansas*, 123 U.S. 623 (1887).

38. *Kidd v. Pearson*, 128 U.S. 1 (1888), following *Mugler.*

39. The Court held that the statute did not deny property without due process of law. In
exercising the police power for the general welfare, the state may diminish the value of an
individual's property as long as it does not completely destroy the property right (123 U.S.,
664, 667, 668–69). There is no guarantee, in perpetuity, that an individual can use his or her
property for a given purpose without reference to the public welfare. However, Harlan warned
that the Court would scrutinize the legislature's intent and examine the substantive reasonableness of economic regulatory legislation. See Ely, *The Guardian of Every Other Right*,
88–89.

40. 123 U.S., 661. Since the legislature had not taken Mugler's property or totally deprived
him of its use, Harlan denied that the plaintiff was due just compensation. In regulating the
use of property, a legislature can deny its owner the right to employ property in the most
profitable manner in order to protect the public's health, safety, welfare, or morals. Since
Mugler could still use his property for other purposes, Harlan reasoned, the regulation was not
tantamount to a total deprivation. *Id.*, 666–69. Dissenting, Field concluded that the prohibition statute amounted to a total destruction or confiscation for which compensation was due.
Id., 678.

the fundamental nature of property rights.[41] Justice Harlan warned that in the future the Court would scrutinize the legislature's intent and the substantive reasonableness of economic regulatory legislation.[42] Thus *Mugler* represented an important step in the development of substantive due process reasoning.

Similarly, in *Powell* v. *Pennsylvania* John M. Harlan justified a prohibition on the sale of oleomargarine as a legitimate means to protect the public against fraud.[43] He acknowledged that the due process clause protects the fundamental liberty to pursue a trade and to sell one's property, but he argued that the statute was reasonably related to a legitimate public purpose.[44] Authority to determine the facts and make a policy judgment belongs to the legislature, and ultimately to the people at the ballot box. However, as Frank Strong observes, Harlan simply ignored the dairy industry's lobbying campaign to monopolize the market through state and federal legislation taxing margarine or prohibiting its sale.[45]

Dissenting, Stephen Field reprised that the prohibition was not a police measure because margarine is a wholesome product. The statute was class legislation that furthered the economic interests of butter producers at the public expense. Inasmuch as the manufacturer had clearly labeled the product, the legislation merely prohibited the sale of a healthy, inexpensive substitute for butter. There was no direct relationship between the prohibition and the state's ostensible purpose of protecting the public against fraud.[46] Moreover, the due process and privileges or immunities clauses conferred a "natural liberty" to sell healthy foods. In contrast to Harlan, Field asserted the courts' authority to scrutinize legislative intent in order to determine whether the majority had arbitrarily deprived a vested property right.[47]

41. *Id.*, 660–61.
42. *Id.*, 661. As Harlan wrote: "It does not at all follow that every statute enacted ostensibly for the promotion of [the public morals, health, or safety] is to be accepted as a legitimate exertion of the police powers of the State."
43. 127 U.S. 678 (1888), 680–81.
44. *Id.*, 684, 685, 686.
45. See Strong, *Substantive Due Process of Law*, 86–88, 89. See also Geoffrey P. Miller, "Public Choice at the Dawn of the Special Interest State: The Story of Butter and Margarine," 77 *Calif. L. Rev.* 83–131 (1989), 103–4, 105–8, 114–15 (hereafter Miller, 77 *Calif. L. Rev.*). As the evidence suggests, the legislation resulted from the butter industry's well-orchestrated campaign to eliminate competition from a cheaper, healthful alternative to whole dairy products.
46. 127 U.S., 692–93, 695.
47. *Id.*, 696, 697–98.

Substantive Due Process, Public Monopolies, and Businesses Affected with a Public Interest

If the states had considerable discretion in regulating laundries, liquor distributors, and oleomargarine manufacturers, surely they could employ the police power to fix rates and establish conditions of service for railroads, ferries, common carriers, public warehouses, and businesses affected with a public interest. During the 1870s, Illinois, Iowa, Minnesota, Wisconsin, Kansas, Mississippi, and other states adopted legislation fixing railroad and public-utilities rates. In a series of cases beginning with *Munn v. Illinois,*[48] railroad, warehouse, and public-utility companies urged the Supreme Court to declare these laws unconstitutional. While the Court generally sustained state regulations as rational or reasonable police measures, these cases gave Field and his judicial allies an opportunity to articulate their theories of constitutional limitations, individual liberty, and the police power.

In *Munn,* Chief Justice Waite sanctioned the state's expansive reading of its police power to fix the maximum rates that public warehouses could charge for storing and handling grain. Speaking for the majority, Waite claimed that the Fourteenth Amendment's due process clause did not prohibit the states from regulating businesses affected with a public interest.[49] Although public grain warehouses did not originally fit the conventional definition of such businesses, Waite contended that they had become devoted to a public purpose.[50] Standing at the gateway of commerce in Chicago, fourteen great warehouses, owned by approximately thirty individuals, had a virtual monopoly over the grain harvest of seven or eight western states passing on its way to eastern ports.[51] Under these conditions, he ob-

---

48. 94 U.S. 113 (1877). Munn & Scott had been convicted in the Criminal Court of Cook County for operating a grain warehouse without the requisite state license and for charging rates in excess of the maximum allowable fee. Munn & Scott claimed that the Illinois statute fixing the maximum rates they could charge for handling and storing grain deprived them of their liberty and property without due process of law. Munn & Scott also claimed that the statute denied them the equal protection of the law and interfered with the power of Congress to regulate interstate commerce. *Id.,* 118–20.

49. *Id.,* 126. When an individual devotes his property to a public purpose, Waite wrote, "he, in effect, grants to the public an interest in that use, and must submit to be controlled by the public for the common good, to the extent of the interest he has thus created." *Id.* See also Ely, *The Guardian of Every Other Right,* 86–87.

50. 94 U.S., 124–25.

51. *Id.,* 131.

served, there was little difference between warehouses and other businesses traditionally devoted to a public purpose.

Since the public has a "direct and positive interest" in regulating grain warehouses, Waite simply extended legal concepts traditionally applicable to common carriers in order to accommodate rapid commercial progress.[52] Even though the plaintiffs had established their private business before the statute was adopted, all property is held subject to regulation for the common good or welfare. Therefore, Waite concluded, the statute was a reasonable regulation rather than a taking of private property. Public regulation was a legitimate antidote to private monopolies that blocked equal access to markets. In effect, the chief justice defined private property as a positive right, subject to legislative control, rather than as a constitutional right beyond the will of ordinary majorities.[53]

In a forceful dissent, Field, with William Strong concurring, characterized the Court's opinion as destructive of property. The mere recitation that a business is affected with a public interest does not "change a private business into a public one," Field asserted.[54] Rejecting Waite's analysis, Field defined property affected with a public interest as "property dedicated by the owner to public uses, or to property the use of which was granted by the government, or in connection with which special privileges were conferred."[55] He drew a line between private business and legitimate public monopolies, which the government could bestow because it has the power to operate means of public transportation such as ferries, highways, and railroads. If the storage of grain is such a business, Field commented, then every private transaction could be clothed with a public interest at a legislative majority's pleasure.

Munn gave Field an ideal opportunity to articulate his view of property rights and the police power.[56] The due process clause, he noted, protects an

52. *Id.* Waite implied but did not state explicitly that businesses, once purely private, could over time become affected with a public interest. In accommodating commercial and technological change, Waite's analysis opened the way to expanding the concept and, ultimately, erasing the distinction between private businesses and businesses affected with a public interest.

53. See Kens, 55 *Rev. of Pol.*, who suggests that the framers of the Constitution anticipated that government would play a role in the creation, protection, use, and transfer of private property. Therefore, their endorsement of protection for property rights should not be interpreted as an open-ended constitutional prohibition of governmental involvement in economic matters.

54. 94 U.S., 138.

55. *Id.*, 139–40.

56. Two years later, in *Union Pacific R.R. Co. v. United States* (the *Sinking Fund Cases*), 99 U.S. 700 (1879), 766–67, Field returned to the defense of property rights. Dissenting, he

owner's use and enjoyment of property, not merely title and possession, as the majority claimed. Field acknowledged that the public could regulate and even prohibit the use of private property to protect the public welfare, but he denied that price-fixing is a legitimate exercise of the police power.[57] Price-fixing simply takes one person's property for the benefit of another. By sustaining the legislative will, the Court had subjected the "fruits of [the owner's] property and the just reward of his labor, industry, and enterprise"[58] to unrestrained majority rule, in derogation of the due process clause. In *Munn*, Field adhered to the traditional theory that the exercise of the police power is restricted to a public purpose. A monopoly grant that merely fosters a group's interest without advancing the general welfare is an expropriation of private property and prohibited by the due process clause.

Stephen Field remained faithful to his Jacksonian belief in equality of economic opportunity. He opposed monopolies and other forms of privilege that interfered with economic liberty. He also believed that individuals had the capacity to make their own economic decisions and take care of themselves. Despite the concentrations of wealth that developed during Reconstruction, Justice Field retained a belief in a neutral state that did not interfere with market forces to benefit particular interests. Like Cooley and Appleton, he sought to keep the public and private spheres distinct. Field employed the due process clause as a constitutional limitation on the police power in order to keep the state from intruding on the private sphere and to prevent private interests from manipulating public authority to their advantage.[59]

During the 1880s the Waite Court sustained most state regulatory policies by interpreting the police, tax, and eminent domain powers broadly.[60] Un-

---

attacked the sinking-fund statute as an impairment of the company's contract (charter) and a destruction of vested property rights. Field characterized the act as violating the taking and due process clauses of the Fifth Amendment, as well as the contracts clause.

57. 94 U.S., 140, 141, 145.

58. *Id.*, 148.

59. However, Field did not advocate unrestrained individualism. See McCurdy, 61 *J. Am. Hist.*, 978–79.

60. Charles Warren, *The Supreme Court in United States History*, rev. ed., 2 vols. (Boston: Little, Brown & Co., 1937), 2:566–67, 568, 571–74, 579, 580–81. Between 1873 and 1880 the Supreme Court generally sustained the states' exercise of the police power. Not until 1888 did the Court begin to employ the due process clause of the Fourteenth Amendment as a substantive restraint on economic and social legislation of the states. *Id.*, 590, 590–91, 592. See also Ely, *The Guardian of Every Other Right*, 88–89. Ely argues that by 1887 *Munn* had lost significance. A majority of justices were prepared to accept the due process clause as an important limitation on the states' police powers.

able to agree with a majority of his brethren, Field, along with Strong and occasionally Bradley, Harlan, and Swayne, characterized various state and congressional regulatory acts as depriving constitutionally protected economic liberty and property rights. Initially, Field rested his dissents on the privileges and immunities clause. Following the Supreme Court's emasculation of this important provision, he turned to the due process clause as a substantive limitation on legislative power. To Stephen Field, the due process clauses embodied unenumerated as well as enumerated rights. Fidelity to constitutional limitations, he believed, was indispensable to preserving individual liberty and advancing the public welfare.

Foremost among the individual's fundamental liberties were the rights to labor and to acquire, use, enjoy, and dispose of property, subject to considerations of the common good. Liberty to pursue a lawful calling, insisted Field, encourages individuals to realize their promise and promotes the wealth, welfare, and progress of the society. Only a very substantial public interest could justify government's restraining individuals from pursuing lawful callings and enjoying the fruits of their labor. Therefore, Justice Field was prepared to subject legislative recitations of the police power to careful judicial scrutiny. During Chief Justice Waite's tenure, Stephen Field and Joseph Bradley prepared the way for the Fuller Court's acceptance of substantive due process as an important element of laissez-faire constitutionalism.

Economic Liberty and the Apotheosis of Substantive Due Process

Between 1888 and 1921 the Fuller and White courts faced an increasing number of cases that pitted the states' use of their police, tax, and eminent domain powers against individual and corporate assertions of liberty and property rights. Although the Court generally sustained state regulations of property, it invoked substantive due process to void laws fixing rates for public utilities and businesses affected with a public interest. The justices were even less deferential to policies that interfered with liberty of contract and the natural forces of the marketplace. In nine important liberty-of-contract cases, the Supreme Court subjected the legislature's judgment and fact-finding to careful judicial scrutiny. In order to survive judicial scrutiny, the legislature had to demonstrate an important public purpose in limiting individual liberty or in interfering with markets.

Similarly, the justices confronted claims that Congress had exceeded its authority to regulate interstate commerce, interfering with the reserved powers of the states and constitutionally protected rights. Although the Supreme Court generally sustained congressional regulations of property, the justices invoked the evolving concept of substantive due process to invalidate regulations of interstate commerce more frequently than state police measures.[61] The Court became increasingly suspicious that Congress was employing the commerce power to centralize decision-making at the expense of the states.[62] Inevitably, the centralization of power would undermine individual liberty, local self-rule, and the federal structure of government.

Property Rights and Substantive Due Process

In twenty of twenty-four cases (1890–1920) that involved the police and tax powers vis-à-vis property rights, the Supreme Court sustained the legislative policy. Writing for the majority in *Lawton* v. *Steele*,[63] for example, Justice Henry Brown noted that the legislature has broad discretion to determine what the public interest requires and "what measures are necessary for the protection of such interests."[64] He then articulated a four-part test for evaluating the constitutionality of police measures. First, the regulation had to promote a public purpose. Second, there had to be a reasonably direct relation between the regulation and the legislature's stated objective. Third, the regulation could not unduly burden a particular individual or class. Fourth, the legislature could not invoke the police power to enrich or advantage a distinct group unless the measure also served a public purpose.[65]

61. But see Cushman, 20 *Mich. L. Rev.*, 741–44. Cushman describes this period as one of judicial ruthlessness regarding the social and economic legislation of the states.

62. See, for example, *Hammer* v. *Dagenhart*, 247 U.S. 251 (1918), infra.

63. 152 U.S. 133 (1894), 133–34. The Court held that a state statute regulating the methods of fishing New York's waters was a reasonable conservation measure and not a deprivation of property without due process.

64. *Id.*, 136.

65. See, for example, Justice Peckham's opinion in *Gundling* v. *Chicago*, 177 U.S. 183 (1900), 188. Employing a reasonableness test, Ely comments, the Court sustained regulations directly related to the public health, safety, and morals but required the states to justify

In a series of decisions following *Lawton*, the Court reiterated its authority to subject legislative determinations of the public interest to judicial review, but the justices usually upheld police measures.

However, in five significant cases the Court voided state police regulations affecting vested property rights.[66] In *Dobbins v. Los Angeles* the Supreme Court overturned the city's decision to prohibit construction of a gas works one month after granting the company a permit. Although Justice William Day conceded that the City of Los Angeles had the authority to prohibit the operation of businesses inimical to the public safety, he denied that the city had demonstrated any change in conditions that would justify the prohibition. The prohibition simply protected the city lighting company's monopoly by excluding private competition. Because the ordinance oppressed a single property owner but did not serve a public purpose, the city's decision was an arbitrary deprivation of property rather than a rational exercise of the police power.[67]

In several other cases, the Court concluded that local ordinances were forms of class legislation that did not serve a valid public objective. Despite the broad nature of the police power, in *Eubank v. City of Richmond* the justices held that a city cannot adopt zoning ordinances for the benefit of a particular group of property owners. Since such ordinances lack a public purpose, Justice Joseph McKenna concluded, they are tantamount to a taking of property without due process of law. While the Supreme Court declined to inquire into the state's or the city's motives, it reexamined the facts upon which the regulation was predicated.[68]

Once again admitting the broad scope of the police power, in *Buchanan v. Warley* (1917) Justice Day characterized a Louisville ordinance prohibiting the sale of houses to "coloreds" in blocks that were more than 50 percent white as an unconstitutional interference with the white property owners' due process rights.[69] Day denied that the ordinance was a reasonable police regulation because it discriminated against a distinct class of property owners but did not promote a valid public purpose. Although he acknowl-

---

measures burdening property rights and economic liberty. See Ely, *The Guardian of Every Other Right*, 90–91.

66. *Dobbins v. Los Angeles*, 195 U.S. 223 (1904); *Eubank v. City of Richmond*, 226 U.S. 137 (1912); *Buchanan v. Warley*, 245 U.S. 60 (1917); and *Brooks-Scanlon Co. v. Railroad Commission*, 251 U.S. 396 (1920).

67. 195 U.S., 237–38. In fact, there was no evidence of any fact-finding to justify the precipitous change in policy. See Strong, *Substantive Due Process of Law*, 214–15.

68. 226 U.S., 142–43.

69. 245 U.S., 78–79.

edged that the state could regulate the use and sale of property for a variety of lawful objectives, he argued that the particular ordinance violated the Fourteenth Amendment and the Civil Rights Acts of 1866 and 1870, which prohibited interference with the right of a white man to sell his property as well as with a "colored" man's right to purchase property without regard to race.[70]

Even though the Supreme Court set aside the legislative policy in the preceding decisions, it gave considerable weight to the legislature's judgment. While the justices avoided inquiring into legislative motives, they did examine the statutes' foreseeable or predictable consequences. Declaring various police measures unconstitutional, a majority found that these laws either promoted a monopoly, favored a special interest, or discriminated against a distinct group. The measures burdened vested property rights and interfered with economic liberty but did not serve any legitimate public objective.

Property Rights of Public Utilities and Businesses Affected with a Public Interest

During the Populist and Progressive Eras the Supreme Court decided numerous cases involving the property rights of railroads, public utilities, insurance companies, and other businesses affected with a public interest. In these cases the companies challenged legislative regulations as a deprivation of property without due process of law. They contested the legislature's authority to fix rates, to delegate rate-making powers to commissions, or to deny judicial review of the reasonableness of the established rates.[71] In some cases the companies disputed the statutory definition of "public utilities" or "businesses affected with a public interest."

Although the Supreme Court expanded the latter concept,[72] in 1890 a

70. Id., 78–79, 81, 82.

71. As the states began to regulate rates through general statutes rather than exclusive franchises and corporate charters, Hovenkamp argues, railroads and public utilities turned toward the due process clause as a means of restraining confiscatory policies. Hovenkamp, *Enterprise and American Law*, 125–30.

72. See *Budd v. New York*, 143 U.S. 517 (1892), and *German Alliance Insurance Co. v. Kansas* 233 U.S. 389 (1914). In the latter case, Justice McKenna claimed that, over time, a private business could become affected with a public interest. Recognizing the risk of fire and catastrophe in modern cities, he noted, the legislature had limited the liberty to write fire

new majority overturned *Munn* v. *Illinois* and the *Granger Cases.* In *Chicago, Milwaukee & St. Paul Ry. Co.* v. *Minnesota,* [73] Justice Samuel Blatchford, joined by Chief Justice Melville Fuller and Justices Stephen Field, David Brewer, and John M. Harlan, used the nascent concept of substantive due process to impose limits on the rate-making authority of the states. "The question of the reasonableness of a rate of charge for transportation by a railroad company," Blatchford wrote, "is eminently a question for judicial investigation, requiring due process of law for its determination." [74] Without an opportunity to challenge the state railroad commission's findings in a court, Blatchford concluded, the company could be deprived of the use of its property in violation of the due process clause. Two years later the railroads suffered a setback in *Budd* v. *New York,* [75] but between 1890 and 1898 the Court generally adhered to the position that the due process clause imposes substantive limits on the reasonableness of state legislation fixing rates for railroads and other public utilities. [76]

As Richard Cortner notes, the *Minnesota Rates Case* of 1890 was far more than a victory for the railroads. It signaled a broader use of due process as a substantive limitation on the power of government. The Minnesota case marked an expansion of judicial review vis-à-vis legislative policymaking. Unless the courts exercised self-restraint, the concept of substantive due process would lead to systemic conflict between the judiciary and republican political institutions. The railroad litigation, writes Cortner, implied profound changes in the Supreme Court's role as a constitutional arbiter of federalism and the separation of powers. [77]

While the Fuller and White Courts acknowledged that the property rights of public monopolies are conditional rather than absolute, they sub-

---

insurance contracts. By regulating rates, the state spread the loss of great conflagrations throughout the community.

73. 134 U.S. 418 (1890).

74. *Id.,* 458.

75. 143 U.S. In *Budd,* Blatchford affirmed *Munn,* holding that persons who devote businesses to a public use subject their property to regulation, which may include fixing maximum rates for goods and services. But he asserted judicial power to review the reasonableness of the scheduled rates. Blatchford cautioned that courts should not intervene unless the maximum allowable rate is so unreasonable that it is confiscatory or deprives a person of property without due process. Thus Blatchford attempted to harmonize *Munn* and the *Minnesota Rates Case,* as well as avoid conflict with legislative policymaking authority.

76. See Richard Cortner, *The Iron Horse and the Constitution: The Railroads and the Transformation of the Fourteenth Amendment* (Westport, Conn.: Greenwood Press, 1993), 126–27, 128–29.

77. *Id.,* xii–xiii, 127.

jected regulatory policies to substantive due process limitations. The Supreme Court admitted that the states could regulate the rates that public monopolies charge for their services, but required legislatures to demonstrate that regulations are reasonable—that is, clearly related to a public purpose and not confiscatory of property rights. Inasmuch as public monopolies are exempt from market forces or result from "market failure," the Court's decisions were consistent with the prevailing laissez-faire economic and legal theories of the day. Between 1890 and 1920, substantive due process became a powerful tool of judicial review of congressional and state legislative policymaking.

Liberty of Contract: The Free World of *Lochner* and *Coppage*

During the same period the Supreme Court decided approximately twenty-five cases that raised significant liberty of contract questions. In most cases the Court sustained state legislation regulating access to the professions, limiting the right to do business, and fixing wages, hours, and conditions of employment. A majority justified these measures as directly related to health, safety, and morals. But beginning with *Allgeyer v. Louisiana*, the justices gradually enlarged judicial review of legislation restricting economic rights. They tended to strike down legislation interfering with access to markets, redistributing income, or favoring one set of economic interests over another.[78] In these cases, the Supreme Court condemned the states' interference in the marketplace without a sufficiently important public purpose. As James Ely notes, however, during the Gilded Age there was never judicial unanimity on the application of laissez-faire principles to economic regulatory legislation.[79]

Speaking for the majority in *Allgeyer*, Justice Rufus Peckham found that a Louisiana statute prohibiting individuals from making valid marine insurance contracts in other states was an unconstitutional interference with the citizen's economic liberty.[80] According to Peckham, the Fourteenth Amend-

---

78. See *New York Life Ins. Co. v. Head*, 234 U.S. 149 (1914); *Blake v. McClung*, 172 U.S. 239 (1901); *Lochner v. New York*, 198 U.S. 45 (1905); *Coppage v. Kansas*, 236 U.S. 1 (1915); *Truax v. Raich*, 239 U.S. 33 (1915); and *Adams v. Tanner*, 244 U.S. 590 (1917).

79. See Ely, *The Guardian of Every Other Right*, 100.

80. 165 U.S., 583–84, 588, 589. Although he acknowledged that the state could regulate

ment embraced the Declaration's promise of liberty and the pursuit of happiness as fundamental civil rights.[81] Although these liberties are conditional, in a free society only a substantial public interest could justify state interference with lawful contractual relationships. Absent such a purpose, legislative interference with the individual's constitutional liberty is a deprivation of due process.[82] Inasmuch as the legislation protected local insurance companies from foreign competition, it amounted to class legislation rather than a police measure. In reality, the statute protected both the public against fraud and local interests from interstate competition.

Once again, in *Lochner v. New York* Justice Peckham argued that liberty of contract is an unenumerated constitutional right.[83] The New York labor law limiting working hours for bakers, he began, interfered unnecessarily with both parties' liberty of contract. "The general right to make a contract in relation to [the bakery] business," Peckham reasoned, "is part of the liberty of the individual protected by the Fourteenth Amendment of the Federal Constitution."[84] However, he acknowledged that the state could regulate the hours and conditions of work for substantial reasons directly related to the public health.

The state could prohibit individuals from making contracts for unlawful purposes, but Justice Peckham denied that the labor law was justified by the public safety, as were regulations in the mining industry. Nor was there a relationship to the public health, as in the case of ordinances requiring smallpox vaccinations.[85] The New York statute interfered arbitrarily with the parties' constitutional freedom to enter and leave the marketplace.[86] As Peckham remarked,

or prohibit the insurance business altogether within its borders, Peckham rejected Louisiana's claim of extraterritorial jurisdiction over contracts executed through the mail or by telegraph.

81. He affirmed Joseph Bradley's opinion in *Butchers' Union Co.* that the right to pursue all lawful callings and make contracts for that purpose is protected by the due process clause.

82. *Id.*, 589–90, 591. See also *New York Life Ins. Co. v. Head*, 234 U.S. 149 (1914), and *New York Life Ins. Co. v. Dodge*, 246 U.S. 357 (1918), affirming *Allgeyer.*

83. 198 U.S. 45 (1905). The New York statute restricted the workweek to sixty hours and prohibited employees from working more than ten hours in any day. For an excellent analysis of *Lochner*, see Paul Kens, *Judicial Power and Reform Politics: The Anatomy of "Lochner v. New York"* (Lawrence: University Press of Kansas, 1990). See also Harry H. Wellington, "Common Law Rules and Constitutional Double Standards: Some Notes on Adjudication," 83 *Yale L.J.* 221–311 (1973), 281–85.

84. 198 U.S., 53.

85. See, for example, *Jacobson v. Massachusetts*, 197 U.S. 11 (1905).

86. 198 U.S., 56, 57, 57–58.

The mere assertion that the subject relates though but in a remote degree to the public health does not necessarily render the enactment valid. The act must have a more direct relation, as a means to an end, and the end itself must be appropriate and legitimate, before an act can be held to be valid which interferes with the general right of an individual to be free in his person and in his power to contract in relation to his own labor.[87]

After subjecting the fact-finding of the New York legislature and courts to careful review, Justice Peckham found that there was no direct relationship among working long hours in the bakery business, developing silicosis and other respiratory diseases, and producing healthy, sanitary bread for public consumption. The bakery industry, he observed, is no more or less injurious to the public health than any other trade or business. Therefore,

> a prohibition to enter into any contract of labor in a bakery for more than a certain number of hours a week, is, in our judgment, so wholly beside the matter of a proper, reasonable and fair provision, as to run counter to that liberty of person and of free contract provided for in the Federal Constitution.[88]

Looking behind the legislature's ostensible justification, Peckham denied that the New York law was a valid police measure. He noted: "It is impossible for us to shut our eyes to the fact that many of the laws of this character . . . are, in reality, passed from other motives."[89] The statute was a labor law that interfered with the right of two legally equal parties to make labor contracts in a free market. It was, Peckham reasoned, a form of class legislation that favored the interests of large bakeries over those of smaller, independent bakers. The New York law was an unjustified intrusion on the individual's autonomy to make personal economic decisions. Unfortunately, the justice did not provide any direct evidence for his "stands-to-reason" argument.[90]

---

87. Id., 57–58. Peckham solidified the doctrine that legislation must have a direct relation to the public welfare in order to override constitutionally protected economic liberties. See Note, 103 Harv. L. Rev., 1366.

88. 198 U.S., 62.

89. Id., 64.

90. See Note, 103 Harv. L. Rev., 1370–71, 1373. Like Peckham, the author argues that the

While Justice Oliver Wendell Holmes criticized the majority's opinion for embodying prevailing laissez-faire economic and Social Darwinist thought,[91] Justice Harlan argued that legislative policy is entitled to great respect if not presumptive validity.[92] Even when the lawmakers' judgment is of doubtful validity, he continued, courts should defer, unless the policy is "plainly and palpably" unconstitutional.[93] Even though Harlan was more deferential to legislative judgment than Peckham, he was willing to reevaluate the facts on which the lawmakers had predicated the policy.[94]

Subsequent generations of scholars have criticized the *Lochner* opinion as fatally flawed because the Court ignored both the legislature's fact-finding and its judgment. Justice Peckham did not ignore the legislative record; he found it a transparent sham for the political interests, which in his opinion were behind the factory law. From his perspective, the facts simply did not support the stated legislative objective. As other contemporaneous decisions indicate, *Lochner* did not preclude the states from justifying regulatory policies that burden economic and other personal liberties. But Peckham's opinion did require the government to show a direct relationship between such regulations and public health and safety.

If *Lochner* was fatally flawed it was because the justices failed to acknowledge that economic conditions had changed dramatically since the Civil

---

unions and large bakeries promoted the law to eliminate competition from nonunion shops, but he too presents no direct evidence to support the claim. See also Miller, 77 *Calif. L. Rev.*, 103–4, 122–25. As Miller suggests, during this era much legislative fact-finding was a farce, a masquerade for interest groups that used the regulatory process to prevent economic competition. Although the Court was unrealistic about the equal bargaining power of labor and business, the justices did not systematically favor the interests of the latter. See Ely, *The Guardian of Every Other Right*, 105. Field's defense of liberty of contract was a broad appeal for individual autonomy and self-determination, rather than a narrow defense of business against labor. See Hovenkamp, 40 *Stan. L. Rev.*, 412–13.

91. In a powerful dissent, Holmes argued that the Constitution does not embody any particular social or economic theory; it "is made for people of fundamentally differing views." 198 U.S., 76. See Richard A. Posner, *Law and Literature: A Misunderstood Relation* (Cambridge, Mass.: Harvard University Press, 1988), 281–89. Holmes's opinion was powerful rhetoric but not well reasoned. Holmes never confronted the principal issue—whether the regulation was an unreasonable interference with due process rights. As Posner notes, his opinion is silent regarding the origins and intent of the Fourteenth Amendment. In fact, the framers of the Fourteenth Amendment and the Civil Rights Act of 1866 imposed constitutional limitations on the states' interference with the individual's economic liberty. See Note, 103 *Harv. L. Rev.*, 1369. Although *Lochner* embodied laissez-faire principles, it did not rest on Social Darwinism, as Holmes claimed.

92. 198 U.S., 68.

93. *Id.*, 68, 72–73.

94. *Id.*, 70–71.

War. Private monopolies and oligopolies had restricted access to markets and undermined competition. Private concentrations of wealth and power had subverted the market freedom necessary for equality of economic opportunity. Some of the justices simply ignored the greed and corruption of the new corporations, which undermined the very liberty that they championed. Nevertheless, the Court continued to vindicate economic autonomy, while state legislatures attempted to promote collective action. The Supreme Court's laissez-faire constitutionalism was beginning to collide with the policies of the emerging welfare state.[95]

The Court's decision in *Coppage v. Kansas*[96] illustrates the growing conflict between the justices' commitment to laissez-faire constitutionalism and legislative attempts to redistribute bargaining power between labor and management. In *Coppage*, Justice Mahlon Pitney concluded that the Kansas law, prohibiting yellow-dog contracts, was an unconstitutional interference with both parties' liberty of contract and therefore prohibited by the Fourteenth Amendment. As legally equal bargaining partners, labor and capital have the same right to enter into and terminate labor contracts. Under this contract, employees had a choice of remaining union members and leaving their jobs, or giving up their union books and keeping their positions.[97]

Although Pitney was not blind to the unequal power and resources of labor and capital, he rejected the argument that the state could employ the police power to redress inequalities of fortune, of wealth and bargaining power.[98] The statute was a form of redistributive legislation that, he asserted, aided unions by limiting the employer's liberty of contract. Absent any evidence of coercion, there was no justification for the law that was related to the public welfare.[99] Just as Field and Bradley had opposed monop-

95. Ely, *The Guardian of Every Other Right*, 102–3.
96. 236 U.S. 1 (1915). The plaintiff had discharged railway switchmen for joining a union in violation of their employment contracts. The statute prohibited employers from placing such conditions on employment contracts. On appeal, the state supreme court declared the statute a valid exercise of the police power sustaining the plaintiff's conviction of a misdemeanor. *Id.*, 6–7.
97. *Id.*, 9–12. See also *Adair v. United States*, 208 U.S. 161 (1908), and *Adams v. Tanner*, 244 U.S. 590 (1917).
98. 236 U.S., 17.
99. *Id.*, 16, 18–19. In a dissenting opinion, Justice Day, along with Charles Evans Hughes, acknowledged the importance of liberty of contract, but he argued that such liberty is subject to the legislature's determination of the public welfare. The legislature is the initial, primary judge of the public welfare. On matters of policy, legislation is entitled to a presumption of validity. In determining the purpose of legislation, Day denied the legitimacy of inquiring into legislators' motives. Day's opinion suggests a minimum-rationality standard that is rather deferential to legislative judgment and factfinding. *Id.*, 35–38.

olies and special privileges for business, Pitney resisted laws favoring labor unions as class legislation. Liberty of contract was essential to free labor, which the framers of the Civil Rights Act of 1866 and the Fourteenth Amendment regarded as a fundamental civil right.

Despite the justices' commitment to liberty of contract, in sixteen cases (1898–1917) they sustained statutes regulating some occupations and professions.[100] The majority concluded that these regulations were directly related to the public health, safety, morals, and welfare, rather than class legislation that redistributed wealth and power or corrected market forces. In *Holden* v. *Hardy*, for example, Justice Brown upheld Utah's power to regulate hours of employment in such dangerous occupations as mining. Denying that the concept of the public welfare is static, Brown noted that the states could use their police powers for purposes that the Constitution's framers and ratifiers had not contemplated. Although miners and their employers are mature adults, competent to make their own economic decisions, Brown concluded that the states have considerable discretion to protect the public health and safety. In regulating inherently dangerous occupations, he observed, the courts should defer to the legislature's judgment and fact-finding.[101]

Similarly, in *Muller* v. *Oregon*[102] and *Miller* v. *Wilson*[103] the Court found an Oregon statute and a California statute regulating women's hours of employment in laundries and hotels valid police measures. In an opinion that depicts women as dependent persons, Justice Brewer argued that limiting women's hours of work is reasonably related to the public health, since the well-being of the race depends on their health as mothers and nurturers. Hence, the public has a direct interest in limiting a woman's right to make

100. In five cases, the Court upheld maximum hour laws: *Holden* v. *Hardy*, 169 U.S. 366 (1898); *Atkin* v. *Kansas*, 191 U.S. 207 (1903); *Muller* v. *Oregon*, 208 U.S. 412 (1908); *Miller* v. *Wilson*, 236 U.S. 373 (1915); and *Bunting* v. *Oregon*, 243 U.S. 426 (1917). The Supreme Court sustained laws regulating payment practices or substituting worker compensation for common-law rules of liability in three cases: *McLean* v. *Arkansas*, 211 U.S. 539 (1909); *Chicago, Burlington & Quincy R.R. Co.* v. *McGuire*, 219 U.S. 549 (1911); and *New York Central R.R. Co.* v. *White*, 243 U.S. 188 (1917). In five cases a majority upheld laws regulating or prohibiting businesses entirely: *Nutting* v. *Massachusetts*, 183 U.S. 79 (1901); *Booth* v. *Illinois*, 184 U.S. 425 (1902); *Otis* v. *Parker*, 187 U.S. 606 (1903); *Williams* v. *Arkansas*, 217 U.S. 79 (1910); and *Rast* v. *Van Deman & Lewis Co.*, 240 U.S. 342 (1916). Finally, in three miscellaneous cases the Supreme Court sustained laws regulating or prohibiting various business practices: *Orient Insurance Co.* v. *Daggs*, 172 U.S. 557 (1899); *In re Helf*, 197 U.S. 488 (1905); and *Rosenthal* v. *New York*, 226 U.S. 260 (1912).

101. 169 U.S. 366 (1898), 386–87, 396–97.

102. 208 U.S. 412 (1908).

103. 236 U.S. 373 (1915).

labor contracts.[104] Unlike minimum-wage laws, maximum-hour regulations did not interfere with the owners' right to manage their businesses by insisting that they reward the least and most productive workers equally. Nor did such laws expropriate employers' property by requiring them to reward workers beyond the market value of their labor.

Similarly, the Court upheld worker compensation laws and regulations governing wage payments as a reasonable exercise of the police power. While a majority asserted the Supreme Court's authority to determine whether the legislature had exceeded its power, the justices eschewed judging the wisdom of legislative policy. The legislature is the primary judge of the necessity of police regulations. In *Chicago, Burlington and Quincy R.R. Co.* v. *McGuire*, Justice Charles Evans Hughes confirmed the established view that the Fourteenth Amendment protects liberty of contract, but he noted that the due process clause prohibits only arbitrary and unreasonable restraints.[105]

Liberty of contract is an unenumerated fundamental right, Hughes argued, subject to lawful restraints that are clearly related to the public welfare. In the area of employer-employee relations, he concluded, state legislatures have considerable discretion in adopting measures to protect the public health.[106] Unless a regulation or prohibition is unrelated to a public purpose, the Court held in several cases involving businesses states deemed a public evil that judges should not second-guess policy judgments of state legislators. Many laws may be silly or unwise, as Justice Harlan observed in *Booth* v. *Illinois*, but they are not palpably unconstitutional.[107]

Congressional Power, Substantive Due Process, and Economic Liberty

During the Populist and Progressive Eras, the U.S. Supreme Court decided sixteen important cases involving the employment of congressional power

104. 208 U.S., 421–22. See also 236 U.S., 380–81. See also *Bunting* v. *Oregon*, 243 U.S. 426 (1917), in which the Court sustained Oregon's ten-hour law for mills and factories.

105. 219 U.S. 549 (1911), 566–67.

106. *Id.*, 570–71, 572–73.

107. 184 U.S. 425 (1902), 431–32. See also *Otis* v. *Parker*, 187 U.S. 606, 608–9, 609–10 (1903); *Williams* v. *Arkansas*, 217 U.S. 79, 88–89 (1910); and *Rast*, 240 U.S., 368 (1916).

vis-à-vis corporate and individual liberty and property interests.[108] In the commerce-clause cases, the Court acknowledged that Congress has plenary power to regulate or even prohibit foreign and interstate commerce. As long as national regulations did not patently interfere with the states' police powers or constitutionally protected property and liberty interests, the justices sustained the authority of Congress to gauge the wisdom of national commercial policy. Even when Congress prohibited the commerce altogether, the Court generally sustained such measures as long as the record established a rational relationship between the regulation and the stated objective. Although the Supreme Court continued to advance liberty of contract as the norm, it conceded that there is no absolute freedom of contract.[109]

In *Adair* v. *United States*[110] and *Hammer* v. *Dagenhart*,[111] however, the Court abandoned self-restraint in several important ways. In *Adair*, Justice Harlan virtually ignored the legislative history of the act of June 1, 1898, that made it a crime to dismiss employees solely because of their union membership.[112] Confining his analysis to the statutory language, he denied that there was any direct (i.e., "real and substantial") relationship between recognizing trade unions, promoting the peaceful settlement of labor dis-

108. In thirteen of these cases the Supreme Court upheld the legislation. Regarding the exercise of the commerce power, see *United States* v. *Joint Traffic Association*, 171 U.S. 505 (1898); *Addyston Pipe & Steel Co.* v. *United States*, 175 U.S. 211 (1899); *Champion* v. *Ames*, 188 U.S. 321 (1903); *Patterson* v. *Bark Eudora*, 190 U.S. 169 (1903); *Northern Securities Co.* v. *United States*, 193 U.S. 197 (1904); *Atlantic Coast Line R.R. Co.* v. *Riverside Mills*, 219 U.S. 186 (1911); *Baltimore & Ohio R.R. Co.* v. *Interstate Commerce Commission*, 221 U.S. 612 (1911); *Second Employers' Liability Cases (Mondou* v. *New York, N.H. & H. R.R. Co.)*, 223 U.S. 1 (1912); *The Pipeline Cases (Ohio Oil Co.* v. *United States)*, 234 U.S. 548 (1914); and *Wilson* v. *New*, 243 U.S. 333 (1917). The Court also found for the government in *Tiger* v. *Western Investment Co.*, 221 U.S. 286 (1911), sustaining the regulation of the sale of Indian lands; *Calhoun* v. *Massie*, 253 U.S. 170 (1920), upholding a limitation on lawyers' fees in claims against the United States; *The National Prohibition Cases (Rhode Island* v. *Palmer)*, 253 U.S. 350 (1920), validating the prohibition amendment; and *Block* v. *Hirsch*, 256 U.S. 135 (1921), sustaining a wartime emergency rent-control act for the District of Columbia.

109. See *Atlantic Coast Line R.R. Co.* v. *Riverside Mills*, 219 U.S. 186 (1911), 202.

110. 208 U.S. 161 (1908). Speaking for the majority in *Adair*, Justice Harlan denied that there was any rational relation between the act prohibiting the dismissal of employees for their union activity and the commerce power. Therefore, the act interfered with the employer's property rights and both parties' freedom to contract.

111. 247 U.S. 251 (1918). In *Hammer*, the child-labor case, Justice Day raised but did not answer the claim that the statute violated the Fifth Amendment's due process clause. Instead, he decided that the statute was a police measure rather than a regulation of interstate commerce. Thus Congress had used the commerce power for purposes that the Tenth Amendment reserves to the states.

112. 208 U.S., 168–69.

putes, and removing obstacles to the free flow of interstate commerce.[113] Wage earners have a right to join unions in order to improve their conditions, he remarked, but "labor organizations have nothing to do with interstate commerce as such."[114]

Dissenting, Justice Joseph McKenna criticized the majority for failing to give adequate consideration to the factual record. Examining the act's legislative history, he observed that Congress has the power to remove all obstructions to interstate commerce, including the causes of labor unrest. By recognizing trade unions and prohibiting lockouts of union members, Congress sought to promote industrial peace in interstate transportation.[115] If the majority had given adequate consideration to the facts, McKenna argued, it could not have escaped the relationship between the statutory means and ends.

In *Hammer* the Supreme Court ignored the legislative record and examined the motives of Congress, despite Justice Day's denial to the contrary.[116] Rather than limiting itself to deciding whether Congress had the authority to restrict the interstate transportation of child-made goods, the majority inquired into the true aim of the act, which was to "standardize the ages at which children may be employed in mining and manufacturing within the States."[117] Since manufacturing is a local activity, Day observed, the regulation of child labor falls within the police power of the states. Congress had exerted its power for illicit motives, transcending the commerce clause and invading the powers reserved to the states under the Tenth Amendment.[118]

Although *Hammer* and *Adair* reflected the Court's disapproval of national regulations that interfere with the marketplace,[119] Justice Day acknowledged the authority of the states to regulate the employment of children in mines and factories. Since children are not equal bargaining partners, Day ad-

---

113. *Id.,* 177–78.
114. *Id.,* 178.
115. *Id.,* 183, 184, 185, 186–87.
116. 247 U.S., 276.
117. *Id.,* 272, 273–74.
118. *Id.,* 276. As Ely argues, the Supreme Court upheld congressional acts designed to prevent state interference with the free flow of interstate commerce. However, the justices remained suspicious of regulations that promoted centralized power or threatened economic liberty. Ely, *The Guardian of Every Other Right,* 108–10.
119. Quoting from Thomas M. Cooley's treatise on *Torts,* Justice Harlan noted in *Adair:* "It is a part of every man's civil rights that he be left at liberty to refuse business relations with any person whomsoever, whether the refusal rests upon reason, or is the result of whim, caprice, prejudice or malice. With his reasons neither the public nor third persons have any legal concern." 208 U.S., 173.

mitted, the states have a legitimate interest in regulating the labor market to protect their welfare.[120] The Supreme Court remained committed to economic freedom, but the majority recognized that liberty of contract is a conditional right that must yield to restrictions directly related to a public purpose.

Despite their differences, a majority of justices rejected interference by the national government with liberty of contract in order to correct market forces and disparities in collective-bargaining power. A judicial majority regarded national wage and collective-bargaining laws as class legislation that expropriated property rights and deprived economic liberty in violation of the due process clause. The Court continued to adhere to nineteenth-century principles of the neutral state and laissez-faire constitutionalism, while the new corporations undermined the market conditions upon which the classical economics and post–Civil War legal canon rested.

During the Reconstruction Era, Justices Bradley and Field articulated a theory of constitutional limitations and unenumerated fundamental rights based on a substantive interpretation of due process. Along with such jurists as Thomas M. Cooley, they believed that the due process and privileges or immunities clauses embodied substantive limitations on the exercise of legislative as well as judicial power. They derived substantive due process from the language and framing of the Fourteenth Amendment and the Civil Rights Act of 1866, which, they believed, embraced the principles of common law and natural law. Field employed the Anglo-American legal tradition to define and protect a core of fundamental rights, largely economic in nature, against unjustified governmental intrusion.

But Justice Field admitted that the states could restrict the exercise of property rights and economic liberty in order to promote the public welfare. When employing the police power, the states had to demonstrate that such restrictions were reasonable—that is, directly related to a public purpose within the authority of the states under the Tenth Amendment. Field, Bradley, Cooley, Appleton, and other advocates of constitutional limitations opposed use of the police power to foster the interests of a particular class or group, whether business or labor. Despite the development of private concentrations of wealth and power, they maintained a belief in the neutral state as the most effective means of promoting both economic liberty and equality of opportunity.

120. 247 U.S., 275.

Beginning in the late 1880s the Fuller Court embraced the views of Justices Bradley and Field on constitutional limitations, unenumerated rights, and the police power. Despite the Fuller Court's acceptance of substantive due process, it employed the doctrine sparingly vis-à-vis state legislation to protect unenumerated property and liberty interests. Both the Fuller and the White Courts recognized the need to reconcile liberty and property claims with the states' essential responsibility to protect the public health, safety, welfare, and morals. The Supreme Court extolled liberty as the norm but admitted that the public could limit or even prohibit contracts that are inimical to the common good. Liberty and property may be fundamental, but they are not absolute rights. In reconciling competing private and public claims, the Supreme Court usually deferred to legislative fact-finding and policymaking.[121]

With relatively few exceptions, the Fuller and White Courts upheld state and national legislation that was directly related to a public purpose. As long as the objective was within the legislature's authority and the means were rationally related to the legislation's legitimate purposes, the Court sustained the regulation or prohibition. Even when a measure burdened property or liberty interests, the justices tended to validate the legislative judgment. However, if policies completely destroyed vested property rights or gave one class or group an advantage at the expense of another, without serving a public objective, the Court condemned legislation as violating the due process clauses.[122]

When the new chief justice, William Howard Taft, assumed office in the autumn of 1921 the United States was an important international actor,

121. Between 1873 and 1912, in 604 cases involving Fourteenth Amendment claims the Supreme Court rendered only fifty-five decisions that were adverse to the states. Six cases involved the equal-protection rights of blacks, fourteen concerned mixed equal-protection and due process claims, and thirty involved due process issues. Of these thirty, two cases dealt with liberty interests and the remaining twenty-eight involved a taking of property without due process. The five remaining decisions concerned other issues. See Charles W. Collins, "Federal Intervention Under the Fourteenth Amendment," 21 *Yale L. J.* 470–88 (1912), 470–71, 484.

122. See Albert M. Kales, "'Due Process,' the Inarticulate Major Premise, and the Adamson Act," 26 *Yale L.J.* 519–49 (1917), 536–39. Kales suggested that the Supreme Court performed a legitimate function as a second chamber, intervening when legislation imperiled the "fundamentals of the social structure." More recently, Michael Perry has argued that the Supreme Court performs a valuable function in translating broadly shared ethical values into constitutional restraints. While he defers to legislative judgments of the public welfare, Perry acknowledges the importance of imposing constitutional limits on utilitarianism. Michael Perry, "Abortion, the Public Morals, and the Police Power: The Ethical Function of Substantive Due Process," 23 *UCLA L. Rev.* 689–736 (1976), 721, 722, 723–24, 725.

capable of projecting its economic and military power in Asia, Europe, and Latin America. The Americans had become a creditor nation, supplying money and commodities to international markets. At the same time, the United States had opened its portals to millions of immigrants seeking work and economic opportunity in the New World. During the Gilded Age the Supreme Court contributed to the creation of a prosperous, dynamic, and polyglot nation stretching from the Atlantic to the Pacific and knitted together by a modern transportation and communications system.

If Stephen Field's laissez-faire constitutionalism had an Achilles' heel, it was the failure to anticipate the abuses of property rights and economic liberty by the new corporations. While Field and Bradley emphasized economic opportunity and free access to markets, predatory trusts fought to achieve monopoly or oligopoly status. In their efforts to entrench themselves, some corporations eliminated competitors ruthlessly, waged war against labor unions, and corrupted public officials. The Supreme Court sustained most regulatory measures, but in some dramatic instances the justices prevented Congress and the states from dealing with these distortions of the marketplace and restoring the conditions necessary for economic liberty and opportunity. In these cases the Taft and Hughes Courts adhered to a narrow definition of the public welfare, which restricted the exercise of the police and commerce powers. By the 1930s the Court's fidelity to laissez-faire constitutionalism clashed with demands for active governmental participation in the economy.

6

The Much-Acclaimed Demise of Substantive Due Process, 1921–1991

During the twentieth century the United States has faced both domestic and international crises that have promoted the growth of governmental power and the imposition of new restraints on liberty, property, and privacy rights. In the 1930s, for example, Americans turned toward government to ameliorate the social and economic effects of the Great Depression. Overwhelmed by the depression, the states pressured the national government for temporary assistance to fifteen million unemployed workers.[1] The limited welfare state that emerged as a temporary response to the depression has since blossomed into a permanent public-service state that redistributes income, provides a great variety of services, and employs more than seventeen million Americans.[2]

1. Richard B. Morris and Graham W. Irwin, eds., *Harper Encyclopedia of the Modern World* (New York: Harper & Row, 1970), 868. In 1932–33 the number of unemployed reached fifteen million.

2. See Charles Reich, "The New Property," 73 *Yale L.J.* 733–87 (1964), 733. Reich argues that government has become "a major source of wealth." By 1990 government accounted for more than 12 percent of the gross national product and employed almost 15 percent of the civilian labor force. The nonmilitary government (local, state, and federal) labor force was 17,373,000, while the national civilian labor force was 121,700,000. Government's share of

After World War II, government assumed permanent responsibility for managing the economy and guaranteeing the welfare of each individual. As employers and providers, government agencies gather, analyze, and control information about the most intimate details of individuals' lives—their incomes, personal habits and tastes, health and mortality, sexual practices and orientations, and their political views. The more Americans rely on government services, largesse, and employment, the more vulnerable they become to intrusions on constitutional liberty, property, and privacy rights. As governmental intrusion becomes more pervasive, judicial protection of fundamental rights becomes more important.

After World War I, the Taft Court (1921–30) continued to employ the due process clauses as a substantive restraint on legislative policymaking. Adhering to established concepts of substantive due process and the police power, the justices required the states and the national government to demonstrate a direct relation between regulatory legislation and the public health, safety, or welfare. During President Franklin Roosevelt's first term (1933–37) the Hughes Court (1930–41) pursued a similar course, but the justices' defense of property and economic liberty collided with New Deal relief and reform policies.[3] While Chief Justice Hughes adopted a conciliatory approach, a narrow majority rejected state and federal interference with property rights and liberty of contract. Risking a confrontation with Congress and the President, Justices Pierce Butler, James McReynolds, George Sutherland, and Willis Van Devanter, sometimes joined by Roberts, held to traditional views of substantive due process and the police power.

Following the Supreme Court's confrontation with Franklin Roosevelt, a new majority virtually abdicated the protection of economic liberty and property rights to Congress and the state legislatures. By adopting a double standard of judicial review, the Stone, Vinson, and Warren Courts relinquished the defense of economic liberty while affording heightened protection to other unenumerated rights. In the area of economic liberty, the Court shifted the burden of proof, requiring those challenging regulatory policies to demonstrate that legislation served no conceivable public purpose. At the same time, the Court made it difficult if not impossible to restrict so-called "preferred freedoms" in order to promote the public wel-

---

the gross national product was $535.3 out of a total of $4,526.7 trillion. See *Statistical Abstract of the United States,* 110th ed. (Washington, D.C.: GPO, 1990), 378, 395, 426.

3. See Ely, *The Guardian of Every Other Right,* 116–17, 119–20, who notes that Progressive and New Deal reformers viewed the Court's defense of property rights as an obstacle to social and economic change.

fare. The Supreme Court abandoned the protection of economic rights to legislative will, but it continued to employ the substantive due process reasoning of *Lochner* in articulating such unenumerated rights as family, marital, and reproductive privacy.

The Court and the Emerging Welfare State

While the Taft Court sustained the national government's exercise of emergency wartime restrictions on property rights,[4] after the emergency had receded it tended to strike down state and federal legislation that interfered with market forces. In areas that were exempt from the marketplace—for example, public monopolies, common carriers, and other businesses affected with a public interest[5]—the Taft and Hughes Courts were more amenable to the exercise of regulatory power. Until 1934, however, the Court restrained the government's reach by refusing to expand the definition of "business affected with a public interest."

Harboring deep reservations about governmental interference in the marketplace, the justices rejected legislative intervention in collective-bargaining disputes,[6] attempts to fix fees and prices in businesses that were not clearly devoted to a public purpose,[7] efforts to protect consumers against alleged fraud,[8] and regulation of wages.[9] The Supreme Court maintained

4. See *Highland v. Russell Car & Snow Plow Co.*, 279 U.S. 253 (1929), sustaining an order fixing the maximum price for coal during World War I, under the Lever Act. Speaking for the Court, Justice Butler acknowledged that liberty of contract must yield to great national purposes, unless the government's exercise of the war power is arbitrary and capricious. *Id.*, 261–62. See also *United States v. MacIntosh*, 282 U.S. 832 (1931), 622.

5. See, for example, *Stafford v. Wallace*, 258 U.S. 495 (1922), 516–17, citing *Munn v. Illinois*, 94 U.S. 113 (1877), to support the proposition that stockyards are businesses affected with a public interest, subject to the commerce power of Congress.

6. *Truax v. Corrigan*, 257 U.S. 312 (1921), holding that an Arizona statute immunizing strikers from civil and criminal proceedings violates the Fourteenth Amendment by depriving their employer's property rights without due process of law. See also *Wolff Packing Co. v. Industrial Court*, 262 U.S. 522 (1923), and *Dorchy v. Kansas*, 264 U.S. 286 (1924).

7. *Tyson & Brothers v. Banton*, 273 U.S. 418 (1927), finding that a state statute fixing the price of theater tickets violates the due process clause of the Fourteenth Amendment. See also *Fairmont Creamery Co. v. Minnesota*, 274 U.S. 1 (1927); *Williams v. Standard Oil Co.*, 278 U.S. 235 (1929); and *New State Ice Co. v. Liebmann*, 285 U.S. 262 (1932).

8. *Burns Baking Co. v. Bryan*, 264 U.S. 504 (1924), concluding that a Nebraska law regulating the standard weight for loaves of bread sold in the state violated the due process clause of the Fourteenth Amendment.

9. *Morehead v. New York ex rel. Tipaldo*, 298 U.S. 587 (1936), ruling that a New York law establishing a minimum wage for women, which sets a fair and reasonable rate for services

that such regulations amounted to class legislation that favored particular economic interests but did not serve a public objective. Therefore, the Court struck these measures as burdensome interferences with economic liberty and property rights. As several recent studies demonstrate, some state and federal regulatory measures were in fact economic protectionism rather than legitimate police regulations.[10]

As the state and national governments attempted to alleviate the social and economic effects of the Great Depression, between 1934 and 1936, the Hughes Court occasionally bowed to congressional and state legislative attempts to restore order to the marketplace.[11] Acknowledging that market forces had failed, Chief Justice Hughes and Justice Owen Roberts conceded that the economic emergency was in some ways comparable to natural catastrophes and the wartime emergency of 1918–19.[12] Nevertheless, by January 1935 the "Old Court" was locked in combat with President Franklin Roosevelt and the Congress.[13] On "Black Monday," May 27, 1935, "a unanimous Court handed Roosevelt three major defeats."[14]

The confrontation between Roosevelt and the Supreme Court continued through 1936.[15] With the administration and the Court at loggerheads, President Roosevelt sent his famous "court-packing plan" to Capitol Hill in February 1937.[16] After the President's address to Congress on March 9,

---

rendered and meets the minimum cost of living to maintain health, interferes with the freedom of contract protected by the Fourteenth Amendment.

10. See, for example, Geoffrey P. Miller, "The True Story of Carolene Products," 1987 *S.Ct. Rev.* 397–428 (1988) (hereafter Miller, 1987 *S.Ct. Rev.*) See also Note, 103 *Harv. L. Rev.*, 1363–83, and Haggard, "Work, Government, and the Constitution," *Liberty, Property, and the Future of Constitutional Development*, ed. Paul, 241–304.

11. See, for example, *Home Building & Loan Ass'n v. Blaisdell*, 290 U.S. 398 (1934); *Nebbia v. New York*, 291 U.S. 502 (1934); and *Hegeman Farms Corp. v. Baldwin*, 293 U.S. 163 (1934).

12. See *Home Building & Loan Ass'n v. Blaisdell*, 290 U.S. 398 (1934), 439–42, 444–45.

13. In a series of decisions the Hughes Court struck down most of Roosevelt's New Deal economic recovery legislation. See Elder Witt, *Guide to the U.S. Supreme Court*, 2d ed. (Washington, D.C.: Congressional Quarterly, 1990), 40. See also *Panama Refining Co. v. Ryan*, 293 U.S. 388 (1935), and *Railroad Retirement Board v. Alton R.R. Co.*, 295 U.S. 330 (1935).

14. Witt, *U.S. Supreme Court*, 40. See also *Schecter Poultry Corp. v. United States*, 295 U.S. 495 (1935), *Louisville Joint Stock Land Bank v. Radford*, 295 U.S. 555 (1935), and *Humphrey's Executor v. United States*, 295 U.S. 602 (1935).

15. *United States v. Butler*, 297 U.S. 1 (1936), and *Carter v. Carter Coal Co.*, 298 U.S. 238 (1936). "The same day," as Elder Witt notes, "the Court, 5–4, struck down the Municipal Bankruptcy Act." See Witt, *U.S. Supreme Court*, 41. See also *Morehead v. New York*, 298 U.S. 587 (1936), striking down New York's minimum-wage law.

16. Roosevelt asked Congress to authorize the appointment of one new justice for every

"Justice Owen Roberts, who had previously cast the crucial vote for over-turning progressive economic legislation, switched sides and voted to up-hold New Deal legislation."[17] Even before Roberts was aware of Roosevelt's court-packing plan, however, he had joined Hughes in a narrow 5–4 major-ity to sustain Washington State's minimum-wage law.[18] To many jurists and scholars, Roberts's "reversal" in *Parrish* signaled the demise of liberty of con-tract. Following that switch and Willis Van Devanter's retirement, the Su-preme Court upheld a series of New Deal social and economic measures, some of which were virtually identical to acts that the justices previously had declared unconstitutional.[19]

A little more than a year after *Parrish*, Justice Stone's *Carolene Products*[20] opinion forecast the Court's abandonment of the protection of economic liberty and property rights to Congress and the state legislatures. Speaking for a bare majority, Stone sustained the authority of Congress under the commerce clause to prohibit the interstate shipment of filled milk. The Fifth Amendment, Stone wrote, does not prohibit Congress from barring filled milk from the marketplace even though the product is a wholesome one containing substitutes for butterfat. Congress may nevertheless presume

member of the Court over the age of seventy. Since six members were then over seventy, Roosevelt could have appointed enough new justices to tip the balance in favor of his New Deal program. See David O'Brien, *Storm Center: The Supreme Court in American Politics*, 2d ed. (New York: W. W. Norton & Co., 1990), 88–94. See also Witt, *U.S. Supreme Court*, 41–42.

17. David M. O'Brien, *Constitutional Law*, vol. 1, *Struggles for Power and Governmental Accountability* (New York: W. W. Norton & Co., 1991), 63.

18. Less than a year after nullifying New York's minimum-wage law for women, in *West Coast Hotel Co.* v. *Parrish*, 300 U.S. 379 (1937), the Court overturned *Adkins* and reversed *Morehead*. David O'Brien notes that "Roberts had switched his vote at conference in Decem-ber 1936, two months before FDR announced his plan." O'Brien, *Storm Center*, 88. See also Witt, *U.S. Supreme Court*, 42.

19. On the same day that the Court decided *Parrish*, it sustained the second Federal Farm Bankruptcy Act, in *Wright* v. *Vinton Branch*, 300 U.S. 440 (1937), and a section of the Railway Labor Act, which promoted collective bargaining, in *Virginia Ry. Co.* v. *System Feder-ation*, 300 U.S. 515 (1937). On April 12 a 5–4 majority upheld the National Labor Relations Act, in *National Labor Relations Bd.* v. *Jones & Laughlin Steel Corp.*, 301 U.S. 1 (1937). Following Van Devanter's announcement that he would retire on June 2, the Supreme Court sustained the unemployment compensation and old-age benefits provisions of the Social Secu-rity Act, in *Steward Machine Co.* v. *Davis*, 301 U.S. 548 (1937), and *Helvering* v. *Davis*, 301 U.S. 619 (1937).

20. 304 U.S. 144 (1938). The first of Franklin Roosevelt's appointees, Justice Hugo Black, concurred in all but the third part of Stone's opinion. Apparently, Black did not subscribe to Stone's views of the judicial function regarding "preferred," noneconomic due process rights that Stone addressed in his famous footnote number four. Justice Butler concurred in the decision, while Justice McReynolds dissented. Justices Cardozo and Reed did not participate.

that such products are harmful because they are indistinguishable from whole-milk products.[21]

Although Stone admitted that there was virtually no factual record to sustain the policy judgment, he argued that the congressional policy was entitled to a presumption of validity. Even absent a factual record, the Court should assume that there are some conceivable facts to support social and economic policy.[22] In fact, Stone ignored considerable evidence that the Filled Milk Act was little more than protectionist legislation designed to favor condensed-milk processors, such as the Borden Company.[23] In the field of social and economic policy, Stone's position foreshadowed judicial abdication to legislative volition rather than deference to reasoned judgments of the public welfare.[24]

But Justice Stone was unwilling to extend the principle of presumptive validity to state and federal policies encroaching on other personal liberties. In his now-famous *Carolene Products* footnote number four, Stone articulated the concept of preferred rights, which would later split the Supreme Court into warring camps.[25] First and Fourteenth Amendment rights guaranteeing equal access to the political process and legal equality to discrete racial and ethnic minorities, Stone argued, are indispensable to ordered liberty. There-

21. *Id.*, 148, 151. But see Miller, 1987 *S.Ct. Rev.*, 398–99. As Miller notes, the Filled Milk Act was in reality an unprincipled example of special-interest legislation. The purported public-interest justification was a transparent masquerade for legislation that protected one segment of the dairy industry against another. The statute expropriated the property of one lawful business to the benefit of another and deprived the public of an inexpensive, healthy alternative to condensed-milk products. See also Haggard, "Work, Government, and the Constitution," in *Liberty, Property, and the Future of Constitutional Development*, ed. Paul, 288–90. Haggard notes that it is often difficult to disentangle efforts to regulate the professions from attempts to put certain groups at a disadvantage.

22. 304 U.S., 152.

23. See Miller, 1987 *S.Ct. Rev.*, 398–99, 401. The Supreme Court simply accepted the specious legislative rationale of the public interest. *Id.*, 411–12.

24. As Ely notes, Stone's opinion depreciated the framers' respect for property rights and the important linkage between property rights and other personal liberties. However, Ely argues that after World War II the post-Roosevelt Court returned, albeit gingerly, to the defense of property rights. Ely, *The Guardian of Every Other Right*, 132–33, 134.

25. For an enumeration of these rights, see Stone's opinion, 304 U.S., 152–53. See also Craig R. Ducat and Harold W. Chase, *Constitutional Interpretation*, 4th ed. (St. Paul, Minn.: West Publishing Co., 1988), 67. See also Harry H. Wellington, "Common Law Rules and Constitutional Double Standards: Some Notes on Adjudication," 83 *Yale L.J.* 221–311 (1973), esp. 277–79. Stone's hands-off minimum-rationality test, as Miller argues, freed interest groups to lobby legislatures without judicial scrutiny. Miller, 1987 *S.Ct. Rev.*, 399.

fore, government policies burdening preferred rights or insular minorities should be viewed as inherently suspect and presumptively invalid.

Justice Stone's dual standard of judicial review assumes that property and economic rights are less important to ordered liberty than other fundamental rights,[26] but there is no constitutional basis for distinguishing among property, economic, or other personal liberties.[27] As William Riker argues, in the Anglo-American legal tradition property rights are inseparable from other civil rights. Property and other civil rights are accorded the same weight in the common law, the Civil Rights Act of 1866, and the Fourteenth Amendment.[28] The amendment's authors regarded property and economic rights as indispensable to liberty and the public welfare. Stone simply ignored the legal-constitutional foundation for property rights and economic liberty.

Justice Stone's *Carolene Products* opinion evidenced the Supreme Court's dramatic turnabout and abandonment of protection for economic liberty and property rights.[29] Moreover, it signaled a significant shift in substantive due process reasoning. Stone's methodology implied that the Court would no longer seriously evaluate whether the public welfare justified burdening preferred rights.[30] These rights would be treated as virtually absolute, rather than conditional rights subject to the reasonable exercise of the police power. Unlike earlier substantive due process reasoning, Stone's double standard would insulate new, unenumerated personal freedoms from governmental intrusion. Simultaneously, Stone's methodology guaranteed the demise of liberty of contract and other unenumerated economic rights.

26. Footnote four implies a two-tiered analysis of governmental actions burdening constitutionally protected rights of individuals. Regarding economic liberty and property rights, Stone's analysis suggests a legitimate public-interest, rational-relation test. Concerning other "fundamental liberties," Stone implies a compelling public-interest, strict-scrutiny standard to justify burdensome state and federal actions.

27. See Christopher Wolfe, *The Rise of Modern Judicial Review: From Constitutional Interpretation to Judge-Made Law* (New York: Basic Books, 1986), 251.

28. See William H. Riker, "Civil Rights and Property Rights," in *Liberty, Property, and the Future of Constitutional Development*, ed. Paul, 49, 50, 55–56, 57. See also Note, 103 *Harv. L. Rev.*, 1376. Employing Justice McReynolds's reasoning in *Meyer*, the author concludes that property rights are an integral element of personhood.

29. Witt, *U.S. Supreme Court*, 42.

30. As Wolfe notes, other than Stone's dictum, the Court has not explicitly adopted the dual standard, but it has done so implicitly by shifting the burden of proof to the states and the federal government in cases involving preferred First and Fourteenth Amendment rights. See Wolfe, *Modern Judicial Review*, 251–55.

The Court and Substantive Due Process, 1921–1937

The Taft and Hughes Courts decided more than fifty cases involving economic due process claims challenging the exercise of state and national
powers. Although these property and liberty claims presented a wide range
of statutory and constitutional issues, until 1937 a majority of justices generally opposed government interference in economic activity unless regulations had a direct, substantial relation to the public welfare. Until 1934 the
majority also adhered to a fairly narrow definition of "business affected with
a public interest" and the public welfare. However, in those areas where
government had granted franchises, monopolies, and licenses, the Supreme
Court was more receptive to employment of states' police, tax, and eminent
domain powers.[31]

Between 1924 and 1930 the justices voided a series of state regulations of
business as burdensome intrusions on property rights that did not advance a
substantial public purpose. In *Burns Baking Co.* v. *Bryan*,[32] for example, a
majority struck down a Nebraska statute establishing maximum and minimum weights for standard loaves of bread. Although the Court acknowledged the state's competence to protect consumers against fraud, it denied
that the maximum-weight provision was a legitimate police measure.[33]
Pierce Butler averred that the statute was a form of expropriation because it
denied the company its property by increasing production costs without justification. But the law had no rational relation to the protection of consumers.[34]

31. In 1922, Robert Cushman forecast, somewhat prematurely, that a new era of judicial
deference to legislative policymaking was emerging. Although the Court remained an active
arbiter of social and economic policy, it was becoming more receptive to legislative fact-
finding. He anticipated that the justices would shift the burden of proof to plaintiffs attacking
legislative policy. See Robert E. Cushman, "The Social and Economic Interpretation of the
Fourteenth Amendment," 20 *Mich. L. Rev.* 737–64 (1922), 757–58.
32. 264 U.S. 504 (1924).
33. *Id.*, 510–11. But see *Pacific States Box & Basket Co.* v. *White*, 296 U.S. 176 (1935),
sustaining an Oregon statute that specified the size and shape of containers for marketing
raspberries and strawberries as a reasonable exercise of the police power. Speaking for the
Court, Brandeis stated that the statute bore a reasonable relation to preventing consumer
fraud and preserving perishable food products, which were legitimate state interests. *Id.*, 182.
However, the evidence suggests that the law gave an advantage to the interests of local con-
tainer manufacturers. See Strong, *Substantive Due Process of Law*, 234.
34. 264 U.S., 513–16, 517. Butler denied that there was any evidence to show that consumers were induced to accept a 10-ounce loaf for a full pound. Dissenting, Brandeis argued
that the law was rational since it prevented consumers from confusing oversize smaller loaves
with larger ones. *Id.*, 518–19.

In two cases concerning restrictions on the use of real property, however, the Taft Court sustained a municipal zoning ordinance and a state pest-control act. Speaking for a majority in *Euclid* v. *Ambler Realty Co.*,[35] Justice Sutherland argued that a zoning ordinance containing use, height, setback, and other restrictions was a reasonable or rational exercise of the police power even though the law reduced land values. Although Sutherland took a broad view of the police power, he argued that there must be a direct relationship to the public health and safety. In this case, there was a substantial relationship between the zoning regulations and municipal authority to relieve congestion, traffic, and fire and safety hazards.[36]

Two years later, in *Miller* v. *Schoene*,[37] the Supreme Court sustained a Virginia statute providing for the compulsory destruction of diseased cedar trees in order to suppress the spread of cedar rust to nearby apple orchards. In an opinion for a unanimous Court, Justice Stone justified the destruction of the trees, without compensation, as a reasonable use of the police power. The police power, Stone reasoned, permits the state to destroy one class of property to save another that, in the legislature's judgment, is of greater public value.[38] In both *Euclid* and *Miller* the Court adhered to the established theory of the police power, which permitted imposing burdens on specific property interests that clearly serve a public purpose.

Between the 1927 and 1932 terms, the Court refused to extend the concept of businesses affected with a public interest to such areas as the sale of theater tickets,[39] the price of such ordinary commodities as ice, gasoline, and dairy products,[40] and the fees of employment agencies.[41] Denying that the sale of theater tickets is a business affected with a public interest, Justice Sutherland argued that the right to determine prices for goods and services "is an inherent attribute of the property itself, and, as such, within the

35. 272 U.S. 365 (1926).

36. Sutherland argued that such ordinances developed from the common-law authority to abate nuisances in order to protect the public welfare. *Id.*, 386–87, 388–90. See also Ely, *The Guardian of Every Other Right*, 113–17.

37. 276 U.S. 272 (1928).

38. "[W]here the public interest is involved," he emphasized, "preferment of that interest over the property interest of the individual, to the extent even of its destruction, is one of the distinguishing characteristics of every exercise of the police power which affects property." *Id.*, 279–80. Insofar as the law was a police measure, it could not be a compensable taking under the due process clause.

39. *Tyson & Brothers* v. *Banton*, 273 U.S. 418 (1927).

40. See *New State Ice Co.* v. *Liebmann*, 285 U.S. 262 (1932); *Williams* v. *Standard Oil Co.*, 278 U.S. 235 (1929); and *Fairmont Creamery Co.* v. *Minnesota*, 274 U.S. 1 (1927).

41. *Ribnik* v. *McBride*, 277 U.S. 350 (1928).

protection of the due process of law clauses of the Fifth and Fourteenth Amendments."[42] While Sutherland recognized that the states could regulate theaters in many ways to protect the public welfare, he denied that selling theater tickets fit any of the traditional classifications of businesses affected with a public interest. Selling theater tickets was no different from any other private commercial transaction, even where an oligopoly might exist.[43]

Dissenting, Stone found the majority's distinction between various kinds of businesses vague. He averred that the questions posed in *Tyson* were questions of expediency or policy, of which the legislature was the best judge. Since the market had failed to work, the legislature was justified in protecting the public against ticket-scalping. Nothing in the Fourteenth Amendment, Stone concluded, prohibited the legislature from regulating private attempts to control markets to the public's detriment.[44] Indeed, the states had long used the police power to prevent private monopolies from undermining free markets.[45]

Responding to the Great Depression, in 1934 the Hughes Court began to expand the definition of "business affected with a public interest" so much that the distinction between such businesses and purely private enterprise became elusive.[46] In *Nebbia* v. *New York* a bare majority sustained a New York law fixing the wholesale price of milk.[47] Justice Owen Roberts argued

42. 273 U.S., 429.

43. *Id.*, 433–35, 436–37, 437, 438. However, in *Stimson Lumber Co.* v. *Kuykendall*, 275 U.S. 207 (1927), the Court held that tow boats kept available for public use are common carriers. By virtue of the function these boats perform, Butler argued for the Court, they are common carriers subject to public regulation of rates. Therefore, a statute prescribing rates does not deprive shippers of their property by preventing them from securing rates lower than those prescribed. Although the state cannot convert a private carrier into a public one, Butler concluded, it does have an interest in preventing common carriers from granting preferential treatment. *Id.*, 211, 212.

44. 273 U.S., 447–48, 451–53.

45. See Kens, 55 *Rev. of Pol.*, and Novak, 18 *Law & Soc. Inquiry*, who document state regulation of commodities and markets in the antebellum era.

46. In *O'Gorman & Young* v. *Hartford Ins. Co.*, 282 U.S. 251 (1931), a five-man majority held that a New Jersey law prescribing rates for fire insurance was a reasonable exercise of the police power as applied to a business affected with a public interest. *Id.*, 257–58. Justices Van Devanter, McReynolds, Sutherland, and Butler dissented. See Ely, *The Guardian of Every Other Right*, 122, on the expansion of the concept of business affected with a public interest.

47. 291 U.S. 502 (1934). Five years later the Supreme Court sustained an order issued pursuant to the Agricultural Marketing Adjustment Act of 1937 regulating the minimum price of milk in the New York City metropolitan area as a reasonable exercise of the power to regulate interstate commerce. Even though the order exempted agricultural cooperatives, the majority averred that it was a reasonable classification consistent with the Fifth Amendment's

that the law was not "unreasonable or arbitrary" or unrelated to the purpose of preventing "ruthless competition from destroying the wholesale price-structure on which the farmer depends for his livelihood, and the community for an assured supply of milk."[48] All due process requires, he continued, is "that the means selected shall have a real and substantial relation" to a valid public purpose.[49]

Roberts acknowledged that, traditionally, the Court had restricted price-fixing to public utilities and monopolies, to businesses possessing public grants and franchises, and to enterprises that the public itself might undertake. But he denied that there was a "closed class or category" of businesses affected with a public interest.[50] In each case, the Court must determine "whether circumstances vindicate the challenged regulation as a reasonable exertion of governmental authority or condemn it as arbitrary or discriminatory."[51]

Under the circumstances, Roberts concluded, the Court should be deferential to the legislature's judgment of the necessity and wisdom of New York's price-fixing law.[52] "With the wisdom of the policy adopted, with the adequacy or practicability of the law enacted to forward it," he wrote, "the courts are both incompetent and unauthorized to deal."[53] However, Roberts insisted that the legislature demonstrate a real and substantial relation between price-fixing and a legitimate state interest. Although Justice Roberts acknowledged the legislature's competence and primacy as a fact-finder and policymaker, he reserved a continuing role for the Supreme Court as a final arbiter of the police power as well as of economic liberty and property rights.

Dissenting vigorously, Justice McReynolds, with Justices Van Devanter, Sutherland, and Butler concurring, protested that emergencies do not confer power on government that otherwise does not exist. Although the Great Depression had caused hardship, Justice McReynolds averred, the Supreme Court should not sacrifice immutable liberty and property rights to a clamorous, impatient majority's demand for relief. The mere assertion of an eco-

---

due process clause. See *United States* v. *Rock-Royal Co-operative*, 307 U.S. 533 (1939), 561–65, 571–72.

48. 291 U.S., 530.

49. *Id.*, 525.

50. *Id.*, 525, 531, 536. See, for example, *Public Service Commission* v. *Utilities Co.*, 289 U.S. 130 (1933).

51. 291 U.S., 536.

52. *Id.*, 537–38.

53. *Id.*, 537.

nomic emergency is not sufficiently compelling to justify fixing prices of a private business.[54] Adhering to the traditional definition of businesses affected with a public interest,[55] McReynolds concluded that the New York statute was not "regulation, but management, control, dictation—it amounts to the deprivation of the fundamental right which one has to conduct his own affairs honestly and along customary lines."[56] The majority opinion, he complained, could justify converting every private business that produces, distributes, or sells ordinary commodities into a public utility.

The Taft and Hughes Courts also opposed governmental policies favoring labor unions, promoting collective bargaining, and imposing wage-and-hour regulations as burdensome interferences with liberty of contract. In *Wolff Packing Co.* v. *Industrial Court*[57] and in *Dorchy* v. *Kansas*[58] the Court found that compulsory arbitration statutes, as applied to businesses not clothed with a public interest, violated employers' and employees' liberty of contract. Rejecting the argument that the Court should grant presumptive validity to legislative declarations that a business is clothed with a public interest, in *Wolff Packing Co.* Chief Justice Taft denied that the nature of the meatpacking business justified intrusion on the individual's liberty of contract.[59] Absent a war or other similar emergency, circumstances did not warrant interference in the business of the butcher, the baker, the tailor, the wood chopper, or the miner and the mine operator.[60] The Court continued to

54. *Id.*, 545–46, 552. See also *Home Building & Loan Ass'n*, 290 U.S. 398 (1934), and *Ex parte Milligan*, 71 U.S. (4 Wall.) 2 (1866).

55. 291 U.S., 552–54.

56. *Id.*, 554–55. As James Bond notes, McReynolds adhered throughout his career to the view that government should not interfere with honest business practices. Believing property rights to be fundamental, Justice McReynolds advocated limited government intervention in free markets. However, he accepted the necessity of government action against monopolies because they interfered with free markets and economic liberty. Thoroughly opposed to the New Deal welfare state, James Clark McReynolds believed that only a free-market economy was compatible with constitutional liberty. See James E. Bond, *I Dissent: The Legacy of Chief Justice James Clark McReynolds* (Fairfax, Va.: George Mason University Press, 1992). Despite the error in the title (McReynolds was never chief justice), Bond's biography is an insightful analysis of the justice's career on and off the Court.

57. 262 U.S. 522 (1923).

58. 264 U.S. 286 (1924). In *Dorchy* the Court found the Kansas law requiring compulsory arbitration unconstitutional as applied to coal mining.

59. 262 U.S., 534, 536–37, 538. See also *Near* v. *Minnesota*, 283 U.S. 697 (1931). Speaking for the Court, Hughes recognized that liberty of contract is not absolute. He emphasized that "the power of the State stops short of interference with what are deemed to be certain indispensable requirements of the liberty assured, notably with respect to the fixing of prices and wages." *Id.*, 707–8.

60. 262 U.S., 537.

view such intrusions in labor contracts as class legislation, which favored the interests of unions at the expense of proprietors and the public.

Despite the Supreme Court's opposition to minimum-wage and collective-bargaining laws, it sustained regulation of employment contracts, hours of employment, and worker compensation as reasonable exertions of the police power. In *Prudential Insurance Co. v. Cheek*[61] the justices upheld Missouri's Service Letter Law, which required insurance companies to provide employees with letters stating the cause for leaving their former employer's service. Rejecting the argument that the law burdened either party's contractual liberty, Mahlon Pitney justified the law as rationally related to the state's legitimate interest in protecting the honest wage-earner's right to secure employment.[62] By removing a barrier to labor markets, the law promoted liberty of contract, which was consistent with the Court's laissez-faire ideology.

Two years later, in *Radice v. New York*,[63] the justices sustained a New York law prohibiting the employment of women between 10:00 P.M. and 6:00 A.M. in restaurants in large cities. Distinguishing the New York law from *Adkins*, Justice Sutherland noted that the "legislature had before it a mass of information from which it concluded that night work is substantially and especially detrimental to the health of women."[64] In such areas of judgment, Sutherland observed, the Court should not overturn legislative policy unless legislative fact-finding is clearly unfounded.[65] As *Radice* suggests, the justices accepted regulations of labor contracts that were related directly to public health.

Just as the Taft Court had rejected the District of Columbia minimum-wage act for women and children,[66] in *Morehead v. New York* the Hughes

61. 259 U.S. 530 (1922).

62. *Id.*, 536–37. Similarly, the Hughes Court upheld a California law conditioning labor contracts made within the state for seasonal work performed by resident fishermen outside the state's jurisdiction. The Court sustained a statutory provision requiring out-of-state employers who hire local fishermen to accept California's compensation provisions as a condition of making local labor contracts for work done in Alaska. See *Alaska Packers Ass'n v. Industrial Accident Commission*, 294 U.S. 532 (1935), 540, 542.

63. 264 U.S. 292 (1924).

64. *Id.*, 294. Of course, Sutherland's reasoning rests on the same gender-based assumptions that the Supreme Court had accepted in *Muller v. Oregon*, 208 U.S. 412 (1908), 422. While such laws were considered to be progressive at the time, today some feminists regard them as denigrating the equal status and rights of women.

65. 264 U.S., 294–95.

66. *Adkins v. Children's Hospital*, 261 U.S. 525 (1923). As an alternative to charity, a District of Columbia statute required employers to pay a minimum wage necessary to provide

Court dismissed a similar state law for female workers.[67] While there were some differences between the two statutes, Justice Butler argued that they were indistinguishable. Both statutes interfered with the liberty of employers and employees to bargain freely and equally over wages, hours, and conditions of employment. Butler examined the background of the New York law but gave little weight to the legislature's fact-finding and to the way the State Court of Appeals had construed the act.[68] The majority held to the view that wage laws are class legislation and merely redistribute wealth and bargaining power in violation of due process.

Dissenting, Chief Justice Hughes asserted that the two statutes were materially different because the New York law provided for a fair wage that was reasonably related to the market value of the services performed. Inasmuch as wages were related to the value of labor, the law was not tantamount to a deprivation of property.[69] Furthermore, Hughes asserted, the law emerged

---

the cost of living, without reference to the services rendered. While Justice Sutherland expressed deference toward congressional factfinding and judgment, he attacked the statute as an unreasonable interference with the liberty of contract. Recognizing that liberty of contract is a conditional rather than an absolute right, Sutherland denied there was any justification for fixing the price of wages. Congress had not demonstrated any rational relation between the rate of compensation and the public health and morals. Since there was no direct relationship between the minimum wage and a worker's productivity, the statute amounted to a compulsory exaction of property without due process. Furthermore, the statute did not apply to dangerous occupations or businesses affected with a public interest, nor was there a temporary emergency to justify the government's interference in the labor market. See also Hovenkamp, 40 Stan. L. Rev., 436–37. For an analysis of Adkins from a feminist perspective, see Joan G. Zimmerman, "The Jurisprudence of Equality: The Women's Minimum Wage, the First Equal Rights Amendment, and Adkins v. Children's Hospital, 1905–1923," 78 J. Am. Hist. 188–225 (1991).

Dissenting, Chief Justice Taft believed that physical differences between men and women justified a minimum wage to protect women's health. 261 U.S., 566. In a separate dissent, Justice Holmes criticized the majority's dogmatic adherence to liberty of contract, for which there was no textual basis. Holmes believed that the law should be sustained as a reasonable police measure. Id., 570, 571.

See also Sutherland's opinion for the majority in Carter v. Carter Coal Co., 298 U.S. 238 (1936), 310, 311, holding a wage-fixing provision of the Bituminous Coal Act of 1935 unconstitutional. Sutherland argued that the act deprived employers of their personal liberty and property under the due process clause of the Fifth Amendment, inasmuch as there was no valid public purpose. But see Sunshine Anthracite Coal Co. v. Adkins, 310 U.S. 381 (1940), sustaining the Bituminous Coal Conservation Act. Denying that the Act deprived the company's property without due process, Justice William O. Douglas argued that because the record supported Congress's judgment the wisdom of the policy was of no concern to the Court. Id., 394–96, 397.

67. 298 U.S. 587 (1936), appellee's brief, 589–93.

68. 298 U.S., 608–9, 610–12, 614–15.

69. Id., 619–21, 622–24. Hughes's argument was similar to the plaintiff's position in Bunt-

from extensive fact-finding regarding the conditions of employment and the exploitation of women and children.[70] Liberty of contract, the chief justice emphasized, is a qualified right, not an absolute right. The Fourteenth Amendment's due process clause protects liberty against arbitrary restraint; it does not prohibit the state from protecting the public welfare.[71]

While Hughes attempted to distinguish *Morehead* from *Adkins*, Stone would have overruled the latter as a vague pronouncement on the due process clause and an unjustifiable limitation on the police power. According to Stone, the police power comprehends the authority to make policy concerning wages, to regulate collective bargaining, and to readjust the bargaining power of labor and management. Articulating a means-ends test, Justice Stone asserted that as long as there is a reasonable relationship between the regulation and a "proper" legislative purpose, and the means are neither arbitrary nor discriminatory, police measures are constitutional. Government, he underscored, has the power to establish "real" liberty of contract by equalizing the bargaining power of labor and management.[72] As Stone's concurring opinion implied, the legislature is the primary judge of the reasonableness of public policy.

Nine months later, in *West Coast Hotel Co. v. Parrish*,[73] the Supreme Court adopted Stone's position. Overruling *Adkins* and distinguishing *Morehead*, Chief Justice Hughes, joined by Justice Roberts in the majority, conceded broad discretion to the Washington legislature in regulating employer-employee relations. Hughes justified the Washington minimum-wage law as a legitimate police measure, protecting the health, safety, and welfare of women.[74] Despite the subterfuge, the majority accepted the legitimacy of governmental intervention in collective-bargaining relationships to adjust economic inequalities. "The legislature of the State," Hughes wrote, "was clearly entitled to consider the situation of women in employment, the fact that they are in the class receiving the least pay, that their bargaining

---

ing v. *Oregon* and *Adkins v. Children's Hospital*, that there was no taking of property because such laws promoted increased efficiency and productivity of labor. See Strong, *Substantive Due Process of Law*, 129–30, 132–34.

70. *Id.*, 625–26, 626–27.
71. *Id.*, 627, 628, 629.
72. *Id.*, 631, 633–35.
73. 300 U.S. 379 (1937).
74. Section two of the Laws of 1913 provided that "it shall be unlawful to employ women workers in any industry in the State of Washington at wages which are not adequate for their maintenance." Section three established an Industrial Welfare Commission to determine wages "which shall be sufficient for the decent maintenance of women." *Id.*, 386–87.

power is relatively weak, and that they are the ready victims of those who would take advantage of their necessitous circumstances."[75] In reality, a majority of justices conceded that profound disturbances in labor markets necessitated government intervention rather than neutrality in order to ensure economic liberty.[76]

Dissenting, Justice Sutherland warned that "the Constitution does not change with the ebb and flow of economic events."[77] By changing the meaning of due process, the Court had usurped the people's right, acting through their representatives, to amend the basic law. In amending the Constitution to meet new conditions, a bare judicial majority had undermined the supremacy of law and transformed enduring constitutional mandates into "mere moral reflections."[78] Sutherland reiterated that liberty of contract is the rule governing wage negotiations between labor and management. The Washington statute was "simply and exclusively, a law fixing wages for adult women who are legally as capable of contracting for themselves as men."[79] Speaking for the dissenters, Sutherland argued that the Court had buried liberty of contract. In contrast to Hughes, Sutherland clung to nineteenth-century principles of laissez-faire constitutionalism. Although the Taft and Hughes Courts had always recognized specific exceptions to the general rule of contractual liberty, with *Parrish* the exceptions swallowed the rule.

In effect, the majority had accepted a minimum-rationality standard for evaluating the constitutionality of economic and social legislation. First, does the policy further a permissible state interest—that is, a subject within the state's constitutional competence? Second, is there a minimally rational relationship between the means employed and the state's ostensible purpose? In answering these questions, Hughes intimated that the Court would pre-

75. *Id.*, 398.
76. *Id.* Jennifer Nedelsky argues that, since *Parrish*, the task of legal scholarship is to develop an alternative to *Lochner*'s property-based limitation on the power of government to promote the public welfare. Indeed, she suggests that since the late 1930s "property" has not been a serious limitation on the welfare state. Unfortunately, Nedelsky does not offer any specific alternatives. See Jennifer Nedelsky, *Private Property and the Limits of American Constitutionalism: The Madisonian Framework and Its Legacy* (Chicago: University of Chicago Press, 1990).
77. 300 U.S., 402. Van Devanter, McReynolds, and Butler concurred in the dissent.
78. *Id.*, 403, 404. Sutherland's reference is to the argument that the supremacy clause of Article Six, section two, makes the Constitution binding law rather than a hortatory document.
79. *Id.*, 407. Sutherland also denied that there were any special circumstances that might justify the state's interference with the fundamental liberty protected by the Fourteenth Amendment. *Id.*, 406–7.

sume the law's validity, unless the legislative record is devoid of support. While the chief justice did not state so explicitly, he implied that plaintiffs challenging social and economic policy bear a substantial burden of proving that the law is so bereft of reason and unsupported by evidence that it is unconstitutional.

If *Parrish* acknowledged the states' broad, discretionary authority to impose restraints on liberty of contract, in *United States* v. *Darby*[80] the Supreme Court legitimized Congress's use of the interstate-commerce power to regulate wages and hours in manufacturing.[81] Explicitly rejecting the rationale of *Hammer* v. *Dagenhart*,[82] Stone emphasized that Congress could regulate business activities antecedent to interstate commerce in order to protect the public health, morals, and welfare. In a brief concluding statement, he dismissed the plaintiff's claim that the wages-and-hours provision of the Fair Labor Standards Act of 1938 violated the Fifth Amendment:

> Since our decision in *West Coast Hotel Co.* v. *Parrish*, it is no longer open to question that the fixing of a minimum wage is within the legislative power and that the bare fact of its exercise is not a denial of due process under the Fifth more than under the Fourteenth Amendment.[83]

Parrish and *Darby* marked the Supreme Court's acceptance *sub silentio* of Stone's double standard. Delivered three days after McReynolds announced his retirement, Stone's *Darby* opinion did not stir a single dissent.

The Premature Burial of Substantive Due Process, 1941–1969

Four months after *Darby*, President Roosevelt nominated Harlan F. Stone to replace Chief Justice Hughes, who announced on June 12, 1941, that he

80. 312 U.S. 100 (1941).
81. *Id.*, 114, 115. See also *National Labor Relations Bd.* v. *Jones & Laughlin Steel Corp.*, 301 U.S. 1 (1937), in which the Court sustained the board's order to reinstate employees who had been dismissed for union activities. While Chief Justice Hughes conceded that manufacturing is not commerce, he argued that the company moved goods in a stream of commerce, beginning with its purchase of raw materials and ending with its sale of steel products at home and abroad.
82. 247 U.S. 251 (1918).
83. 312 U.S., 125.

planned to retire at the end of the term.[84] Beginning with Stone's tenure as chief justice, the Supreme Court rarely used the due process clauses to defeat the regulation of businesses, professions, and the use of property. As Stone had forecast in *Carolene Products*, social and economic policies would be entitled to a presumption of validity unless they are clearly devoid of any rational basis.[85] If there were some judicially conceivable basis for the policy, henceforth, the Supreme Court would sustain the legislature's judgment.

During the Stone, Vinson, and Warren eras, the Court entertained relatively few due process challenges to social and economic policies implicating property or economic liberty interests. In deciding these cases, the justices almost invariably applied a minimum-rationality test to sustain state and national regulatory legislation. Although Justices Hugo Black and Felix Frankfurter disagreed on many issues involving the exercise of jurisdiction and judicial power, they apparently shared the view that the substantive due process, liberty-of-contract philosophy of *Lochner* was dead and deserved a decent burial.

Three cases decided between 1942 and 1968 illustrate the deference of the Roosevelt and post-Roosevelt Courts to congressional policymaking. In *Federal Power Commission v. Natural Gas Pipeline Co.*[86] the Supreme Court sustained the Natural Gas Act of 1938. Citing *Carolene Products*, *Sunshine Coal Co.*, and *Darby*, Chief Justice Stone argued that the Federal Power Commission (FPC) had not denied the company its procedural or substantive due process property rights under the Fifth Amendment. Although Stone reviewed the reasonableness of the FPC's rate-making, he exhibited to the Commission virtually the same degree of deference he had exhibited toward Congress, a co-equal institution.[87] Concurring, Felix Frankfurter agreed entirely with Stone's opinion, inasmuch as the Natural Gas Act authorized judicial review of the FPC orders fixing "just and reasonable rates."[88] Justices Black, Douglas, and Frank Murphy also concurred in the decision,

84. See O'Brien, *Storm Center*, 74. O'Brien reports that Felix Frankfurter preferred Robert Jackson but agreed with Roosevelt "that Stone, a Republican, would inspire confidence in him 'as a national and not a partisan President.'"
85. 304 U.S. 144 (1938), 152.
86. 315 U.S. 575 (1942).
87. For an excellent discussion regarding the presumptive validity of regulatory agencies' fact-finding and decision-making, see Justice Douglas's opinion (of the Court) and Justice Robert Jackson's dissenting opinion in *Federal Power Commission v. Hope Natural Gas Co.*, 320 U.S. 591 (1944).
88. 315 U.S., 609.

but they criticized Stone's assumption that the Fifth Amendment's due process clause authorizes the Supreme Court "to invalidate an order as unconstitutional because it finds the charges to be unreasonable."[89]

Separated by almost twenty-four years, *Carolene Products Co. (II)* v. *United States*[90] and the *Permian Basin Area Rates Case*[91] underscored the Court's new deference to congressional policymaking. As Justice Stanley Reed wrote in *Carolene Products (II)*, the plaintiff bears the burden of proving in a clear and convincing way "that there is no rational basis for the legislation; that it is an arbitrary fiat."[92] Similarly, in the *Permian Basin Case*, John Marshall Harlan (II), claimed that, since Congress had invested broad rate-making authority in the FPC,

> [a] presumption of validity therefore attaches to each exercise of the Commission's expertise, and those who would overturn the Commission's judgment undertake "the heavy burden of making a convincing showing that it is invalid because it is unjust and unreasonable in its consequences."[93]

As both decisions reveal, the Stone, Vinson, and Warren Courts abandoned any serious effort to distinguish between economic regulatory legislation that served a valid public purpose and class legislation that advanced a distinct group's interests.

Despite continuing conflict between the Supreme Court's liberal and conservative wings, the consensus on social and economic policy extended to the states' use of the police power. Here too the Vinson Court usually sustained state legislation against substantive due process attacks. In *Lincoln Federal Labor Union*, for example, Justice Black argued that a Nebraska constitutional amendment and a North Carolina statute guaranteeing nonunion employees' right to work did not violate the liberty of employers, employees, or union members. If the states have the power to prohibit discrimination against nonunion employees, Black noted, they also have authority under

89. *Id.*, 599.

90. *Carolene Products (II)*, 323 U.S. 18 (1944).

91. 390 U.S. 747 (1968). See also *Berman* v. *Parker*, 348 U.S. 26 (1954), 33. Sustaining the District of Columbia Redevelopment Act, Justice Douglas asserted that the Fifth Amendment is not a barrier to social policy even when the legislature takes property for a broad public purpose—namely, urban redevelopment—rather than a direct public use.

92. 323 U.S., 31–32.

93. 390 U.S., 767.

the police power to prohibit the making of union contracts that obligate employers to "refuse to hire or retain nonunion workers."[94] Black specifically rejected the substantive due process, liberty-of-contract reasoning of *Allgeyer*, *Lochner*, and subsequent cases. Since *Nebbia*, he emphasized, there has been little doubt about the states' authority to regulate labor contracts without regard to whether businesses are clothed with a public interest.[95]

If the Vinson Court left any doubt about its views on liberty of contract, Justice William O. Douglas dispelled the ambiguity in *Day-Bright Lighting, Inc. v. Missouri.*[96] Sustaining a Missouri statute that encouraged employees to exercise the franchise, Douglas brushed aside the company's claim that the law, which required that it pay employees up to four hours' wages for voting during the workday, interfered with the liberty of contract. While conceding that the "legislative power has limits," Douglas retorted: "Our recent decisions make plain that we do not sit as a super-legislature to weigh the wisdom of legislation nor to decide whether the policy which it expresses offends the public welfare."[97] Douglas reiterated the majority's view that the public welfare is a "broad and inclusive concept" that comprehends the community's moral, social, economic, physical, and political well-being. For emphasis, Justice Douglas added that the only way to invalidate the law was to return "to the philosophy of the *Lochner*, *Coppage*, and *Adkins* cases,"[98] which the Court refused to do.

In *Williamson v. Lee Optical Co.*[99] Justice Douglas confirmed the Warren Court's rejection of substantive due process review of economic regulatory policy. He denied that an Oklahoma law, making it a crime for persons (opticians) other than licensed optometrists and ophthalmologists to fit,

94. *Lincoln Federal Labor Union v. Northwestern Iron & Metal Co.*, 335 U.S. 525 (1949).

95. *Id.*, 536–37. See also Black (dissenting) in *Hood & Sons v. Du Mond*, 336 U.S. 525 (1949), and his opinion for the Court in *Travelers Health Ass'n v. Virginia*, 339 U.S. 643 (1950). See also Frankfurter's concurring opinion in the companion case to *Lincoln Federal Labor Union*, *American Federation of Labor v. American Sash & Door Co.*, 335 U.S. 538 (1949). Supporting Black's deference to legislative authority, Frankfurter took the opportunity to engage in a discourse on judicial self-restraint. Echoing Holmes, Justice Frankfurter attacked the early concepts of economic liberty and substantive due process as an attempt to enshrine laissez-faire thinking in the Constitution. *Id.*, 543.

96. 342 U.S. 421 (1952).

97. *Id.*, 423.

98. *Id.*, 424–25.

99. 348 U.S. 483 (1955). For an analysis of the use of the courts to protect the economic position of optometrists in this case, see Mark Tushnet, "Public Choice Constitutionalism and Economic Rights," in *Liberty, Property, and the Future of Constitutional Development*, ed. Paul, 37–40.

duplicate, or place eyeglass lenses in frames, violated either the due process clause or the equal protection clause.[100] The Oklahoma law, wrote Douglas, may be needless and wasteful, but the legislature, not the Court, must determine the wisdom or utility of the policy. "The day is gone," he continued, "when this Court uses the Due Process Clause of the Fourteenth Amendment to strike down state laws, regulatory of business and industrial conditions, because they may be unwise, improvident, or out of harmony with a particular school of thought."[101] Quoting from Chief Justice Waite's opinion in *Munn v. Illinois* (1877), Douglas advised aggrieved persons to resort to the polls, not to the courts.[102]

Approximately eight years after *Williamson*, Justice Black delivered another body blow to substantive due process review of state commercial and business regulations. In the U.S. constitutional system, Black wrote, "it is up to legislatures, not courts, to decide on the wisdom and utility of legislation."[103] The time had long since passed, he continued, when the Court would use the due process clause to void laws that it believed unreasonable, "that is, unwise or incompatible with some particular economic or social philosophy."[104] Once again proclaiming the doctrine of *Lochner* dead, Hugo Black observed: "We have returned to the original constitutional proposition that courts do not substitute their social and economic beliefs for the judgment of legislative bodies, who are elected to pass laws."[105] If the people seek relief from unwise or uncommonly silly laws, they must do so in the legislature. As long as legislative polices do not run afoul of specific constitutional prohibitions, Black asserted, the Supreme Court will not exploit

100. 348 U.S., 484–88.
101. *Id.*, 488. See also Ely, *The Guardian of Every Other Right*, 139–40.
102. 348 U.S., 488. See also Black's opinion for the Court in *Brotherhood of Locomotive Firemen v. Chicago, R.I. & P. R.R. Co.*, 393 U.S. 129 (1968). But see the conflict between Justices Black and Harold Burton in *Morey v. Doud*, 354 U.S. 457 (1957). Black hinted that the reasoning behind *Lochner* was not dead, but merely its application to economic interests.
103. *Ferguson v. Skrupa*, 372 U.S. 726 (1963), 729.
104. *Id.*
105. *Id.*, 730. "Whether the legislature takes for its textbook Adam Smith, Herbert Spencer, Lord Keynes, or some other is no concern of ours." *Id.*, 732. But see Justice Stewart's opinion for the Court in *Lynch v. Household Finance Corp.*, 405 U.S. 538 (1972), 542–43, which explicitly rejects the dichotomy on which Black's opinion in *Skrupa* and Stone's view in *Carolene Products* rests. As Stewart argues, the framers of the Civil Rights Act of 1866 did not make a distinction between property rights and other personal liberties. Inasmuch as people own property, the dichotomy between property rights and personal rights is absurd. However, according to Ely, there is no move to openly repudiate the *Carolene Products* double standard. Ely, *The Guardian of Every Other Right*, 141.

the "vague contours" of the due process clause to frustrate social and economic experimentation.[106]

In cases involving substantive due process property and economic liberty claims, the Rehnquist Court adheres to the Stone-Black-Douglas line of reasoning that social and economic policies are entitled to presumptive validity. Expressing deference to legislative fact-finding and policymaking, the justices claim to have buried the *Lochner* reasoning that earlier courts used to censor social and economic policies. Since the vague contours of the due process clause do not yield explicit economic rights, the Court has applied a minimum-rationality standard to substantive due process property and economic-liberty claims. If there is a judicially conceivable rational relationship between the policy and some imaginable legitimate public purpose, the Supreme Court will usually exercise self-restraint and validate the statute or regulation. Only when the deprivation is egregious—that is, patently arbitrary and without any rational foundation or imaginable public purpose—is the Court willing to use the due process clauses to restrain the legislature's economic policymaking.

In an article that appeared in October 1920, just before the presidential election, William Howard Taft wrote: "There is no greater domestic issue in the election than the maintenance of the Supreme Court as the bulwark to enforce the guaranty that no man shall be deprived of his property without due process of law."[107] During the next fifteen years, under Taft and Hughes the Supreme Court generally adhered to the view that the due process clauses impose substantive limits on legislative power vis-à-vis property rights and economic liberties. A majority opposed government interference with liberty of contract and vested property rights unless the states and the national government could demonstrate a direct and substantial relationship to the public welfare. The Taft and Hughes Courts also opposed collective-bargaining and minimum-wage laws as class legislation that advanced the

106. While Justice Harlan concurred in the decision, he did not necessarily share Black's absolutist views concerning the demise of substantive due process. In a one-line concurrence, Harlan agreed that the state legislation bore "a rational relation to a constitutionally permissible objective." 372 U.S., 733. In 1968, Harlan, with Black and Potter Stewart concurring, dissented in *Glona v. American Guarantee & Liability Ins. Co.*, 391 U.S. 73 (1968). In classifying individuals for economic regulatory purposes, Douglas maintained, the state need only show a rational relation between the objective and the classification. However, where fundamental rights are at stake the state must meet a higher test. See Douglas (opinion of the Court), 391 U.S. , 69–72.

107. William Howard Taft, "Mr. Wilson and the Campaign," 10 *Yale Rev.* 1–25 (1921), 19–20.

interests of labor at the expense of business and the public. Although the Court added little to the evolution of substantive due process, its laissez-faire constitutional ideology clashed with the emerging welfare state.

By 1936 the Supreme Court's defense of economic liberty and property rights collided with the Roosevelt administration's economic and social policies. Sitting "as a continuous constitutional convention," complained Robert H. Jackson, Roosevelt's former solicitor general and attorney general, a majority used the Court "to cripple other departments of government and to disable the nation from adopting social or economic policies which were deemed inconsistent with the Justices' philosophy of property rights."[108] Employing the due process clauses, judicial majorities "seriously contracted the interstate commerce power" and "cut down the effective power of the states."[109] The same justices, Jackson criticized, "were strict and niggardly in construing *powers* of government and liberal to the point of extravagance in construing *limitations*—even inventing such limitations as 'freedom of contract' where none existed in the Constitution."[110] Despite Jackson's complaint, the Court did not invent liberty of contract or invariably "cut down" state and national economic regulatory policies.[111] In fact, the Supreme Court generally sustained policies that had a direct relationship to some legitimate public purpose.

Although the Taft and Hughes Courts were wary of governmental attempts to interfere with market forces, the justices conceded legislative authority under the war, commerce, tax, eminent domain, and police powers to respond to temporary international and domestic emergencies. Despite the majority's opposition to price-fixing, the Hughes Court strained the concept of "business affected with a public interest" so that eventually the term lost all practical meaning. In areas where markets had failed to operate or where government had granted monopolies and franchises, the justices acknowledged legislative authority to limit property and economic liberty.

Between 1933 and 1935 a majority of the Hughes Court became increasingly skeptical of legislative fact-finding and policymaking. As the Roosevelt administration and state governments stretched their powers to consti-

108. Robert H. Jackson, *The Struggle for Judicial Supremacy: A Study of a Crisis in American Power Politics* (New York: Vintage Books, 1941), x–xi.

109. *Id.*, xii–xiii.

110. *Id.*, xiii.

111. As Ely observes, the Court was fairly receptive to state efforts to deal with the depression. Ely, *The Guardian of Every Other Right*, 120–21. However, Sutherland was opposed to class legislation that favored one group's economic interests over another. See, for example, his opinion in *Home Building & Loan Ass'n v. Blaisdell*, 290 U.S. 398 (1934).

tutional limits, the majority subjected governmental social and economic policies to rigorous standards of judicial review. In areas where it believed market forces were operating effectively, the Court applied what amounted to a strict-scrutiny, compelling-interest standard. In other areas, the justices continued to employ either a minimum-rationality or a substantial-relation standard, sustaining legislation that was directly related to a legitimate public purpose.[112]

If the Taft and Hughes Courts were skeptical toward economic regulation and welfare policy, the Stone, Vinson, and Warren Courts were virtually obsequious to Congress and the state legislatures. In the hands of Hugo Black and William O. Douglas, Harlan F. Stone's doctrine of presumptive validity guaranteed that few attacks on social and economic policies would survive the Court's review. When social and economic policy rested on such suspect classifications as race or implicated noneconomic personal liberties (preferred rights), however, the Warren Court applied strict-scrutiny, compelling-interest standards of judicial review. In the absence of such claims, unless the policy challenged was wholly devoid of reason, unsupported by any conceivable facts, and without some imaginable public purpose, the due process clauses offered little hope for plaintiffs with property and economic-liberty claims.[113]

Simultaneously, the Warren Court was becoming increasingly receptive to substantive due process claims presenting noneconomic personal liberty interests. As the Supreme Court's decision in *Griswold* v. *Connecticut* (the contraception case)[114] indicates, the justices had not abandoned the funda-

---

112. See Strong, 15 *Ariz. L. Rev.*, 428–29 and passim. Strong claims that in the thirty-five years following *Lochner* the Supreme Court's objective in the domain of economic regulatory legislation was "to forbid legislative tinkering with the free play of market forces absent proof that despite a policy of enforcing competition the rigor mortis of monopoly had manifested itself in the body economic." *Id.*, 435.

113. For a critical evaluation of the Court's dual standard, see Stephen Macedo, "Economic Liberty and the Future of Constitutional Self-Government," in *Liberty, Property, and the Future of Constitutional Development*, ed. Paul, 91–126, esp. 91–95. Macedo criticizes the Roosevelt and Warren Courts for their failure to see the connection between economic and other liberties.

114. 381 U.S. 479. Following *Roe* v. *Wade*, 410 U.S. 113 (1973), a spate of articles appeared in the nation's law journals arguing that between *Griswold* and *Roe* the Supreme Court had returned to the substantive due process thinking underlying *Lochner*. See, for example, Philip B. Heymann and Douglas E. Barzelay, "The Forest and the Trees: *Roe* v. *Wade*," 53 *B.U. L. Rev.* 765–84 (1973) (hereafter Heymann, 53 *B.U. L. Rev.*); Laurence H. Tribe, "Forward: Toward a Model of Roles in the Due Process of Life and Law," 87 *Harv. L. Rev.* 1–53 (1973) (hereafter, Tribe, 87 *Harv. L. Rev.*); Louis Henkin, "Privacy and Autonomy," 74 *Colum. L. Rev.* 1410–33 (1974) (hereafter Henkin, 74 *Colum. L. Rev.*); and Michael Perry,

mental-rights, substantive due process reasoning of *Lochner*. The Court shifted its focus from economic rights to other unenumerated liberties or preferred rights, which a majority regarded as fundamental. Stone's double standard of judicial review ensured that few government policies that encroached on preferred rights would survive judicial review. At the same time, his approach guaranteed that few plaintiffs raising economic due process claims could vindicate their rights.

"Abortion, the Public Morals, and the Police Power: The Ethical Function of Substantive Due Process," 23 *U.C.L.A. L. Rev.* 689–736 (1976) (hereafter Perry, 23 *U.C.L.A. L. Rev.*).

While the former authorities approved of the Court's analysis, John Hart Ely warned of the dangers implicit in *Roe*, which was a far more dangerous precedent than *Lochner*, since the Court demanded that the state show a compelling interest in restricting the right to an abortion in the first trimester of a pregnancy. In *Roe*, Ely warned, the Supreme Court decided policy questions that are legislative in nature. Ely concluded that *Roe* was not bad constitutional law; it simply was not constitutional law. See John Hart Ely, "The Wages of Crying Wolf: A Comment on *Roe v. Wade*," 82 *Yale L.J.* 920–49 (1973), 940–41, 943, 944, 947 (hereafter Ely, 82 *Yale L.J.*).

7

Liberty and Privacy— Marriage and the Family

Despite Justice Hugo Black's funeral oration for the substantive due process philosophy[1] that informed *Lochner v. New York*, since 1923 the Fifth and Fourteenth Amendments have become prolific sources of personal liberty and privacy rights.[2] Two years after Black pronounced the "second death of substantive due process," Justices John Marshall Harlan (II) and Byron

1. See *Ferguson v. Skrupa*, 372 U.S. 726 (1963), 731–32.
2. For an overview of the origins and evolution of noneconomic substantive due-process rights, see Ira C. Lupu, "Untangling the Strands of the Fourteenth Amendment," 77 *Mich. L. Rev.* 981–1077 (1979) (hereafter Lupu, 77 *Mich. L. Rev.*). See also Jeffrey S. Koehlinger, "Substantive Due Process Analysis and the Lockian Liberal Tradition: Rethinking the Modern Privacy Cases," 65 *Ind. L.J.* 723–76 (1990) (hereafter Koehlinger, 65 *Ind. L.J.*); Daniel O. Conkle, "The Second Death of Substantive Due Process," 62 *Ind. L.J.* 215–42 (1987) (hereafter Conkle, 62 *Ind. L.J.*); Harry H. Wellington, "Common Law Rules and Constitutional Double Standards: Some Notes on Adjudication," 83 *Yale L.J.* 221–311 (1973) (hereafter Wellington, 83 *Yale L.J.*); Thomas·L. Emerson, "Nine Justices in Search of a Doctrine," 64 *Mich. L. Rev.* 219–34 (1965) (hereafter, Emerson, 64 *Mich. L. Rev.*); Robert B. McKay, "The Right of Privacy: Emanations and Intimations," 64 *Mich. L. Rev.* 259–82 (1965); Arthur E. Sutherland, "Privacy in Connecticut," 64 *Mich. L. Rev.* 283–88 (1965); and John R. Green, "Liberty Under the Fourteenth Amendment," 27 *Wash. U.L.Q.* 497–562 (1942) (hereafter Green, 27 *Wash. U.L.Q.*).

White resurrected the doctrine in *Griswold* v. *Connecticut*.[3] Although they disagreed on the scope of the liberty that due process protects, Harlan and White believed that the Fourteenth Amendment was broad enough to include a married couple's decision to prevent conception.[4] Dissenting, Black replied that the majority's conception of liberty, "based on subjective considerations of 'natural justice,' is no less dangerous when used to enforce this Court's views about personal rights than those about economic rights."[5]

While Black's criticism of *Griswold* is well taken, in earlier due process cases involving personal autonomy and privacy rights the Supreme Court had relied primarily on the framers' common-law understanding of liberty and property rights. As Samuel Warren and Louis Brandeis wrote in 1900, the common-law "right to liberty secures the exercise of extensive civil privileges."[6] According to Warren and Brandeis, liberty and privacy are complementary aspects of personal autonomy, which the common law protects against governmental burdens unjustified by a need to advance the public welfare.[7] As the common law evolved in response to important social, economic, and technological changes, this personal realm expanded far beyond physical security and bodily integrity.[8] It now includes the individ-

3. 381 U.S. 479 (1965). For an analysis of *Griswold* and the right to privacy, see William M. Beaney, "The Griswold Case and the Expanding Right to Privacy," 1966 *Wis. L. Rev.* 979–95 (1966) (hereafter Beaney, 1966 *Wis. L. Rev.*). Beaney argues that until Congress and the executive become more sensitive to threats to personal dignity and privacy there is a need for judicial intervention. *Id.*, 994–95. See also Robert G. Dixon, "The *Griswold* Penumbra: Constitutional Charter for an Expanded Law of Privacy?" 64 *Mich. L. Rev.* 197–217 (1965) (hereafter Dixon, 64 *Mich. L. Rev.*).

4. 381 U.S., 481–86. See also Beaney, 1966 *Wis. L. Rev.*, 983, 984. For an analysis of the justices' views, see Notes, "On Privacy: Constitutional Protection for Personal Liberty," 48 *N.Y.U. L. Rev.* 671–773 (1973), 673–86 (hereafter Notes, 48 *N.Y.U. L. Rev.*).

5. 381 U.S., 522. On the difficulty of developing a consistent, general theory of substantive due process, see Robert G. Dixon, "The 'New' Substantive Due Process and the Democratic Ethic: A Prolegomenon," 1976 *B.Y.U. L. Rev.* 43–88 (1976). Dixon specifically rejects the argument that the framers intended to incorporate natural law directly into the Constitution, yet he admits that the due process clause is even more elastic than the commerce clause. *Id.*, 43, 44.

6. Samuel D. Warren and Louis D. Brandeis, "The Right to Privacy," 4 *Harv. L. Rev.* 193–220 (1900), 193 (hereafter Warren, 4 *Harv. L. Rev.*). For a more recent attempt to define the concept of privacy in terms of the specific dignitary interests at stake, see Hyman Gross, "The Concept of Privacy," 42 *N.Y.U. L. Rev.* 34–54 (1967).

7. Warren, 4 *Harv. L. Rev.*, 216–17. While the due process clauses afford a right to individual privacy, this right would not shield an individual from the right of the judiciary or the legislature to use otherwise private information for a legitimate public purpose—for example, in a criminal trial or legislative investigation.

8. *Union Pacific R.R. Co.* v. *Botsford*, 141 U.S. 250 (1891). Speaking for the Court, Justice Horace Gray noted that no right is more sacred than the individual's right to control his own

ual's intellectual and emotional life. "Thoughts, emotions, and sensations," Warren and Brandeis wrote, "demanded legal recognition, and the beautiful capacity for growth which characterizes the common law enabled the judges to afford the requisite protection, without the interposition of the legislature."[9]

With its emphasis on precedent, the evolutionary character of the common law inhibits judges from engaging in the freewheeling, natural-law jurisprudence that Hugo Black criticized. Moreover, as Brandeis recognized, constitutionally protected common-law rights are subject to the states' exercise of the police power. While legislators have a primary function of determining the general welfare—that is, balancing competing interests—judges have a responsibility to decide whether regulations seriously burden or destroy personal liberty and privacy rights without advancing a valid public purpose. This subtle interplay tends to restrain judges from interfering with legislative policymaking and to prevent intemperate legislative majorities from unduly burdening the exercise of fundamental liberty and privacy rights. Properly understood, today, judges can employ this common-law, police-power jurisprudence to reconcile claims of personal liberty and privacy with the republican principle of majority rule.

Turning to the common-law, police-power reasoning of earlier economic due process cases, in *Meyer v. Nebraska* Justice McReynolds extended constitutional protection to noneconomic liberties. He argued that due process includes a bundle of personal rights, defined in the common law, which the framers of the Constitution, the Bill of Rights, and the Fourteenth Amendment recognized as "essential to the orderly pursuit of happiness by free men."[10] McReynolds's interpretation implies that liberty includes all of the fundamental rights, both enumerated and unenumerated, requisite for personal development and fulfillment, subject only to those regulations and

---

person, to be free from the restraint or interference of others, except through the clear and unquestioned authority of the standing law. In other words, there must be some public interest to justify such an intrusion. *Id.*, 251, 252, 252–53. Fourteen years later, in *Jacobson v. Massachusetts*, 197 U.S. 11 (1905), Justice John M. Harlan acknowledged that the state of Massachusetts had the authority to require inoculations against smallpox as a means of protecting the public health. The overriding need to protect the public health justified the intrusion on Jacobson's right to personal liberty, to his bodily integrity, and to the right to care for his own health. *Id.*, 26–27, 37, 38.

9. Warren, 4 *Harv. L. Rev.*, 195.

10. 262 U.S. 390 (1923), 399. See also George E. Garvey, "Unenumerated Rights—Substantive Due Process, the Ninth Amendment, and John Stuart Mill," 1971 *Wis. L. Rev.* 922–38 (1971), 925 (hereafter Garvey, 1971 *Wis. L. Rev.*).

prohibitions that promote the public welfare.[11] Not unlike liberty of contract and the right to pursue the common callings, Justice McReynolds recognized that privacy is a conditional right that the legislature can circumscribe to promote a valid public purpose.

However, in the period following *Carolene Products (I)* the Court abandoned serious efforts to reconcile the exercise of "preferred" liberty and privacy rights with valid uses of the police power. As the Supreme Court's recent decisions on marriage, the family, and procreation suggest, the justices have manipulated the standard of judicial review to achieve the results that a majority or plurality favor. In some areas the Court has made it difficult, if not impossible, to sustain otherwise valid state regulations that circumscribe unenumerated rights. In other areas a majority has deferred to legislative judgments of the public welfare. While earlier decisions emphasized the conditional nature of unenumerated rights, some recent decisions stress the virtually absolute nature of liberty and privacy rights.

Family Privacy and Individual Autonomy

Beginning with *Meyer*, the Court has attempted to define a bundle of personal substantive due process rights that limit the authority of the states and the national government over the individual.[12] Today this bundle of personal rights[13] includes three basic dimensions, two of which rest on explicit constitutional limitations or can be inferred from specific provisions. The first

11. As James Bond observes, McReynolds's opinions in *Meyer* and *Pierce* have become the foundation for the Supreme Court's recent liberty and privacy decisions. See Bond, *I Dissent*, 130. Although McReynolds was not a systematic jurist who clearly articulated the reasons for his opinions, the "implicit rationale" of *Meyer* and *Pierce v. Society of Sisters*, 268 U.S. 510 (1925), has influenced the evolution of personal liberty and privacy jurisprudence. "In the last two decades the Court, expanding the category of fundamental rights even further to include privacy rights, has revived the doctrine of substantive due process whose use by McReynolds subjected him to the bitterest criticism." *Id.*

12. Note, "The Constitution and the Family," 93 *Harv. L. Rev.* 1157–383 (1980) (hereafter Note 93 *Harv. L. Rev.*), provides an excellent overview and analysis of substantive due process, family privacy, and the state's interests in regulating aspects of family and other intimate relationships.

13. See Paul Kauper, "Penumbras, Peripheries, Emanations, Things Fundamental, and Things Forgotten: The *Griswold* Case," 64 *Mich. L. Rev.* 235–58 (1965), 258 (hereafter Kauper, 64 *Mich. L. Rev.*). Kauper employs the term "bundle of rights" in the context of rights associated with the home, family, and marriage. Although he acknowledges that these rights are deeply rooted in American society, he is skeptical of the Court's exercise of judicial power in *Griswold*.

encompasses liberty of thought, belief, conscience, and speech, which the First Amendment explicitly enumerates. A second dimension embraces the liberty or security of the person within the context of the home, which the Fourth Amendment protects by prohibiting unreasonable searches and seizures. Since these rights are either explicit or can be inferred from specific constitutional provisions, they do not require extraordinary justification.

The third dimension includes rights of personal liberty and privacy that have no specific textual basis. Moreover, some scholars and jurists argue, these rights are judicial inventions that cannot even be inferred from the Fifth or the Fourteenth Amendment's due process clause. This domain of unenumerated personal liberty now includes the right to marry, to choose a marital partner, to establish a family, to define family relationships, to procreate, to rear and educate one's children, to determine one's sexual relationships, to prevent conception, to terminate a pregnancy, and to seek medical treatment and care for oneself.

Although these personal rights have no explicit textual foundation, they can be derived from the same Anglo-American legal and constitutional traditions as economic liberties.[14] It is neither necessary nor desirable to appeal to vague or absolutist principles of natural justice to define and vindicate specific liberties protected by the due process clauses. To the contrary, the valid use of the police power conditions the exercise of both enumerated and unenumerated liberty and property rights. As late nineteenth-century exponents of constitutional limitations argued, the exercise of all liberty and property rights is subject to legislative determinations of the public welfare. The traditional theory of the police power suggests that due process rights can be circumscribed by reasonable regulations—that is, measures that are directly related to a public purpose. The task of contemporary jurisprudence is to reconcile the exercise of specific liberties with particular expressions of the public welfare in individual cases.

Today's conflicts over family privacy, sexual intimacy, and procreation are quite different from the economic focus of the Gilded Age. But the attempt to distinguish between regulations that advance a public purpose and others that merely burden fundamental rights or promote purely class interests remains of vital importance. In making such distinctions, nineteenth-century police-power jurisprudence suggests that courts should examine the legislative record in order to establish the foreseeable consequences of a policy. Does the record demonstrate a clear relationship between the regulation

14. On the need to identify and define the constitutional values underlying the concept of unenumerated fundamental rights, see Ely, 82 *Yale L.J.* 920–49.

(the means) and the stated policy objectives (the ends) that are within the legislature's competence? Or is the legislation little more than an attempt to impose a particular group's will on the public through government. Does the regulation or prohibition unduly burden or destroy a constitutionally protected right without clearly serving the putative purpose? In some of the following cases involving family relationships, marital privacy, sexual intimacy, and procreation the record simply did not support the stated purpose of the legislation. The policy was an unwarranted intrusion on a fundamental liberty.

Parents, Children, and the Nuclear Family

Until *Eisenstadt v. Baird*[15] the Supreme Court attempted to anchor personal liberty and privacy decisions in the nuclear family, which it portrayed as antecedent to the Constitution and essential to a free society.[16] In *Meyer*, Justice McReynolds argued that the nuclear family is essential to maintaining "both [the] letter and spirit of the Constitution."[17] He also recognized the state's legitimate interest in fostering good citizenship, ensuring American ideals, and promoting English as the mother tongue. But McReynolds denied that the Nebraska law prohibiting instruction in other languages to children who had not passed the eighth grade served a valid public purpose. Therefore, he concluded that the measure was devoid of any rational basis; the statute was an arbitrary interference with the liberty of parents to direct their children's education.[18]

Two years later, in *Pierce v. Society of Sisters*, McReynolds again confronted a state's attempt to limit parents' liberty to make educational deci-

15. 405 U.S. 438 (1972). See Notes, 48 *N.Y.U. L. Rev.*, 693, suggesting that *Eisenstadt* marked a turning point in the privacy cases by emphasizing the right of autonomous individuals to make decisions about their personal lives.

16. Bruce C. Hafen, "The Constitutional Status of Marriage, Kinship, and Sexual Privacy—Balancing the Individual and Social Interests," 81 *Mich. L. Rev.* 463–574 (1983), 472 (hereafter Hafen, 81 *Mich. L. Rev.*). See also Note, 93 *Harv. L. Rev.*, 1351–57, and Notes, 48 *N.Y.U. L. Rev.*, 751–52, for a discussion and analysis of the cases dealing with the parental right to direct the rearing and education of children.

17. 262 U.S., 402.

18. *Id.*, 400–401, 402, 403. The state simply had not demonstrated that the statute promoted any of the objectives it sought to advance through the exercise of the police power. Dissenting in the companion case, *Bartels v. Iowa*, 262 U.S. 404 (1923), Justice Holmes argued that, since reasonable people might disagree about the desirability of requiring primary instruction in the English language, the Constitution does not prevent the states from experimenting in the field of education, which falls within the police power. *Id.*, 412.

sions for their children. He characterized an Oregon law requiring children between the ages of eight and sixteen to attend public schools as an arbitrary interference "with the liberty of parents and guardians to direct the upbringing and education of children under their control."[19] Justice McReynolds acknowledged the state's legitimate interest in regulating all schools, supervising and examining the qualifications of teachers, prescribing a basic curriculum, and prohibiting instruction of matter clearly inimical to the public welfare, but he claimed that the legislation had no "reasonable relation to some purpose within the competency of the State."[20] While McReynolds believed that, insofar as possible, individuals should be left free to exercise their fundamental liberty and property rights, he never exalted individual rights "so as to render government ineffectual to those purposes which were its legitimate ends."[21] Both in *Meyer* and in *Pierce*, McReynolds insisted that the state demonstrate a clear and direct relationship between the law and a valid public purpose.

Nineteen years later, in *Prince v. Massachusetts*,[22] the Roosevelt Court sustained a Massachusetts law prohibiting minors from selling printed matter or other merchandise on the streets or in public places.[23] Speaking for the Court, Wiley Rutledge noted the importance of family life but argued that the state, as *parens patriae*, "may restrict the parent's control by requiring school attendance, regulating or prohibiting the child's labor and in many other ways."[24] Although parents have authority within their own

19. The law applied only to children who had not completed the eighth grade. 268 U.S. 510 (1925), 534–35.

20. *Id.*, 535. He denied that the state has "any general power . . . to standardize its children by forcing them to accept instruction from public school teachers only." *Id.*

21. *Id.* McReynolds's opinions in *Meyer* and *Pierce* stand as testimony to his abiding faith in individualism, the inherent nature of personal rights, limited constitutional government, and the importance of such traditional institutions as the family. Furthermore, McReynolds had a fixed, narrow view of governmental power. Bond, *I Dissent*, 131.

22. 321 U.S. 158 (1944).

23. *Id.*, 160. The law applied to boys under twelve and girls under eighteen. Mrs. Prince, a Jehovah's Witness, claimed that the enforcement of the statute interfered with her religious belief and her duty to spread the Gospel by distributing religious tracts, *Watchtower* and *Consolation*. She averred that the statute, as enforced, violated her religious liberty and that of her minor children and ward, Betty M. Simmons, also a minor, under the First and Fourteenth Amendments. Mrs. Prince's claims rested on the "free exercise" clause of the First Amendment, applicable to the state under the due process clause of the Fourteenth Amendment, and a closely related parental liberty interest protected by the due process clause. *Id.*, 161–63.

24. *Id.*, 166 (notes omitted). The state's wide-ranging power to protect children's welfare, Rutledge continued, includes the authority to limit parental freedom, even in areas of "conscience and religious conviction." *Id.*, 167.

household to rear their children and impart their religious beliefs, the state has a special responsibility to protect the health, safety, welfare, and morals of the children. This special responsibility gives the state greater latitude in restricting the liberty interests of children than in restricting those of adults.[25] While sustaining the restriction of parental authority, Rutledge required that the state demonstrate some discernible public purpose to justify the intrusion on family life.[26]

Upholding a New York law that prohibited the sale of "girlie" magazines containing nude pictures to minors, in *Ginsberg v. New York*,[27] Justice William Brennan affirmed the authority of the state to restrict the liberty interests of minors. Since the First Amendment does not protect "obscenity," Brennan reasoned, New York has greater discretion in restricting the rights of minors than it does in restricting the rights of adults.[28] Absent a First Amendment claim, the Supreme Court required the state to show that the prohibition merely had a perceptible relation to protecting minor children from harm. As in earlier decisions involving minors, the Court continued to adhere to traditional views of the police power. After determining that the prohibition was within the state's authority, the Court left the legislature considerable discretion to weigh the competing interests and the desirability of restricting a minor's access to "obscene" publications.

More recently, however, the Burger Court has applied rigorous standards of judicial review in balancing assertions of public authority against the liberty interests of parents and children. In *Wisconsin v. Yoder*,[29] for example, several Amish families successfully challenged Wisconsin's compulsory school-attendance law, which required parents to send their children to

25. *Id.*, 167–68. In the field of employment, the state has considerable discretion in limiting child labor, Rutledge continued, since a democratic society has a strong interest in promoting the healthy growth and development of young people into fully mature citizens. *Id.*, 168. But see *Bellotti v. Baird* (*Bellotti II*), 443 U.S. 622 (1979), 634, in which Justice Powell argues that the minor's Fourteenth Amendment right to decide to have an abortion is virtually as extensive as that of an adult's.

26. Dissenting, Justice Frank Murphy argued that laws encroaching on First Amendment freedoms were presumptively invalid. Employing a minimum-rationality test, he denied that the state had shown any danger to the children or the public safety that would justify the restriction on religious liberty. *Id.*, 171–72, 173, 173–74, 175.

27. 390 U.S. 629 (1967). The New York penal code made it a crime knowingly to sell pictures depicting nudity and magazines containing such pictures to minors under seventeen, which taken as a whole, may be harmful to such minors.

28. *Id.*, 637–43. If the magazines were obscene and the First Amendment does not protect "obscenity," there is no need to distinguish between minors and adults, since the knowing sale of such materials is not a protected activity under the First and Fourteenth Amendments.

29. 406 U.S. 205 (1972).

school until age sixteen. They claimed that the law interfered with their religious liberty and right to prepare their children for a meaningful life in Amish society. Balanced against these claims was the state's interest, as *parens patriae*, in requiring two additional years of secondary education to prepare children for citizenship and to equip them to care for themselves in the larger society.

In the context of an explicit First Amendment claim, Chief Justice Warren Burger denied that the state's interest in one or two additional years of education was sufficiently important to burden the liberty interests of parents and children. Conceding the state's authority to promote universal education, Burger observed, only public interests of the "highest order" could override "legitimate claims to the free exercise of religion."[30] Because few Amish children leave their communities, which have functioned successfully for more than two centuries in the United States, there was little evidence to support the state's claim.[31]

Absent a showing of harm to the physical or psychological health of children or a threat to the public health, safety, peace, order, or welfare, Wisconsin simply had not justified severely burdening an explicitly protected fundamental right.[32] As Burger's analysis suggests, in cases involving "preferred freedoms" the Court will require the state to demonstrate a compelling public purpose in restricting the exercise of explicit First Amendment rights. Conversely, absent preferred rights, the state need only show a reasonable relationship to the public welfare in restricting the general liberty interests of parents and children.[33]

If *Yoder* left doubts about the relative standing of enumerated, implied, and unenumerated rights, Justice Stewart attempted to clarify the majority's

30. *Id.*, 215.
31. *Id.*, 227.
32. *Id.*, 230. Paraphrasing Thomas Jefferson, Burger noted that the Amish way of life promoted values essential to preserving a democratic society. Even if they are a bit eccentric, he remarked, the Amish "reflect many of the virtues of Jefferson's ideal of the 'sturdy yeoman' who would form the basis of what he considered as the ideal of a democratic society." Indeed, Amish separateness contributes to a diverse or pluralistic society, which the Constitution encourages. *Id.*, 225–26.
33. *Id.*, 233–34. In separate concurring opinions, Justices Stewart and White did not take exception to the chief justice's analysis suggesting that the Court's standard of judicial review would vary according to the specificity and/or importance of the constitutional claim asserted. *Id.*, 236–41. Dissenting, Justice Douglas criticized the majority for failing to distinguish between the religious liberty interests of parents and children, but failed to show that the children's testimony regarding their religious convictions differed from that of the parents. *Id.*, 241–46. But he too did not differ with Burger concerning appropriate standards of judicial review.

position in *Runyon v. McCrary*.[34] In *Runyon* the Court sustained the application of the Civil Rights Act of 1866 to contracts between parents and racially segregated private schools.[35] While the majority acknowledged the parents' right of privacy and freedom of association as well as the right to direct the education of their children, it denied that the application of the Civil Rights Act infringed any parental rights previously recognized.[36] Endeavoring to distinguish *Runyon* from earlier decisions, Stewart argued that parents do not have a "constitutional right to provide their children with private school education unfettered by reasonable government regulation."[37]

Although parents and children have an implied First Amendment right to freedom of association, which may include attending schools that promote a belief in racial segregation, the right is subject to the reasonable exercise of congressional power to protect legal equality. Stewart denied that the Civil Rights Act, as applied, interfered with any rights the Court had recognized in *Meyer, Pierce,* or *Yoder.* These cases merely established a parental right to send a child to a private rather than public school. By interpreting *Meyer* and *Pierce* narrowly, Stewart circumscribed the parental liberty interest and expanded the scope of congressional authority to promote equality. Implicitly, Justice Stewart ranked legal equality higher than freedom of association, with reference to the specific, competing claims. Some may quarrel with his ranking, but adjudicating conflicting claims of textually based rights is eminently a judicial function.

Turning to the right to privacy, Justice Stewart distinguished decisions concerning children's education from decisions involving procreation. Unlike *Roe* and *Griswold,* he noted, *Runyon* did "not represent governmental intrusion into the privacy of the home or a similarly intimate setting."[38] Simply because the government cannot burden a woman's decision to bear children, does not mean that "it is similarly restricted by the Constitution from regulating the implementation of parental decisions concerning a child's education."[39] Although Stewart asserted the distinction, he did not

34. 427 U.S. 160 (1976).

35. 42 U.S.C. § 1981 provides that "[a]ll persons within the jurisdiction of the United States shall have the same right in every State . . . to make and enforce contracts . . . as is enjoyed by white citizens." *Id.,* 160. As interpreted in *Johnson v. Railway Express Agency,* 421 U.S. 454 (1975); *Tillman v. Wheaton-Haven Recreation Assn.,* 410 U.S. 431 (1973); and *Jones v. Alfred Mayer Co.,* 392 U.S. 409 (1968), the Civil Rights Act of 1866, as reenacted in 1870, prohibits racial discrimination in making private contracts.

36. 427 U.S., 176–77.

37. *Id.,* 178.

38. *Id.*

39. *Id.*

provide a rationale for differentiating the two privacy rights, unless he believed that governmental intervention in procreative decisions is inherently more intrusive on personal liberty and privacy than interference with a parent's educational decisions. The Court's failure to articulate a credible distinction among various unenumerated privacy rights illustrates the manipulability of its post–*Carolene Products* approach to fundamental rights.

Despite Justice McReynolds's character flaws, his opinions for the Court in *Meyer* and *Pierce* provide a credible constitutional foundation for unenumerated liberty and privacy rights. More by instinct than by reasoning, McReynolds employed the economic due process line of precedent from *Allgeyer* through *Coppage* to expand the meaning of personal liberty. Beginning with *Meyer* and *Pierce* the Supreme Court has recognized that the parental right to nurture and direct a child's education is a conditional liberty subject to reasonable regulations that promote the public welfare. In reconciling these unenumerated privacy interests with the public welfare, the Court has employed a minimum-rationality standard similar to that used in economic-liberty decisions since 1937. The justices left the states considerable discretion to balance competing interests in public eduction but required the legislature to demonstrate that regulations actually served the policy's stated objectives. As long as the regulation was clearly related to a valid public purpose, the justices did not question the wisdom or desirability of limiting unenumerated parental liberty interests.

However, when parents buttressed generalized liberty claims with assertions that state laws burden their religious freedom, the justices applied a close-scrutiny, compelling-interest standard in weighing competing public and private claims. In balancing parental liberty interests against congressional authority to further racial equality, under the Thirteenth Amendment, the Court has deferred to legislative judgment. Compared with decisions involving marriage and procreation, the justices have left Congress and the state legislatures considerable discretion in regulating parental rights. While there is a credible basis for affording explicit textual rights heightened protection, thus far the Supreme Court has failed to provide a convincing rationale for distinguishing among various unenumerated rights.

Procreation, Marriage, and Family Relationships

Since 1942 the Supreme Court has included the rights to marry, procreate, and establish family relationships as fundamental personal liberties protected by the Fourteenth Amendment's due process and equal protection clauses.[40] The Court's early decisions rest on traditional views of marriage and the family in American society. Its recent decisions expand the concept of "family" and focus on the right of autonomous individuals to make personal choices concerning procreation, contraception, family relationships, and sexual intimacy. Although the justices have expanded the range of unenumerated rights, they have failed to develop coherent rationales for according varying degrees of protection to personal decisions involving marriage, procreation, and family life.[41] In these areas, the Supreme Court's substantive due process jurisprudence appears manipulable and result oriented.

Procreation and the Survival of the Race

Beginning with Skinner v. Oklahoma,[42] the Court has viewed procreation as a basic civil right inextricably related to marriage and the family.[43] "Marriage and procreation," observed William O. Douglas, "are fundamental to the very existence and survival of the race."[44] While the Court disposed of Skinner on equal-protection grounds, Douglas's, Stone's, and Jackson's opinions reveal the justices' differing views of unenumerated fundamental rights rooted in the Fourteenth Amendment. As Douglas concluded, the Oklahoma law, which mandated sterilization for certain defined classes of habitual criminals, imposed an irreparable injury. The statute "forever deprived [Skinner] of a basic liberty."[45] Given the risk of irreparable harm to a fundamental right, Douglas subjected the legislative policy to strict scrutiny.

40. On the "right to marry cases" see Hafen, 81 Mich. L. Rev., 507–11. See also Note, 93 Harv. L. Rev., 1248–57.

41. See Jennifer Jaff, "Wedding Bell Blues: The Position of Unmarried People in American Law," 30 Ariz. L. Rev. 207–42 (1988) (hereafter Jaff, 30 Ariz. L. Rev.). Jaff argues that, given the increasing number of unmarried people in American society, there is a need to reexamine rights of personal privacy and intimacy based on marriage and the traditional family.

42. 316 U.S. 535 (1942). An Oklahoma statute provided for mandatory sterilization of habitual criminals—that is, persons convicted two or more times under Oklahoma law for felonies involving moral turpitude. However, the statute exempted persons convicted for violations of "prohibitory laws, revenue acts, embezzlement, or political offenses." Id., 537. Since the statute impinged on a fundamental right, the Court subjected the classificatory distinction to strict scrutiny. The law could not pass muster because the state failed to show even a rational basis for the classification. It could not demonstrate that larceny is an inheritable biological characteristic, while embezzlement is not. Id., 541. On the subject of sterilization and privacy, see Notes, 48 N.Y.U. L. Rev., 713–17, and Note, 93 Harv. L. Rev., 1296–1303.

43. 316 U.S., 541.

44. Id. (opinion of the Court).

45. Id.

Concurring, Chief Justice Stone argued that Oklahoma had a constitutional duty, under the due process clause, to afford Skinner a meaningful hearing before depriving someone of a fundamental right.[46] Stone did not object to mandatory sterilization; he opposed a statute that deprived an individual of a fundamental right without adequate process. Also concurring, Jackson argued that the Fourteenth Amendment imposes substantive limitations on the legislature's power over personal liberty.[47] While the Court disposed of *Skinner* on equal-protection grounds, apparently there was a consensus that the right to procreate is fundamental. However, the majority failed to agree on a doctrinal basis for the right or to articulate the conditions that would justify restricting procreation in order to promote the public safety and welfare.

In a decision far removed in time and substance from *Skinner,* the Supreme Court examined the degree of protection that the due process clause affords to procreative decisions. Speaking for a majority in *Cleveland Board of Education* v. *LaFleur,*[48] Justice Potter Stewart first identified the specific due process right that the Fourteenth Amendment protects. Relying on *Skinner* as well as on *Roe* and *Eisenstadt,* Stewart noted, first that the due process clause protects a woman's decision to bear children from unwarranted governmental intrusion. Second, he examined the burden that the Cleveland, Ohio, and Chesterfield County, Virginia, school boards' maternity-leave regulations imposed on a teacher's decision to bear children.[49] Third, he asked whether the public interests that the school boards had advanced justified the burdens imposed.

Since the boards' policies affected a fundamental right, Stewart wrote, "the Due Process Clause of the Fourteenth Amendment requires that such rules must not needlessly, arbitrarily, or capriciously impinge upon this vital area of a teacher's constitutional liberty."[50] Examining the competing claims of the teachers and the school boards, Stewart found that several of the

46. *Id.,* 544.
47. *Id.,* 546.
48. 414 U.S. 632 (1979). Several pregnant public school teachers brought these actions challenging mandatory maternity-leave rules of the Cleveland, Ohio, and Chesterfield County, Virginia, boards of education. The Cleveland rules required pregnant teachers to take leave five months before the anticipated birth of a child. The Chesterfield County rules required teachers to provide at least six months' notice, and to take leave four months before the anticipated birth. The Cleveland rules provided that teachers were not eligible to return to work until three months after the birth of a child. Both boards required teachers to obtain a physician's certificate of physical fitness prior to returning. *Id.,* 634–38.
49. *Id.,* 640, 641, 650.
50. *Id.,* 640.

regulations lacked minimum rationality. He conceded that although Ohio and Virginia had a legitimate interest in ensuring the continuity of instruction, the mandatory termination of teachers who are four or five months pregnant creates a conclusive and irrebuttable presumption that every such woman is physically unfit to teach. Inasmuch as a pregnant woman's ability to work is very much an individual matter, Stewart concluded, the rule did not further the state's interest in keeping unfit teachers out of the classroom. Admittedly, the regulation was administratively convenient, but it simply did not serve the board's legitimate interests in promoting continuity of instruction and ensuring that classroom teachers are physically competent.[51] It was an entirely arbitrary and irrational regulation that served no legitimate public purpose.

As *LaFleur* indicates, the Court can protect substantive liberty interests without subjecting legislation to a close-scrutiny, compelling-interest standard of judicial review. After identifying the specific rights implicated, Justice Stewart determined that the school board regulations burdened the constitutionally protected interests of the plaintiffs. When no rational basis for the regulations can be identified, it is unnecessary to subject the regulations to close scrutiny or to require the state to show a compelling interest. Using the same rational-relation standard, the Court could easily sustain other regulations that were drawn up to serve the Cleveland school board's legitimate interests—for example, requiring a medical certificate or supplemental physical examination before certifying a teacher as "fit" to return to the classroom.[52] As the majority's opinion in *LaFleur* implies, a teacher's liberty interest in childbearing is an important but conditional right that the state can reasonably limit to protect the educational needs of school-children.

Both *LaFleur* and *Skinner* demonstrate that the Court need not balance competing public and private interests in order to protect unenumerated due process rights from unjustified intrusions. In both cases a careful examination of the regulations and the record revealed that the policy did not actually serve objectives within the state's competence. The Oklahoma law did not protect the public against habitual offenders; the Cleveland regulation

51. *Id.*, 643, 645, 647–48, 651. Powell concurred on equal-protection grounds, but he too applied a minimum-rationality standard. Dissenting, Justice Rehnquist (with whom Chief Justice Burger concurred) argued that the majority's opinion would prevent legislatures from drawing lines based on age. All legislation of a general character, he observed, involves drawing lines. The Court's preference for individualized decision-making would undermine the legislature's ability to enact general and impartial public policies. *Id.*, 657–59.

52. *Id.*, 648–49.

did not further the city's interest in children's education. In these cases, the justices were able to protect unenumerated rights without intruding unnecessarily on the states' exercise of the police power. They left the states an opportunity to devise regulations that actually serve valid objectives.

Marriage: A Basic Civil Right

If procreation is fundamental to the survival of the race, the Supreme Court has characterized marriage as the foundation of the traditional nuclear family and American society. Marriage, observed Justice Field, "is the foundation of the family and of society, without which there would be neither civilization nor progress."[53] Since the 1880s the Court has viewed marriage as a fundamental civil right that is essential to the orderly pursuit of freedom and vital to the political and constitutional order. Accordingly, it has extended the protection of the due process clause to the rights to marry, to choose a marital partner, and to privacy in the marital relationship.

Although Stephen Field noted that marriage is a fundamental right, he acknowledged the authority of the states to regulate various aspects of the marital relationship.[54] As in cases involving parental and procreative liberties, police-power jurisprudence recommends that the Court should first decide whether the Fifth or Fourteenth Amendment protects a specific aspect of the marital relationship. Second, it ought to determine whether a particular governmental regulation burdens the protected marital right. Third, the Court should examine the degree to which the regulation burdens the right. Fourth, the justices should determine whether the regulation or prohibition actually advances the public welfare. Unless the legislation clearly serves a valid purpose, the state would be barred from unduly burdening or destroying marital rights. In contrast to this restrained approach, the Supreme Court's recent decisions on marital rights require judges to balance

53. *Maynard v. Hill*, 125 U.S. 190 (1888) (opinion of the Court), 211. In *Griswold*, Justice Douglas described marriage as "a coming together for better or for worse, hopefully enduring, and intimate to the degree of being sacred. It is an association that promotes a way of life, not causes; a harmony in living, not political faiths; a bilateral loyalty, not commercial or social projects." 381 U.S., 486.

54. 125 U.S., 205. Marriage, Field wrote, creates "the most important relationship in life," but it "has always been subject to the control of the legislature." The legislature, he continued, "prescribes the age at which parties may contract to marry, the procedure or form essential to constitute marriage, the duties and obligations it creates, its effects upon the property rights of both, present and prospective, and the acts which may constitute grounds for its dissolution." *Id.*

competing public and private interests, which is a legislative rather than a judicial function.

In *Loving* v. *Virginia*[55] the Warren Court decided unanimously that a Virginia law prohibiting interracial marriages violated both the due process and the equal protection clause of the Fourteenth Amendment. Speaking for the Court, Chief Justice Earl Warren observed that the "freedom to marry has long been recognized as one of the vital personal rights essential to the orderly pursuit of happiness by free men." Since the racial classification was insupportable and implicated a fundamental right, it deprived "the State's citizens of liberty without due process of law." The statute could not survive judicial scrutiny because it had no conceivable purpose within the state's competence. Under the U.S. Constitution, Warren concluded, "the freedom to marry, or not to marry, a person of another race resides with the individual and cannot be infringed by the State."[56] The right to choose a marital partner without regard to race is a fundamental, unenumerated liberty that the Fourteenth Amendment covers.

Relying on *Loving*, *Griswold*, *LaFleur*, and other recent decisions, Justice Thurgood Marshall, in *Zablocki* v. *Redhail*, restated the Supreme Court's view that "the right to marry is part of the fundamental 'right of privacy' implicit in the Fourteenth Amendment's Due Process Clause."[57] Although the Court decided *Zablocki* on equal-protection grounds, it employed a fundamental-rights, substantive due process argument masquerading in disguise. Basically, Marshall argued that the Wisconsin law requiring a divorced father to obtain a court order granting him permission to remarry unconstitutionally burdened his fundamental liberty "of personal choice in matters of marriage and family life."[58] Marshall found the state's interests insufficient to impose a virtual prohibition on Redhail's personal autonomy.

55. 388 U.S. 1 (1967). After having been married in the District of Columbia, the Lovings, an interracial couple, returned to their home in Virginia. They were subsequently convicted for violating the state's prohibition of interracial marriages. However, the sentence was suspended for twenty-five years on the condition that they not return to Virginia together during that period. *Id.*, 2–3.

56. *Id.*, 12.

57. 434 U.S. 374 (1978), 384.

58. *Id.*, 385. In an effort to foster child-support and counseling before assuming additional parental responsibilities, the Wisconsin law required divorced, noncustodial parents who had not met their court-ordered support responsibilities to obtain a court order before marrying. The statute required such parents to show that their support obligations had been met and that their children would not become public charges in the future. The state had the power to deny marriage licenses to persons who did not meet these requirements. Furthermore, persons who obtained marriage licenses without a court's permission were subject to criminal penalties. *Id.*, 375.

Marshall confirmed "the fundamental character of the right to marry," but he denied that every state regulation relating "in any way to the incidents of or prerequisites for marriage must be subjected to rigorous scrutiny."[59] To the contrary, the state can impose reasonable regulations that do not "significantly interfere" with an individual's decision to marry.[60] Justice Marshall implied that the Court's standard of judicial review should vary according to the degree that state regulations burden a fundamental right. In this case, he noted, "the statutory classification . . . clearly does interfere directly and substantially with the right to marry."[61] Furthermore, Wisconsin had other, less intrusive means to satisfy its ostensible purposes, including "wage assignments, civil contempt proceedings, and criminal penalties."[62]

Concurring in the Court's decision, Justice Stewart argued that the Wisconsin law was "an unwarranted encroachment upon a constitutionally protected freedom," rather than invidious discrimination.[63] Although the states have the authority to regulate and even prohibit marriage under some circumstances, the due process clause of the Fourteenth Amendment imposes limits on the states' exercise of their police powers.[64] As Stewart recognized, the Constitution does not enumerate the right to marry, but the Court's prior decisions have made it "clear that freedom of personal choice in matters of marriage and family life is one of the liberties so protected."[65] The only issue is whether the state's objectives in restricting Redhail's liberty interests were sufficiently important to justify the prohibition, which he denied.

Attacking the majority's equal-protection analysis, Stewart claimed that "the doctrine is no more than substantive due process by another name."[66]

59. *Id.*, 386

60. *Id.*, 394. Similarly, Justice Powell argued that the state may impose various legitimate preconditions on marriage. However, he argued, regulations and prohibitions must have some rational relation to the state's ostensible objectives. Since the measure was unrelated to any alleged purpose, Wisconsin simply had not justified foreclosing marriage to many indigent citizens. *Id.*, 397 and passim. The state failed to demonstrate that the prohibition on future marriages would advance its ostensible objective of promoting financial responsibility for the children of previous marriages.

61. *Id.*, 387.

62. *Id.*, 390.

63. *Id.*, 391–92.

64. *Id.*, 392. In fact, Stewart denied that there is a right to marry in a constitutional sense. The right or privilege, he observed, is defined and limited by state law—for example, statutes requiring persons to pass a blood test, prohibiting individuals under fourteen from marrying, or prohibiting siblings from marrying.

65. *Id.*, 393.

66. *Id.*, 395. See also Lupu, 77 *Mich. L. Rev.*, 992–95, 1024.

The only purpose this masquerade serves is to conceal the Court's reluctance "to rely on substantive due process."[67] As a result, the Supreme Court's doctrine had shifted

> the focus of the judicial inquiry away from its proper concerns, which include "the nature of the individual interest affected, the extent to which it is affected, the rationality of the connection between legislative means and purpose, the existence of alternative means for effectuating the purpose, and the degree of confidence we may have that the statute reflects the legislative concern for the purpose that would legitimately support the means chosen."[68]

Stewart was calling for a candid discussion of the Court's use of the due process clause to invalidate legislative decisions implicating unenumerated fundamental liberties. Rather than abandoning the concept of substantive due process, he implied, the Supreme Court should develop an explicit methodology for determining whether there is a direct relationship between the regulation or prohibition and the state's ostensible purpose.

Nine years later, in *Turner v. Safley*,[69] the Supreme Court reiterated its approach of balancing marital rights and the state's interest in prohibiting marriage. Relying on *Zablocki*, Justice Sandra Day O'Connor acknowledged that the right to marry may survive even in a prison setting, where the state's legitimate penological objectives severely diminish a prisoner's expectations of liberty and privacy. Speaking for the Court, O'Connor explicitly recognized the obligation to develop specific standards of judicial review for

67. 434 U.S., 395.

68. *Id.*, 396, quoting from Harlan (concurring), *Williams v. Illinois*, 399 U.S. 235 (1970), 260. Like Stewart, Harlan objected to such subterfuge: "The 'equal protection' analysis of the Court is, I submit, a 'wolf in sheep's clothing,' for that rationale is no more than a masquerade of a supposedly objective standard for *subjective* judicial judgment as to what state legislation offends notions of 'fundamental fairness.' " *Id.*, 259. Harlan claimed that the adherents of the new equal-protection and the old substantive due process doctrines were substituting their own "enlightened judgment" on social and economic philosophy for that of the legislature. For his part, Harlan preferred to determine whether legislation arbitrarily infringes the individual's constitutionally protected interests. *Id.*

69. 482 U.S. 78 (1987). A class of inmates had challenged two regulations that the Missouri Department of Corrections had adopted. One regulation restricted the rights of certain prisoners within the system to communicate through the mail, unless prison officials deemed such communication in the prisoners' best interests. A second regulation limited the right of prisoners within the system to marry, except for compelling reasons, with the permission of prison superintendents.

balancing the state's interest in managing prisons and "the need to protect constitutional rights."[70]

The Missouri Department of Corrections permitted prisoners to marry for compelling reasons, with the prison superintendent's permission. In practice, prison officials granted permission in cases of pregnancy or the birth of an illegitimate child.[71] Although Missouri conceded that *Zablocki* and *Loving* established a fundamental right to marry, it denied that the right applies to prisoners. Rejecting the state's claim, O'Connor argued that many attributes of the marriage relationship survive incarceration, including emotional support, property and inheritance rights, receipt of government benefits, and consummation of a marriage following release from prison.[72] Characterizing the state's response to security problems as "exaggerated," she noted that there were "obvious, easy alternatives to the Missouri regulation that accommodate the right to marry while imposing a *de minimis* burden on the pursuit of security objectives."[73] While O'Connor admitted Missouri's legitimate interests in security and rehabilitation, she denied that the state's regulations were reasonably related to these penological interests.[74]

As the Supreme Court's decisions on marriage reveal, the justices have employed a balancing approach to unenumerated marital rights, but they have failed to develop a credible methodology for weighing the relative importance of competing public regulations and personal liberty. While a majority has sustained "rational" regulations in some cases, in others it has required the state to demonstrate either a "substantial" or a "compelling" purpose in limiting marital rights. The Supreme Court's failure to develop a coherent methodology has imparted a perception of manipulability to its personal liberty and privacy decisions, which undermines the credibility of

70. *Id.*, 85.

71. Missouri prison officials generally permitted both male and female prisoners to marry civilians. The ban applied to marriages between female and male prisoners within the same prison. *Id.*, 97–99.

72. *Id.*, 96.

73. *Id.*, 98. Missouri claimed that female prisoners' requests were denied because their marriage to other prisoners or ex-felons fostered "excessive dependency." *Id.*, 98–99. While Stevens, with Brennan, Marshall, and Blackmun, agreed with the majority's decision concerning the marriage regulation, they rejected O'Connor's use of a minimum-rationality standard. Stevens argued that a trial judge would likely accept any plausible security concern. Therefore, a mere logical connection would justify most incursions on constitutionally protected rights. *Id.*, 100–101. Furthermore, Justice Stevens criticized the majority for sifting the trial record and making a *de novo* judgment without an adequate record on the marriage regulation. *Id.*, 101–2, 112–15.

74. *Id.*, 97.

substantive due process jurisprudence. Its balancing approach to rights is sometimes indistinguishable from the legislative process in which elected representatives weigh competing interests when determining the public welfare. Finally, in *Zablocki* and *Turner* it was unnecessary to balance anything, since the states had not demonstrated that the regulations served their ostensible purposes.

Family Relationships

Similarly, the Supreme Court's decisions concerning the right to establish family and other intimate relationships reveal its failure to develop a coherent methodology in the face of new demands for constitutional protection.[75] The Court's earlier decisions focused on parental and marital rights in relation to the traditional nuclear family as the foundation of American society. Since the late 1960s, however, various social and economic forces have undermined the traditional nuclear family. Today, a significant number of children live in single-parent homes, with members of an extended family, or with foster families.[76] A marked increase in the number of unmarried couples (both heterosexual and homosexual) living together[77] in long-term, stable, and significant relationships has eroded the traditional definition of marriage and the family. As state legislatures revise definitions of "marriage" and "the family," should the Supreme Court's protection for family privacy extend to these new "families"? If so, should the Court balance the use of the police power against claims of family liberty and privacy rights?

In *Moore v. East Cleveland*[78] the Supreme Court expanded the protection of the Fourteenth Amendment's due process clause to include the extended

75. For an analysis of traditional family and other intimate relationships, see Notes, 48 *N.Y.U. L. Rev.*, 740–50. See also Note, 93 *Harv. L. Rev.*, 1271–96, for a definition of the family and the protected relationships therein.

76. As the Census Bureau reports, between 1970 and 1990 the percentage of children under eighteen living with only one parent doubled, from 12 percent to 25 percent. Among single-parent children, the percentage living with a parent who had never married increased from 4 percent to 31 percent. In 1990, 5 percent of all children lived with their grandparents. Another 2 percent lived with persons other than a relative. U.S. Department of Commerce, Bureau of the Census, *Current Population Reports: Marital Status and Living Arrangements, March 1990* (Washington, D.C.: GPO, 1991), 4–7.

77. In 1990 there were 5.7 million unmarried partners living together. *Id.*, 14.

78. 431 U.S. 494 (1977). See also Lupu, 77 *Mich. L. Rev.*, 1015–16, 1017. Lupu notes that *Moore* is the first decision since 1937 to invalidate legislative policy on naked substantive due process grounds.

family.[79] Speaking for a plurality, Justice Lewis Powell argued that the extended family is entitled to protection because it is deeply rooted in the American tradition.[80] Concurring, Justice Brennan observed that for generations millions of Americans had grown up and flourished in extended immigrant families that provided social, economic, and emotional support.[81] For Justices Powell and Brennan, the extended family was functionally equivalent to the nuclear family, since both fulfilled similar needs and were "deeply rooted in this Nation's history and tradition."[82]

Whether grandparents choose to share their home with children and grandchildren for reasons of economic necessity, social support, or emotional attachment, Powell concluded, the decision to establish close family ties in a common household is constitutionally protected. As Justice Powell commented, "the choice of relatives in this degree of kinship to live together may not lightly be denied by the State."[83] Therefore, the City of East Cleveland had to demonstrate a more substantial interest in interfering with this private choice than "preventing overcrowding, minimizing traffic and parking congestion, and avoiding an undue financial burden on East Cleveland's school system."[84]

Powell conceded that these are legitimate goals, but he argued that the regulation served the city's putative interests only marginally. The East Cleveland law permitted a mother who had a single dependent son with twelve dependent school-age children or a family with "a half dozen licensed drivers, each with his or her own car" to live together,[85] but it prevented a mother, a son, and two grandchildren who were cousins from living in the same home. Thus the housing law established arbitrary and capricious boundaries that unconstitutionally burdened a fundamental liberty.

Although Powell admitted the dangers inherent in expanding the contours of substantive due process, he could not "avoid applying the force and rationale of [previous decisions] to the family choice involved in this case."[86]

---

79. Mrs. Inez Moore had been convicted for violating an East Cleveland housing ordinance that limited residents of a dwelling unit to members of a single family. The law contained a restrictive definition of the term "family." As applied to Mrs. Moore, the ordinance prohibited her from living together with her dependent son and two grandsons, who were cousins. The second grandson came to live with Mrs. Moore after his mother died. 431 U.S., 496–97.

80. Id., 504.

81. Id., Powell (plurality opinion), 504–5; Brennan (concurring, with Marshall), 508.

82. Id., 503. Moreover, both blood and kinship link the nuclear and extended families.

83. Id., 505–6. But see Lyng v. Costello, 477 U.S. 635 (1986).

84. 431 U.S., 499–500.

85. Id., 500.

86. Id., 501.

The liberty that the due process clause guarantees, Powell remarked, is not limited to the Constitution's specific prohibitions on the exercise of governmental power.[87] Liberty "is a rational continuum which, broadly speaking, includes a freedom from all substantial arbitrary impositions and purposeless restraints."[88] Following Harlan's advice in Poe, Powell urged his colleagues to exercise reasonable and sensitive judgment in scrutinizing a state's justification for limiting fundamental liberties.[89] However, as Powell added quickly, judicial self-restraint does not compel the Court to abandon the concept of unenumerated fundamental rights.

Dissenting, Stewart (with Rehnquist) denied that the ordinance intruded on any constitutionally protected right to privacy or freedom of association. In the private realm of family life, Justice Stewart conceded that the Fourteenth Amendment protects the family from many unwarranted intrusions. However, the Constitution does not create a right to share one's home with whomever one pleases, whether a kin or a perfect stranger. Unless an ordinance intrudes substantially on some protected right, Stewart concluded, a city is free to decide how to enforce its laws. While he denied that Mrs. Moore's interests rose to the level of a constitutional right, Stewart did not reject Powell's substantive due process reasoning.[90]

In a separate dissenting opinion, Justice Byron White denied that the due process clauses have a substantive component. Inasmuch as substantive due process is nothing more than a judicial construct,[91] he argued, the Court should exercise caution and self-restraint in finding state legislation arbitrary or unreasonable. But he did not recommend abandoning the concept.[92] Unlike Harlan and Stewart, White urged the Court to adopt a variable standard of review in balancing competing public and private interests. He claimed that some rights might deserve "a heightened degree of protection under the Due Process Clause."[93] While White identified liberties that deserved heightened protection, he did not provide a method for distinguishing among various fundamental rights.[94] Thus White's appeal for variable

87. Lupu, 77 Mich. L. Rev., 1019.
88. 431 U.S., 502, quoting from Harlan (dissenting), Poe v. Ullman, 367 U.S. 497 (1961), 543.
89. 431 U.S., 502.
90. Id., 536–37, 537–38.
91. Id., 543–44.
92. Id., 544–45. Indeed, Justice White acknowledged that the Court had not overruled or rejected its definition of liberty in Meyer v. Nebraska.
93. 431 U.S., 546.
94. Id., 548. Among the liberties requiring heightened judicial scrutiny are the freedoms of

standards of judicial review suffers from the same flaw as Harlan Stone's *Carolene Products* approach.

Although the Supreme Court has expanded the substantive protection of the due process clause to the extended family, it has thus far refused to provide similar protection to unmarried heterosexual couples who live together in long-term, stable, or significant relationships.[95] The Court also has denied protection to intimate relationships between consenting adult homosexuals. Speaking for a narrow majority in *Bowers* v. *Hardwick,* Justice White rejected Michael Hardwick's claim that "his homosexual activity is a private and intimate association that is beyond the reach of state regulation" and protected by the Ninth and Fourteenth Amendments.[96]

White denied that Hardwick's privacy claim resembled any of the rights that the Supreme Court had articulated in previous due process cases con-

---

speech, press, and religion, the freedom from cruel and unusual punishment, the right to vote, the right of association, and the right to privacy. As White interpreted Justice Stewart's position, these are among the liberties implicit in the concept of ordered liberty. *Id.,* 548–49. However, White was unwilling to include all of those substantive interests that are deeply rooted in the history and traditions of the American people. Powell's approach would lead to a massive invasion of state and congressional authority. Like *Lochner,* he concluded, Powell's approach would inhibit legislatures from responding to social and economic change. *Id.,* 548–49.

95. See, for example, Thurgood Marshall's dissent from the Court's denial of *cert., Hollenbaugh* v. *Carnegie Free Library,* 439 U.S. 1052 (1978). The library had dismissed Rebecca Hollenbaugh, a librarian, and Fred Philburn, a custodian, who were living together with their infant child. Even employing a minimum-rationality test, Marshall argued, the Court could not sustain the public library's action. The dismissal represented a direct intrusion on Hollenbaugh's and Philburn's privacy rights. The library had attempted to dictate its employees' sexual conduct and family living arrangements, without showing any meaningful impact on their job performance. *Id.,* 1052, 1053, 1054–56.

96. 478 U.S. 186 (1986). The Supreme Court denied that the due process clause protects the right of an adult male to engage in sodomy with another consenting adult male in the privacy of his bedroom. Justice White argued that, since most states had long criminalized sodomy, *Bowers* involved no fundamental right deeply rooted in the nation's history and traditions or implicit in the concept of ordered liberty. Therefore, he refused to extend the contours of substantive due process to create new fundamental rights. *Id.,* 191–94. Inasmuch as the law did not burden any fundamental liberty or privacy interest, Justice White noted, the state need only demonstrate that the prohibition is rational. White concluded that Georgia had a rational basis for enacting the law on "the presumed belief of a majority of the electorate . . . that homosexual sodomy is immoral and unacceptable." *Id.,* 196. For a further analysis of *Bowers* see Conkle, 62 *Ind. L.J.,* who argues that *Bowers* represents the beginning of the second death of substantive due process and that, as a result, *Roe* v. *Wade* was in serious jeopardy. *Id.,* 215, 237–41. Indeed, he argues that the two decisions are inconsistent and that this discrepancy undermines the foundation of the Court's substantive due process decisions. For a discussion of sexual behavior and privacy see Notes, 48 *N.Y.U. L. Rev.,* 732–37.

cerning marriage, procreation, or family relationships. However, in *Eisen-stadt v. Baird*[97] the justices had extended equal protection to the intimate decisions of unmarried persons to use contraceptives. Having admitted that there is an intimate private realm that encompasses unmarried as well as married persons, White's reasoning in *Bowers* is at odds with *Eisenstadt* and with some of the abortion cases.[98] Moreover, some commentators criticize the majority's opinion as result-oriented jurisprudence that reflects and legitimizes "homophobic violence on the part of public officials and private citizens alike."[99] Admittedly, the due process clauses do not protect every conceivable claim, but the Court's failure to develop a neutral rule that can be applied consistently vitiates the substantive due process doctrine in the realm of sexual intimacy and privacy.

As long as the Rehnquist Court adheres to definitions of fundamental rights based on the principles of ordered liberty or the traditions and conscience of the American people, it is not likely to expand the contours of substantive due process to include homosexuals' intimate relationships.[100] From the perspective of the narrow (5–4) *Bowers* majority, neither homosexual nor unmarried heterosexual partnerships are deeply rooted in the traditions or the conscience of the American people. To include these intimate relationships within the substantive meaning of the due process clauses would require the Rehnquist Court to abandon its understanding of the framers' original intent. From Justice White's position, neither the values of the framers nor the historical context for the drafting of the original

97. 405 U.S. 438 (1972).

98. Indeed, there has been an avalanche of scholarly commentary criticizing the methodological inconsistency between *Bowers* and the Court's contraception and abortion decisions. See, for example, Conkle, 62 *Ind. L.J.* 215 (1987); Mark H. Kohler, "History, Homosexuality, and Homophobia: The Judicial Intolerance of *Bowers v. Hardwick*," 19 *Conn. L. Rev.* 129 (1986); David A. J. Richards, "Constitutional Legitimacy and Constitutional Privacy," 61 *N.Y.U. L. Rev.* 800 (1986); and Thomas B. Stoddard, "*Bowers v. Hardwick*: Precedent by Personal Predilection," 54 *U. Chi. L. Rev.* 648 (1987).

99. See, for example, Kendall Thomas, "Beyond the Privacy Principle," 92 *Colum. L. Rev.* 1431 (1992), 1435. However, it is possible to interpret *Bowers* as merely standing for the proposition that the Supreme Court is not prepared to extend the protection of the due process clause to every conceivable claim, which is consistent with the majority's appeal for self-restraint.

100. See Michael R. Engleman, "*Bowers v. Hardwick*: The Right of Privacy—Only Within the Traditional Family?" 26 *J. Fam. L.* 373–93 (1987–88). Engleman argues that the Court has restricted the right of privacy to such areas as the family, procreation, and contraception. On *Bowers*, see also Laurence H. Tribe and Michael Dorf, 57 *U. Chi. L. Rev.* 1057–1108 (1990), 1065–68 (hereafter Tribe, 57 *U. Chi. L. Rev.*).

Constitution, the Bill of Rights, or the Fourteenth Amendment would support such an expansive reading of due process.[101]

By "balancing" the competing public interests and individual rights at stake in recent privacy cases, the Supreme Court has intruded unnecessarily on the policymaking authority of the state legislatures. In many of the above privacy and personal liberty cases, the regulation or prohibition simply did not further the ostensible objectives of the states. To paraphrase Justices Harlan and Powell, the statute was a purposeless restraint that seriously burdened or destroyed a protected right without advancing the stated purpose. In some cases—for example, *LaFleur* and *Bowers*—the regulation or prohibition was probably a form of partial (class) legislation that sought to impose the norms of some groups on other groups.[102]

By first determining whether various regulations and prohibitions actually serve a purpose within the state's authority, the Court could have employed a renewed police-power jurisprudence to protect liberty and privacy rights, without impairing the legislative function. In most cases, the justices could have avoided dubious attempts to balance indivisible private rights and divisible public interests. If dignitary rights are indivisible values and public policies are divisible resources, as the Court's opinions indicate, private rights and the public welfare cannot be balanced on the same scale. As the plurality opinion in *Planned Parenthood of Southeastern Pennsylvania* v. *Casey* suggests, Justices O'Connor, Kennedy, and Souter have made an initial but only partially successful effort to circumvent this flawed methodology.

The Supreme Court's decisions on marriage and the family reveal that the justices have not abandoned the concept of unenumerated fundamental rights rooted in the due process clauses.[103] With the exception of *Bowers*,

101. But see David A. J. Richards, "Liberalism, Public Morality, and Constitutional Law: Prolegomenon to a Theory of the Constitutional Right to Privacy," 51 *Law & Contemp. Probs.* 123–150 (1988). Richards argues that the framers' values support a constitutional right to privacy that goes beyond traditional family relationships.

102. The Cleveland school board's regulation reflected little more than an attempt to shield children from pregnant teachers. Aside from the unequal enforcement of Georgia's antisodomy statute, since the 1970s revisions of state laws regulating sexual acts between consenting adults of the same gender indicate that public morality is changing. As of January 1, 1991, twenty-three states had repealed statutes criminalizing such conduct, while another nine states had reduced the crime to a misdemeanor. The laws of three states punishing sexual relations between consenting adults of the same gender had been declared unconstitutional. Fifteen states still punished such conduct as a felony. See Ducat, *Constitutional Interpretation*, 608–9.

103. Ira Lupu argues that the Burger Court breathed new life into substantive due process

the Court subscribes to substantive due process as a restraint on legislative policymaking.[104] Therefore, as Justice Powell has argued, it should clarify its objectives and make its methodology explicit. If constitutional liberty means "freedom from all substantial arbitrary impositions and purposeless restraints,"[105] as John Marshall Harlan (II) has written, the justices have an obligation to explain and justify their reasons for including and/or excluding specific liberty interests from the ambit of the due process clauses. The Court should abandon pretense and engage in a candid dialogue about its use of due process to restrain the exercise of legislative power in matters of marriage, procreation, the family, and sexual intimacy.

Since these liberty interests are judicial constructs that the justices derive from their reading of American constitutional history, Harlan's and Powell's advice of caution and restraint in overturning legislative policy is well taken. As they suggest, the Court should adopt an approach that gives appropriate weight both to the public's interest in regulation and to the individual's liberty and privacy rights. With some important exceptions, the Supreme Court has taken the position that substantive due process rights are conditional rather than absolute rights. Despite his recent assertions to the contrary, in *Roe v. Wade* even Justice Harry Blackmun conceded that a woman's right to terminate her pregnancy "is not unqualified and must be considered against important state interests in regulation."[106] Blackmun insists, however, that the state demonstrate a compelling interest in virtually any regulation that implicates a fundamental right.[107]

Dissenting in *Akron v. Akron Center for Reproductive Health*,[108] Sandra Day O'Connor argued that "not every regulation that the State imposes must be measured against the State's compelling interests and examined with strict scrutiny."[109] Since fundamental rights are not absolute, she suggested, the

---

after the Warren Court signed its death certificate in *Ferguson v. Skrupa.* See Lupu, 77 *Mich. L. Rev.*, 984.

104. See Brett J. Williamson, "The Constitutional Privacy Doctrine After *Bowers v. Hardwick*: Rethinking the Second Death of Substantive Due Process," 62 *S. Cal. L. Rev.* 1297–1330 (1989).

105. Quoted from Harlan, J. (dissenting), *Poe v. Ullman*, 367 U.S. 497 (1961), 543.

106. 410 U.S. 113 (1973), 154.

107. *Id.*, 155–56. Even John Stuart Mill recognized that, insofar as an individual's conduct has a direct effect on others, society can legitimately limit the exercise of liberty and property rights. See John Stuart Mill, "On Liberty," in *Utilitarianism, On Liberty, and Essays on Bentham*, ed. Mary Warnock (Cleveland, Ohio: Meridian Books, 1962), 226–29.

108. 462 U.S. 416 (1983).

109. *Id.*, 461.

Court should use an "'unduly burdensome' standard" in abortion cases.[110]
Only when legislation poses an absolute bar, infringes substantially, or
heavily burdens a fundamental right would Justice O'Connor apply strict
scrutiny and require the states to demonstrate a compelling interest in the
regulation or prohibition.[111] In all other cases, O'Connor would pay greater
deference to legislative judgment. While she claimed that the "unduly burdensome standard" is appropriate in the abortion context, she did not specify how this standard would apply to specific claims. In 1992, *Casey* gave
the Court an important opportunity to further articulate and apply O'Connor's approach to various abortion and privacy rights.

110. *Id.*
111. *Id.*, 462.

8

Reproductive Liberty and Individual Autonomy— Contraception and Abortion

Since 1965 the Supreme Court has employed the Fourteenth Amendment to create a new fundamental right to reproductive liberty. Similar to liberty of contract, reproductive liberty is an unenumerated right that the Warren and Burger Courts have read into the due process clause. As the framing of the amendment suggests, however, there is no greater justification for inferring reproductive liberty than liberty of contract from the due process clause. Nor is there any persuasive rationale, derived from the Constitution's language or history, for giving privacy rights greater protection than unenumerated economic liberty and property rights. In fact, the authors of the Fourteenth Amendment and the Civil Rights Act of 1866 regarded economic liberty and property rights as indispensable to personal freedom.

Nevertheless, after 1937 the Supreme Court denigrated economic liberty and property rights, while granting heightened judicial protection to reproductive freedom. Refusing to invalidate state limitations on economic liberty, between 1965 and 1990 the Court struck various prohibitions and regulations of contraception and abortion as burdensome interferences with personal liberty. In 1983, Sandra Day O'Connor began criticizing the majority's approach as unnecessarily intrusive on the states' police power.[1] Jus-

---

1. O'Connor (dissenting) in *Akron v. Akron Center for Reproductive Health*, 462 U.S. 416

tice O'Connor has attempted to forge a principled compromise that reconciles the conflict between reproductive liberty, conceived as an indivisible right of individual autonomy and privacy, and the public welfare, viewed in utilitarian terms. However, the Court's recent abortion decision, *Planned Parenthood of Southeastern Pennsylvania v. Casey,* is a pragmatic compromise that reflects the public mind,[2] rather than a principled resolution of the conflict between the Supreme Court's substantive due process jurisprudence and republican principles of government.

As an analysis of the abortion and contraception decisions demonstrates, the justices have employed a balancing methodology to reconcile the competing public and private interests at stake. In striking the balance, the justices have manipulated the standard of judicial review to achieve the results that a plurality or majority found desirable in particular cases. Sometimes, the justices have applied a "compelling interest" standard to invalidate state prohibitions and regulations of abortion and contraception that, in their judgment, either destroyed or severely impaired the decisional liberty of women. At other times, they have used an "unduly burdensome" standard to sustain legislation that impinged on but did not vitiate the reproductive liberty of women. Whatever the result, the Court's methodology is flawed precisely because it requires judges to balance indivisible dignitary rights against divisible public goods. The majority's methodology invites judges to behave like legislators who weigh competing interests and allocate scarce values or resources.

Contraception and Individual Autonomy

In 1961, dissenting in *Poe v. Ullman,*[3] Justice Harlan inferred a right to reproductive liberty and privacy from the due process clause of the Four-

---

(1983); (dissenting) in *Thornburgh v. American College of Obstetricians and Gynecologists,* 476 U.S. 747 (1986); and (concurring in part) in *Webster v. Reproductive Health Services,* 109 S.Ct. 3040 (1989).

2. In 1992 Mansfield State University's Rural Services Institute conducted a random sample survey of Pennsylvanians, which showed that 78 percent agreed with the basic premise of *Roe* that a woman should have the right to terminate a pregnancy in consultation with her physician. However, at least 75 percent agreed with all of the major provisions of the 1989 amendments to Pennsylvania's Abortion Control Act, which the Court sustained in *Casey.* The author is indebted to Marilyn A. Bok, director of the Rural Services Institute, and to Mansfield University for permission to use the data published in "The Public Mind: Views of Pennsylvania Citizens," Report No. 4 (May 1992).

3. 367 U.S. 497 (1961). *Poe* was the first of two challenges to a Connecticut statute prohibiting physicians from prescribing contraceptives and patients from using them.

teenth Amendment. Arguing that a Connecticut law prohibiting married couples from obtaining or using contraceptives was an unjustifiable invasion of their most intimate and private decisions, Harlan stated that due process had evolved into more than a procedural safeguard. In the United States due process had developed into a guarantee against arbitrary and burdensome legislation.[4] The due process clause, he observed, extends beyond the specific protections of the first eight amendments; it embraces all of the rights that are fundamental to citizens in a free society. Due process, he averred, is "a discrete concept which subsists as an independent guarantee of liberty *and* procedural fairness, more general and inclusive than the specific prohibitions [of the Bill of Rights]."[5]

Justice Harlan acknowledged Connecticut's legitimate interest in protecting public morality, but he emphasized that the states exercise their sovereign powers within the limits imposed by the due process clause. Since the Fourteenth Amendment does not define specific liberty interests, with each new claim the Court must determine whether the nation's constitutional tradition warrants including the rights asserted. Should the justices decide that a specific right is protected, Harlan remarked, they must employ reasonable and sensitive judgment in determining whether the government's stated objectives justify abridging an individual's liberty. As Harlan also acknowledged, the exercise of personal liberty and privacy rights is subject to regulations and prohibitions that promote a compelling public purpose. However, the states cannot use the police power merely to burden protected rights or to impose a particular group's values on individuals.

Turning to the specific claims in *Poe*, Justice Harlan conceded the state's authority to promote marital fidelity by prohibiting various forms of illicit sex, but he denied that the total ban on a married couple's use of contraceptives advanced Connecticut's expressed interest in promoting marriage and the family. In order to enforce its ban, the state would have to enter the marital bedroom. Since the statute invaded a fundamental aspect of liberty,

4. *Id.*, 539, 540–41. In a separate dissent, Justice Douglas conceded that the due process clauses could be used to restrain unreasonable invasions of marital privacy, but he was reluctant to revive the "discredited" substantive due process reasoning of *Lochner. Id.*, 517, 519–20, 521. See also Kauper, 64 *Mich. L. Rev.*, 241, and Kenneth L. Karst, "Invidious Discrimination: Justice Douglas and the Return of the 'Natural-Law–Due-Process' Formula," 16 *U.C.L.A. L. Rev.* 716–50 (1969), 727–28, 729.

5. 367 U.S., 542 (italics added). The liberty of the due process clauses, Harlan continued, protects the individual's "freedom from all substantial arbitrary impositions and purposeless restraints." *Id.*, 543. See also Karst, 16 *U.C.L.A. L. Rev.*, 743–44, who argues that the due process clauses comprehend all of the citizen's civil rights, including marital and procreative rights.

the marital relationship in the privacy of the home, it had to pass a rigorous test. Harlan argued that the law should be subject to strict scrutiny, rather than minimum rationality, in determining whether the state had a sufficiently compelling interest to destroy a fundamental right of privacy.[6] The law was an irrational prohibition that undermined Connecticut's ostensible objective of promoting marital relationships.

Four years later, in *Griswold* v. *Connecticut*,[7] the Supreme Court struck two Connecticut laws prohibiting physicians from prescribing and married couples from using contraceptives. Although a majority decided that the Constitution protects a married couple's intimate decision to prevent conception, there was considerable disagreement about the doctrinal basis for the specific right to privacy. Speaking for the Court, Justice Douglas asserted that the First, Third, Fourth, and Fifth Amendments, as applied to the states through the due process clause of the Fourteenth Amendment, create various "rights of 'privacy and repose'" that encompass a married couple's decision to prevent conception.[8] Justice Goldberg concurred in the decision, but he relied on the Ninth Amendment as a source of unenumerated fundamental rights.[9] Also concurring were Justices Harlan and White, who relied exclusively on the due process clause as an independent limitation on legislative authority to burden the individual's fundamental liberties without a compelling public interest.[10] Despite their different approaches, Douglas, Harlan, and White employed a balancing approach and "compelling interest" standard in finding the Connecticut law unconstitutional.

6. 367 U.S., 548–49. While Harlan required the state to show an important purpose, he denied that privacy rights are absolute. As he observed, the home is not a haven for crime. He argued that adultery, fornication, incest, and homosexual conduct were not immune from the state's reach simply because these practices occurred in the home. *Id.*, 552–53. See also Karst, 16 *U.C.L.A. L. Rev.*, 743–44.

7. 381 U.S. 479 (1965).

8. *Id.*, 482–85, 485. As Douglas argued, these rights emanate from various other rights that the Constitution explicitly protects. Although the First Amendment does not mention freedom of association, this right is indispensable in vindicating such explicit rights as freedom of speech, petition, and assembly. In turn, freedom of association requires a degree of associational privacy.

9. In defining which rights are fundamental, Justice Goldberg turned to the traditions and collective conscience of the American people to determine whether a principle is so rooted in American society "as to be ranked as fundamental." *Id.*, 493, quoting *Snyder* v. *Massachusetts*, 291 U.S. 97, 105.

10. 381 U.S., Harlan (concurring), 493. Inasmuch as the statute applied indiscriminately to married and unmarried persons alike, White noted, Connecticut simply could not demonstrate that the law advanced the stated goal of prohibiting all forms of promiscuous or illicit sexual relationships. *Id.*, 503–4, 505–6.

If *Griswold* lacked doctrinal clarity, a majority nevertheless believed that the Constitution creates a fundamental right to privacy that includes a married couple's decision to prevent conception. As in earlier cases, the justices continued to confine reproductive rights to marriage and the family. When a state intrudes in this private realm, totally banning contraception, its prohibition is subject to strict scrutiny. As Justice Black's dissent suggested, *Griswold* marked a return to the reasoning of *Lochner*, despite the reluctance of the majority to rest the decision squarely on the substantive due process philosophy that had informed the liberty-of-contract cases between 1897 and 1923.[11] But the *Griswold* Court subjected the law to a standard of review that few regulatory policies could survive.

In *Eisenstadt v. Baird*[12] the Supreme Court relied on the equal protection clause to extend *Griswold* to unmarried persons. The Court voided a Massachusetts law prohibiting physicians and pharmacists from prescribing and dispensing contraceptives to anyone but married persons. It could not be sustained as a valid health measure, designed to control disease, because the classification had no rational relation to preventing the spread of sexually transmitted diseases. The law contained so many exceptions that it could not be regarded as a deterrent to premarital sex, which *would* be within the state's competence. Unless the real purpose of the statute was to punish unmarried persons for illicit sex by requiring women to give birth to unwanted children, Brennan concluded, the classification did not serve any other conceivable valid public purpose.[13]

As *Griswold* and *Eisenstadt* demonstrate, the Court expanded rather than retreated from the concept of substantive due process in several significant ways. First, the justices discovered a new substantive liberty—namely, the right to prevent conception. Second, the Supreme Court extended the right to unmarried as well as married persons. Third, it concluded that women, as autonomous individuals, have a right to decide whether to have children.

11. *Id.*, Black (dissenting), 514–16, 522–24. See also Justice Stewart's separate dissenting opinion, 528, and Kauper, 64 *Mich. L. Rev.*, 257, for a discussion of Black's criticism of *Griswold*.

12. 405 U.S. 438 (1972). Speaking for a plurality, Justice Brennan argued that the law violated the equal protection clause of the Fourteenth Amendment because it was irrational, riddled with many exceptions, and did not serve the state's ostensible purpose of protecting public health. *Id.*, 440–42.

13. *Id.*, 446–53. Although the Court declined to conclude that a total ban on contraception would conflict with fundamental human rights, Justice Brennan observed that "whatever the rights of the individual to access to contraceptives may be, the rights must be the same for unmarried and married alike." *Id.*, 453.

In contrast to economic liberty, when the state destroys or seriously impairs reproductive rights it must show a compelling interest in restricting the individual's choice. Thus the Court perpetuated Stone's constitutionally flawed double standard by applying a higher standard of judicial review to privacy rights than to economic liberty.

By balancing competing interests, in the contraception cases the Warren and Burger Courts once again intruded unnecessarily on the legislative function. In *Poe* and *Griswold* the state of Connecticut did not demonstrate that the prohibition advanced its stated purpose of promoting marital fidelity. Similarly, in *Eisenstadt* Massachusetts failed to show that the law prevented either premarital sex or the spread of sexually transmitted diseases. The statutes encroached on a private sphere protected by the due process clause without serving any valid public purpose. By requiring the states to demonstrate a public objective, the Court could have protected personal liberty without balancing competing interests, which is a legislative task, or employing a heightened standard of scrutiny, which is a questionable methodology.

Abortion and a Woman's Right to Decide

Despite important differences between contraception and abortion, Justice Brennan's opinion in *Eisenstadt* was only a step or two removed from *Roe v. Wade*. For the first time, in *Roe* the Supreme Court decided that the due process clause of the Fourteenth Amendment encompasses a woman's decision to terminate an unwanted pregnancy by abortion.[14] A woman may make this difficult decision in consultation with her physician, noted Justice Blackmun, but her decision is personal. As a free, equal, and autonomous person, a woman possesses the fundamental liberty to make procreative choices for herself.[15] However, Harry Blackmun denied that the right is abso-

14. 410 U.S. 113 (1973), 153. Joining Blackmun in the opinion of the Court were Chief Justice Burger and Justices Douglas, Brennan, Stewart, Marshall, and Powell. Justice Stewart also wrote a concurring opinion. Justice Rehnquist dissented. Chief Justice Burger and Justice Douglas filed concurring opinions in the companion case, *Doe v. Bolton*, 410 U.S. 179 (1973), while Justice White filed a dissenting opinion in that case.

15. Although Blackmun framed the constitutional issue as a matter of privacy, *Roe* is about personal liberty—the liberty of women to decide for themselves whether to have children. See Estrich and Sullivan, 138 *U. Pa. L. Rev.*, 125–27, 129, and Jed Rubenfeld, "On the Legal Status of the Proposition That 'Life Begins at Conception,'" 43 *Stan. L. Rev.* 599–635

lute. He rejected Norma McCorvey's claim "that she is entitled to terminate her pregnancy at whatever time, in whatever way, and for whatever reason she alone chooses."[16]

Having recognized the conditional nature of the right, Blackmun conceded that the state may have legitimate, overriding public interests in regulating the performance of abortions.[17] He identified three legitimate state interests that might become compelling at various points during a woman's pregnancy: (1) safeguarding maternal health, (2) maintaining medical standards, and (3) protecting potential life.[18] In determining the point at which the state could legitimately regulate the performance of abortion, Justice Blackmun articulated his now famous trimester analysis.

During the first trimester, Blackmun began, the state could not enact regulations that burdened the woman's decision. Since having an abortion was safer than carrying to term, he reasoned, Texas could not demonstrate a rational health interest that would justify restricting the right. In consultation with a physician, a woman is free to terminate her pregnancy without the state's interference. Beginning in the second trimester the state could adopt policies to protect maternal health and regulate medical practice, as long as these policies did not burden the woman's decisional liberty by substantially increasing the costs and risks of abortion. At the point of viability, the state may even prohibit abortion in order to preserve potential life, "except when it is necessary to preserve the life or health of the mother."[19]

Much of Blackmun's trimester analysis is beside the point of *Roe*, how-

---

(1991), 602. See also Allen, 56 *U. Cin. L. Rev.*, 468, 478–79, who argues that *Roe* is about decisional privacy and freedom from coercion.

16. 410 U.S., 153. But see Andrew Koppelman, "Forced Labor: A Thirteenth Amendment Defense of Abortion," 84 *Nw. U. L. Rev.* 480–535 (1990), 515–16, who argues that the Thirteenth Amendment is a virtually absolute bar to state interference with women's abortion decisions. The major problem with Koppelman's position is that no other prohibition of servitude requires the sacrifice of potential or actual life.

17. 410 U.S., 154 (citations omitted).

18. *Id.*, 154, 155. See Laurence H. Tribe, "Forward: Toward a Model of Roles in the Due Process of Life and Law," 87 *Harv. L. Rev.* 1–53 (1973), 27–28; Henkin, 74 *Colum. L. Rev.*, 1420–21; and David J. Zampa, "The Supreme Court's Abortion Jurisprudence: Will the Supreme Court Pass the 'Albatross' Back to the States?" 65 *Notre Dame L. Rev.* 731–80 (1990), 731–32 (hereafter, Zampa, 65 *Notre Dame L. Rev.*). See also Edward Keynes with Randall K. Miller, *The Court vs. Congress: Prayer, Busing, and Abortion* (Durham, N.C.: Duke University Press, 1989).

19. 410 U.S., 163–64. For a detailed discussion of Blackmun's trimester analysis, see Keynes, *The Court vs. Congress*, 251–57.

ever, because the Texas statute was not a regulation of abortion. It prohibited and criminalized the performance of abortion at any stage in pregnancy, except to save the woman's life.[20] Having identified Norma McCorvey's liberty interest, Blackmun could have employed a reasonableness test to void a statute that virtually destroyed the right.[21] There was no justification for balancing competing interests or subjecting the Texas criminal abortion statute to strict scrutiny, since the law simply did not have a rational relation to any legitimate state interest. In reality, Harry Blackmun employed strict scrutiny in *Roe* to challenge the abortion regulations of most states.

Following *Roe*, the Supreme Court invalidated a wide variety of state laws that impinged directly on women's decisions to end their pregnancies.[22] These statutes included provisions requiring married women to inform their spouses or obtain their consent, regulations requiring minor dependent women to inform or obtain the consent of their parents or guardians before obtaining an abortion, informed-consent provisions requiring physicians to recite a litany or parade of horribles to patients, and regulations imposing fixed waiting periods on women. At the same time, the Court sustained some laws expressing the states' interests in ensuring that women make informed decisions or that minor women notify a parent or guardian who can provide essential medical information and advice at a stressful time. In deciding whether these laws advance the states' legitimate interests in protecting the health, marriage, family relationships, and parental rights of women, the justices have attempted to distinguish between laws that are coercive or that give third parties a veto over a woman's decision, and those

20. 410 U.S., 146–47. The statute provided that any person who performs or procures an abortion in violation of the act is guilty of a felony punishable by a fine of up to $1,000 and/or a prison sentence not exceeding five years.

21. Inasmuch as most subsequent cases involved regulation rather than a prohibition of abortion, *Roe* is of limited precedential value. Many of these cases could have been disposed of by requiring the legislature to demonstrate that the regulation served a purpose within the state's constitutional authority.

22. Since 1977, however, the Supreme Court has held that neither the states nor the national government has a constitutional obligation to fund elective or therapeutic abortions for poor women. Because the Court has concluded that state and national funding policies do not deny equal protection or burden a fundamental right, government need only demonstrate that regulations and restrictions are rationally related to the constitutionally permissible goals of preserving health and potential life. See *Beal v. Doe*, 432 U.S. 438 (1977); *Poelker v. Doe*, 432 U.S. 519 (1977); *Maher v. Roe*, 432 U.S. 464 (1977); *Harris v. McRae*, 448 U.S. 297 (1979); and *Rust v. Sullivan*, 111 S.Ct. 1759 (1991). But see C. Andrew McCarthy, "The Prohibition on Abortion Counseling and Referral in Federally-Funded Family Planning Clinics," 77 *Calif. L. Rev.* 1181–1210 (1989), and Alexandra A. E. Shapiro, "Title X, the Abortion Debate, and the First Amendment," 90 *Colum. L. Rev.* 1737–1778 (1990).

that express valid state interests and impose less than an undue or substantial burden.

Beginning in 1976 the Supreme Court invalidated a series of laws that required married adult women to obtain a spouse's written consent before having an abortion. Speaking for the majority in *Planned Parenthood* v. *Danforth*, for example, Justice Blackmun acknowledged that the states may have a valid interest in preserving potential life and the marital relationship, but that they cannot seriously impair a woman's right to obtain an abortion without demonstrating a sufficiently compelling interest.[23] By granting husbands a veto, the state of Missouri had virtually destroyed women's right to decide. However, the state had not shown that a spousal veto in any way furthered its expressed interest in promoting sound marital relationships.

The Supreme Court also has invalidated various consent statutes that give parents, guardians, and spouses a veto over the decisions of minor women seeking an abortion. Despite significant differences among state laws, in *Danforth*, *Bellotti* v. *Baird* (*Bellotti II*),[24] and *Akron* v. *Akron Center for Reproductive Health*[25] the justices voided statutes that gave parents and guardians a veto during the first trimester. In these cases, the Court found the statutes constitutionally defective because they imposed "an absolute limitation on the minor's right to obtain an abortion."[26] While a state can treat minors differently from adults, it cannot seriously impair or virtually destroy the exercise of their constitutional liberty without a compelling public interest. However, as Stewart implied in *Danforth*, less sweeping parental-consent laws could pass judicial muster, even during the first trimester.[27]

Seven years after *Danforth*, in *Planned Parenthood Association* v. *Ashcroft*,[28] a bare majority sustained a revised Missouri law containing a parental-consent provision. Unlike the previous statute, the new law provided for a judicial proceeding in which a minor woman could establish that she is "sufficiently mature to make the abortion decision herself or that, despite her immaturity, an abortion would be in her best interests."[29] Although the

---

23. 428 U.S. 52 (1976) (opinion of the Court), 69–71.

24. 443 U.S. 622 (1979).

25. 462 U.S. 416 (1983).

26. 428 U.S., Stewart (concurring), 90. See also *Bellotti II*, 443 U.S., 634, 635, 637. The majority found the Missouri and Massachusetts statutes constitutionally flawed because the states failed to distinguish between mature and immature minor women in drafting the parental-consent provisions. 428 U.S., 69, 75; 443 U.S., 643–44.

27. 428 U.S. (Stewart, with Powell, concurring), 86–90.

28. 462 U.S. 476 (1983).

29. *Id.*, 491. Dissenting in part, Justice Blackmun maintained that the statute gave parents

majority opinion was fragmented, five justices (White, Powell, Burger, Rehnquist, and O'Connor) upheld the provision as a legitimate expression of the state's interest in maternal health and potential life. Concurring, Justice O'Connor supported the parental-consent provision because it did not impose an "undue burden on any right that a minor may have to undergo an abortion."[30] The Supreme Court also has sustained parental notification laws that, in its judgment, do not seriously burden or destroy a minor's right to obtain an abortion.[31] As the Court's decisions suggest, if the states draw parental consent and notification statutes carefully, they can advance legitimate public interests in protecting maternal health and potential life.[32]

Similarly, the Court has attempted to distinguish between informed-consent regulations that are coercive and those ensuring that a woman's choice is voluntary and informed. In obtaining a woman's permission to perform an abortion, some statutes required physicians to read a detailed statement informing each woman about abortion and childbirth.[33] Speaking for the ma-

---

and judges an absolute veto over an unemancipated woman's decision to have an abortion. *Id.*, 503–4.

30. *Id.*, 505.

31. See *H.L. v. Matheson*, 450 U.S. 398, which involved a Utah statute providing that before performing an abortion a physician must "*[n]otify, if possible, the parents or guardian of the woman upon whom the abortion is to be performed, if she is a minor* or the husband of the woman, if she is married." *Id.*, 400 (emphasis in the original); Utah Code Ann. § 76-7-304 (1981). As applied to H.L., an unmarried, immature dependent minor, the Utah law did not impose an absolute veto on the young woman's decision.

32. See *Hodgson v. Minnesota*, 110 S.Ct. 2926 (1990), in which apparently six justices believed that a single-parent notification law, with a judicial bypass procedure, could survive judicial muster. For a comprehensive analysis of the abortion rights of minor women, see Christopher M. Kelly, Tracy D. Knox, and Randolph R. Rompola, "*Hodgson* and *Akron II*: The Supreme Court's New Standard for Minor's Abortion Statutes," 66 *Notre Dame L. Rev.* 527–54 (1990), esp. 535–53, for an analysis of the Minnesota statute's provisions. On the same day, in *Ohio v. Akron Center for Reproductive Health*, 110 S.Ct. 2972 (1990), 2984, the Court sustained a one-parent notification provision as a reasonable expression of the state's interest in "ensuring that, in most cases, a young woman will receive guidance and understanding from a parent." The Ohio law made it a crime for a physician to perform an abortion on an unmarried, unemancipated woman (under eighteen) without notifying one parent at least twenty-four hours before the procedure. However, the statute included several important exemptions and a judicial bypass procedure. *Id.*, 2977–78.

33. 462 U.S., 422–24. The law required that physicians inform a patient (1) that she is actually pregnant, (2) the time that had elapsed since conception, (3) that the fetus is a human life from the time of conception, (4) that the physician has a duty to preserve the life of a viable fetus, (5) that serious physical and psychological consequences might result from an abortion, and give a detailed description of the fetus's anatomical and physical characteristics, and provide lists of agencies that provide birth-control information or that can assist her during pregnancy, including adoption agencies.

jority in *Akron*, Powell found that the city's informed-consent procedure attempted to coerce women into giving birth by suggesting that abortion is a "particularly" dangerous procedure.[34] Writing for the Court three years later, in *Thornburgh v. American College of Obstetricians & Gynecologists*[35] Justice Blackmun concluded that Pennsylvania's informed-consent provision was "nothing less than an outright attempt to wedge the Commonwealth's message discouraging abortion into the privacy of the informed-consent dialogue between the woman and her physician."[36] The Akron ordinance and the Pennsylvania statute were the antithesis of the states' professed interest in promoting informed consent because they inhibited a genuine dialogue between physicians and their patients.[37]

In addition to determining the burdensome effects of various consent and notification laws, the Supreme Court has examined the burdens that fixed waiting periods and other dilatory procedures impose on a woman's decision to have an abortion. In *Akron*, for example, the Court found a twenty-four-hour waiting period unduly burdensome because there was no discernible medical basis for an inflexible requirement. By requiring women to make several trips to abortion facilities, Powell reasoned, the ordinance increased the cost and the risk of performing abortions. Therefore, the City of Akron could not demonstrate that the regulation advanced its stated interests in safeguarding women's health.[38] Dissenting, Justice O'Connor conceded that

34. *Id.*, 443–45.

35. 476 U.S. 747 (1986).

36. *Id.*, 762. As Blackmun emphasized, "the Commonwealth does not, and surely would not, compel similar disclosure of every possible peril of necessary surgery or of simple vaccination, reveals the anti-abortion character of the statute and its real purpose." *Id.*, 764.

37. In separate dissenting opinions, Burger, White, and O'Connor claimed that the provision was a legitimate measure ensuring that women would make informed, knowledgeable judgments; that the law did not directly infringe on the right to choose an abortion; and that the law was "rationally related to the State's interests in ensuring informed consent and in protecting potential human life." O'Connor (dissenting), 462 U.S., 831. Unless a law unduly burdens a fundamental right, O'Connor argued, courts should determine whether the regulation has a rational relationship to legitimate objectives. Only when a law imposes an undue burden should courts impose strict scrutiny. *Id.*, 828. Although some commentators heralded the majority's opinion as a decisive reaffirmation of *Roe*, others noted that four justices either questioned its validity or called for an outright reversal. See David Fernandez, "*Thornburgh v. American College of Obstetricians*: Return to Roe?" 10 *Harv. J.L. & Pub. Policy* 711–27 (1987), 721–26. But see Fulks, 26 *J. Fam. L.*, 771–72, 780–81, who notes that support for *Roe* had eroded in *Akron*.

38. 462 U.S., 449–51. By contrast, in *Hodgson* the Court found a forty-eight-hour waiting period to be a reasonable means of ensuring that a minor's decision is knowing and intelligent. The waiting period, Powell concluded, was a reasonable burden on the minor's right to terminate her pregnancy. 110 S.Ct., 2944.

the requirement increased the cost, but denied that the effect was unduly burdensome. The waiting period, she noted, was a reasonable means of "ensuring that a woman does not make this serious decision in undue haste."[39]

Prior to *Casey* the Supreme Court had failed to forge a consensus on the regulation of abortion. As the increasingly fragmented nature of its decisions reveals, the Court could not agree on an appropriate balance between reproductive liberty and the scope of the states' authority to regulate abortion. Nevertheless, a plurality sustained laws that affected but did not destroy or substantially burden a woman's right to decide whether to have an abortion. In overturning unduly burdensome consent laws, the plurality generally used a "compelling interest" standard. Otherwise, it employed a lower standard of review when sustaining various consent and notification statutes. To this extent, the justices varied the standard of review according to how intrusive they found state regulations. Whatever the standard of review, the Court attempted to balance indivisible rights and divisible public goods on the same scale.

In contrast to the Supreme Court's post–*Carolene Products* balancing approach, a renewed police-power jurisprudence would protect unenumerated rights without encroaching unnecessarily on the policymaking authority of the states. Undoubtedly, the states can use the police power to ensure that physicians have their patients' informed consent before performing medical procedures, including abortions. In the case of minors, the states have a special responsibility to ensure that minor women are mature enough to make such decisions for themselves, without informing their parents or obtaining their consent prior to an abortion. As the above informed-consent cases indicate, the Court could have preserved the right to decide by ascertaining whether the regulation actually furthered the stated interests of protecting the woman's health and ensuring that the decision would be informed and voluntary. By examining the legislative record it would have been possible to decide whether the regulation promoted a knowing decision or simply coerced women into continuing their pregnancies. Moreover, the Burger Court could have afforded protection to unenumerated liberties without varying the standard of review according to subjective evaluations of the relative importance of various due process rights.

---

39. 462 U.S., 474.

The Physician's Rights and the Regulation of Medical Practice

While the states cannot destroy or severely impair a woman's fundamental right to decide in favor of abortion, the courts have long acknowledged the public's legitimate authority to regulate the medical professions and safeguard medical standards. Since 1973 the justices have attempted to reconcile women's right to decide with the states' authority to regulate the medical profession. These decisions involve the power to (1) license medical personnel,[40] (2) restrict the performance of abortions to certified physicians,[41] (3) limit an attending physician's discretion to provide information that individual women need to make intelligent decisions, (4) regulate the methods that physicians use to induce abortions at various stages of pregnancy, (5) restrict the physician's judgment in determining whether a fetus is viable, and (6) intrude on the physician's primary duty to protect a woman's health and life. As with consent and notification provisions, the Supreme Court has sought to distinguish laws that express the states' legitimate interest in regulating medical practice from those that severely impair or destroy women's liberty. Here too the justices have varied the judicial standard according to their evaluation of the burden imposed.

In balancing the competing and distinct interests of protecting maternal health and preserving potential human life, many states have adopted laws regulating the methods or techniques that physicians can use to induce an abortion. Several states require physicians to determine whether a fetus is viable before inducing an abortion. Some states also have enacted laws requiring physicians to preserve the life of a viable or potentially viable fetus in the later stages of pregnancy. These laws require physicians to make difficult judgments about fetal viability and to take measures to save the

40. See *Rosen v. Louisiana State Board of Medical Examiners*, 419 U.S. 1098 (1975), voiding a statute that authorized the revocation or suspension of a doctor's license for performing abortions in the first trimester unless necessary to save a woman's life. As applied to the first trimester, the Court found that the law unduly burdened women's liberty without advancing a valid state interest in promoting health. However, the district court admitted that after the first trimester Louisiana could enact regulations that are narrowly tailored to express its legitimate interests, which the court did not define. 380 F. Supp. 875 (D. E.D. La. 1974), 876, 877.

41. *Connecticut v. Menillo*, 423 U.S. 9 (1975). In a *per curiam* opinion, the Court affirmed the state's legitimate interest in assuring that only qualified persons perform abortions under conditions that make the procedure safer than normal childbirth. Since prosecuting unlicensed persons for performing abortions does not burden any constitutional right, there was no need to subject the law to a strict-scrutiny, compelling-interest test. *Id.*, 10–11.

unborn child's life. Some laws proscribe the use of particular abortifacients; others require the presence of a second physician to deliver and care for the newborn child. While acknowledging the states' interest in preserving potential life and regulating medical practice, the Court has evaluated such laws in terms of their burdensome effects on women's liberty.

Speaking for a majority in *Danforth*, Justice Blackmun denied that Missouri could prevent doctors from using amniocentesis, a safe abortion technique then commonly employed after the twelfth week of pregnancy, under the pretext of promoting maternal health.[42] He concluded that the legislature's outright proscription of a safe technique simply did not advance Missouri's stated interests.[43] Similarly, in *Colautti* v. *Franklin*[44] the Supreme Court found a provision of Pennsylvania's abortion law, requiring physicians to determine whether a fetus is or may be viable before performing an abortion, unduly burdensome.[45] Since the Pennsylvania Abortion Control Act imposed criminal penalties on doctors who failed to perform such tests without defining "potential viability," Blackmun concluded that the law intruded impermissibly on the physician's procedural due process rights and consequently on the pregnant woman's substantive liberty.[46] By interfering with the physician's best clinical judgment, both statutes reduced access to abortions and imposed a substantial burden on some pregnant women.

In two other cases, *Ashcroft* and *Thornburgh*, the Supreme Court faced the issue of postviability care due unborn children. While a majority sus-

42. Inasmuch as the law required physicians to use prostaglandin injection, a method not widely available in Missouri, the state could not justify the regulation as a reasonable health measure. 428 U.S., 76, 79.

43. *Id.*, 79. However, Blackmun noted that after the first trimester a state can regulate abortion procedures "in ways that are reasonably related to maternal health." *Id.*, 76. Disputing the majority's finding, Justice White denied that the statute burdened women significantly. *Id.*, 96–99. White criticized the majority for behaving like a continuous constitutional convention as well as the nation's medical board "with powers to approve or disapprove medical and operative practices and standards throughout the United States." *Id.*, 99.

44. 439 U.S. 379 (1979).

45. The statute subjected physicians to charges of criminal homicide for "intentionally, knowingly, recklessly or negligently caus[ing] the death of another human being." *Id.*, 394. However, more recently, in *Webster* v. *Reproductive Health Services*, 109 S.Ct. 3040 (1989), the Court sustained a provision of a Missouri law that requires physicians to determine whether a fetus is viable. In effect, the statute creates a presumption of viability in the twentieth week, which the physician can rebut before performing an abortion. The statute requires that, prior to performing an abortion on any woman whom a physician has reason to believe is twenty or more weeks pregnant, the physician ascertain whether the fetus is viable by performing "such medical examinations and tests as are necessary to make a finding of the gestational age, weight, and lung maturity of the unborn child." *Id.*, 3054.

46. 439 U.S., 395, 396, 397–401.

tained Missouri's "second-physician requirement,"[47] the Court found that
Pennsylvania's postviability standard of care significantly increased the risks
to the mother in order to preserve the life and health of the unborn child.[48]
As Justice Blackmun interpreted the Pennsylvania statute, the provision ex-
posed women to increased medical risks that were not justified by a sufficiently compelling state interest. By failing to provide explicitly for third-
trimester emergencies, he argued, the requirement of a second attending
physician to care for the newborn chilled the performance of abortions.[49]

Dissenting, Justice White denied that a woman's right to decide whether
to have an abortion is fundamental—that is, essential to ordered liberty or
deeply rooted in the traditions and conscience of the American people.
White took the position that a woman's right to favor abortion over childbirth is "a species of 'liberty' that is subject to the general protections of the
Due Process Clause," but he denied that the right is so fundamental that
state regulations are subject to more than minimal judicial scrutiny. Therefore, he rejected the application of strict scrutiny to most state regulations
of abortion.[50]

Also dissenting, O'Connor rejected both Blackmun's "compelling interest" analysis and White's conclusion that a woman's right to terminate her
pregnancy is less than fundamental. Unless a statute imposes an undue burden on women's abortion decisions, she wrote, the Supreme Court should
decide whether the law "bears a rational relationship to [the state's] legitimate purposes."[51] Even if a law triggers strict scrutiny, it is still possible that
the regulation will survive a heightened level of judicial review. Because
there had not been a full factual inquiry in the district court, the Supreme
Court could not evaluate the degree to which various provisions impinged
on women's abortion decisions. Absent a factual record, the justices could

47. The Missouri law required the attendance of a second physician in the delivery room to
preserve the unborn child's life, provided that this requirement did not "pose an increased risk
to the life or health of the woman." 462 U.S., 483. As Powell interpreted the second-physician requirement, it could be waived in the event of increased risk to the life or health of the
woman. Thus the Missouri statute was rational because it advanced the state's compelling
interest in preserving life without posing a significant added risk to the woman. Id., 485–86.

48. Section 3210(b) of the Pennsylvania Abortion Control Act of 1982 required physicians
to exercise the same degree of care to preserve the life of the fetus in performing late abortions
as in normal childbirth procedures. 476 U.S., 768.

49. Id., 770–71. It should be noted, however, that the Missouri law did not contain an
explicit waiver. The difference between the two states' provisions seems elusive.

50. Id., 789–93.

51. Id., 828. O'Connor adhered to her position that an undue burden is one that poses
"absolute obstacles or severe limitations on the abortion decision." Id.

not possibly decide whether the postviability requirement either burdened a fundamental right or advanced the state's alleged purpose.

In evaluating the regulation of abortion facilities by states, the Supreme Court has sought to determine whether specific regulations significantly increase the costs of obtaining abortions or reduce access to abortion facilities.[52] In both *Akron* and *Ashcroft*, for example, the Court invalidated regulations requiring doctors to perform all second-trimester abortions in critical-care hospitals. Speaking for a majority, Lewis Powell denied that either Akron or Missouri had demonstrated a compelling interest in mandating full-service, acute-care hospitals throughout the second trimester.[53] However, after evaluating the medical evidence, Powell concluded that a law requiring late second-trimester abortions to be performed in hospitals would rationally express a compelling state interest.

Dissenting, Justice O'Connor denied that the regulation imposed a significant obstacle because it only marginally increased the cost of abortions. Therefore, there was no apparent justification for applying heightened judicial scrutiny or a more exacting standard of review.[54] In effect, O'Connor suggested that trial judges should apply a highly quantitative analysis to decide whether mandatory hospital confinements, pathology reports, or other regulations increase the costs significantly and therefore reduce access to abortions substantially.[55] Although O'Connor and Powell came to different conclusions regarding the law's burdensome effects, their approach was similar. Each examined the legislative record to decide whether the regulation advanced the law's stated purpose.

52. Some states have adopted legislation mandating that first- and second-trimester abortions be performed in critical-care hospitals rather than clinics or physicians' offices. Other laws require abortion facilities to file pathology reports on fetal tissue. And some statutes mandate that clinics and hospitals file statistical reports on abortions they have performed. Many of these provisions differ significantly from regulations governing the performance of other medical and surgical procedures.

53. *Akron*, 462 U.S., 432–34, 434–38. See also *Ashcroft*, 462 U.S., 481–82. On the same day, in *Simopolous v. Virginia*, 462 U.S. 506 (1983), Justice Powell sustained a Virginia statute that required doctors to perform second-trimester abortions in hospitals, including outpatient clinics, as a reasonable means of promoting women's health. After evaluating the medical evidence, Powell apparently concluded that the statute did not burden the fundamental rights of women.

54. 462 U.S., 466–67.

55. See, for example, opinion of Stapleton, Circuit Judge, in *Casey*, 947 F.2d 682 (3d Cir. 1991), 698. "A review of the abortion case law, and *Webster* and *Hodgson* in particular," Stapleton observed, "suggests that no undue burden is caused by abortion regulations that do not have a 'severe' or 'drastic' impact upon time, cost, or the number of legal providers of abortions." In reference to the abortion procedure, Judge Stapleton's analysis attempts to quantify the effects of specific regulations for pregnant women as a group. See also Estrich and Sullivan, 138 *U. Pa. L. Rev.*, 133, 134–35.

The Challenge to *Roe* v. *Wade*

In a series of decisions since 1983, Sandra Day O'Connor has attempted to develop a new approach to the abortion controversy. Beginning with her dissent in *Akron*, Justice O'Connor has urged judicial self-restraint in evaluating the regulation of abortion by states. As she articulated her approach in *Akron*, *Thornburgh*, and *Webster* v. *Reproductive Health Services*, trial judges would evaluate abortion policies in two stages. In the first stage, a trial judge would ask whether the governmental policy (either a regulation or prohibition) challenges burdens or impinges on a right that is fundamental—that is, unenumerated but protected. If the answer to this threshold question is no, the court's inquiry should cease, because the policy is within the legislature's constitutional discretion. Should the people find the policy uncommonly foolish or politically unacceptable, they can reject the legislature's judgment in the polling booth.

If a trial court finds that an abortion law implicates a woman's reproductive freedom, it must then determine whether the regulation or prohibition either destroys or severely burdens the liberty interest asserted. At this second stage, the trial court should make a factual inquiry into the nature of the burden. Is the policy only minimally burdensome or is it unduly burdensome? In order to guide state and federal trial judges, Justice O'Connor has prodded the Court to develop explicit standards for measuring just how burdensome specific regulations are in relation to the individual plaintiff's claims. As she argued in *Akron*, an unduly burdensome statute is one that either destroys or interferes substantially with a woman's right to decide in favor of abortion. In the context of the Supreme Court's fundamental-rights jurisprudence, O'Connor suggests that strict scrutiny should be applied to such abortion regulations.[56]

Finally, the trial court would balance the competing private and public claims. If a statute totally destroys the right or imposes substantial risks and costs that tend to destroy the right to decide, the trial court should determine whether the regulation serves a public interest that is compelling enough to restrict performing an abortion. As Justice Brennan conceded in

---

56. *Akron*, 462 U.S., 462–63. Or, as Justice Brennan observed in *Carey* v. *Population Services International*, the Court should apply strict scrutiny to "state regulations that burden an individual's right to decide to prevent conception or terminate pregnancy by substantially limiting access to the means of effectuating that decision" as well as "to state statutes that prohibit the decision entirely." According to Brennan, a law that prohibits abortions entirely or substantially limits access to abortions should trigger strict scrutiny and a compelling-interest standard of judicial review. 431 U.S. 678 (1977), 688.

Carey v. *Population Services International,* "even a burdensome regulation may be validated by a sufficiently compelling state interest"[57] in safeguarding maternal health, medical standards, and potential life. Even though a majority found the Akron ordinance unduly burdensome, as Justice O'Connor noted, the Court acknowledged that "even a 'significant obstacle' can be justified by a 'reasonable' regulation."[58] If *Roe* protects women against absolute obstacles, official interference, or coercive restraint, O'Connor concluded, it is unnecessary to find that every state regulation inhibiting abortions to some degree is invalid.[59] While Justice O'Connor's approach is in some ways more deferential to legislative authority than Justice Blackmun's, both methodologies require the Supreme Court to balance competing private and public interests, which is a function that legislative institutions usually perform in a republican society.

Casey and the Promise of Liberty

Adhering to Justice Blackmun's compelling-interest standard, in *Casey* District Court Judge Daniel Huyett found six sections of the Pennsylvania Abortion Control Act unconstitutional.[60] Huyett concluded that the informed-consent, parental-consent, spousal-notification, reporting, and pub-

57. *Id.,* 686.

58. 462 U.S., 463. As she noted, Powell had followed this approach. *Id.,* 434, 435, 438. For further analysis and criticism of O'Connor's argument, see Estrich and Sullivan, 138 *U. Pa. L. Rev.* 132–33, and Zampa, 65 *Notre Dame L. Rev.* 748–55. See also Ann E. Fulks, "*Thornburgh:* The Last American Right-to-Abortion Case?" 26 *J. Fam. L.* 771–92 (1987–88), and Nancy K. Rhoden, "Trimesters and Technology: Revamping *Roe* v. *Wade,*" 95 *Yale L.J.* 639–97 (1986).

59. 462 U.S., 464.

60. *Planned Parenthood of Southeastern Pennsylvania* v. *Casey,* 744 F.Supp. 1323 (E.D. Pa. 1990). The 1988 and 1989 amendments to the act provided that in a medical emergency a physician could waive the consent and notification requirement only if there was "a serious risk of substantial and irreversible impairment of [a] major bodily function or death." In all other cases, physicians were required to wait at least twenty-four hours before performing an abortion. Physicians, rather than trained counselors, were required to provide women with information on the nature, risks, and alternatives to abortion, the probable gestational age of the fetus, and the medical risks of continuing pregnancy. Although the statute contained a parental-consent provision, it also provided for a judicial bypass procedure. The spousal-notification section required women to inform the spouse unless (1) he was not the father, (2) he could not be found after a diligent effort, (3) the pregnancy resulted from sexual abuse, or (4) there was a danger of bodily injury. The public-disclosure provision required abortion providers to release statistical information on the performance of abortions in cases involving the use of public funds.

lic-disclosure sections were coercive, substantially increased the risks and costs of abortion, imposed significant burdens, or erected serious obstacles to women seeking an abortion. The state, he observed, had not offered a sufficiently compelling reason to justify burdening women's decisions. Applying a minimum-rationality standard, however, Judge Huyett sustained a provision requiring physicians to determine the gestational age of the fetus. Since all of the plaintiffs perform such tests to determine whether the fetus is viable as well as the risks and the most appropriate method of performing an abortion, the court concluded that the requirement conforms to accepted medical practice.[61]

Speaking for the court of appeals, Judge Walter Stapleton largely reversed the lower court's decision, sustaining all but the statute's spousal-notification provision.[62] Inasmuch as Roe involved the outright prohibition of abortion, Stapleton distinguished Casey from the Supreme Court's 1973 decision. Unless a regulation impinges directly on a woman's fundamental right to decide in favor of abortion, Stapleton reasoned, courts should employ less than a strict-scrutiny, compelling-interest standard of judicial review. Denying that most of the Pennsylvania regulations unduly burdened women's right to decide, Stapleton applied the deferential minimum-rationality standard of recent economic-liberty decisions. Apparently, he believed that O'Connor had articulated a consensus in earlier cases that a Supreme Court plurality would accept.[63]

In contrast to all other provisions of the Pennsylvania law, the court of appeals found that the spousal-notification section unduly burdened married women who chose not to consult their husbands because they feared physical violence or economic and psychological coercion to continue their preg-

61. Id., 1388–90.

62. *Planned Parenthood of Southeastern Pennsylvania* v. *Casey,* 947 F.2d 682 (3d Cir. 1991).

63. Id., 693–94. Judge Stapleton reasoned that a statute could infringe on the right by "(1) causing a delay before the abortion is performed; (2) raising the monetary cost of an abortion; (3) reducing the availability of an abortion by directly or indirectly causing a decrease in the number of legal abortion providers; (4) causing or forcing the woman to receive information she has not sought; (5) causing the woman to find the person or persons whom the state has required that she notify or obtain consent from; (6) causing the woman to endure any negative or hostile response from a person whom the state has required the woman to notify or obtain consent from; and (7) taking away the power to decide whether to have an abortion by giving another person, usually a parent or spouse, a veto power on the abortion decision." Id., 698. As Stapleton's criteria suggest, he relied on empirical evidence to determine the costs and risks that specific regulations impose on the majority of women for whom the regulations are not burdensome. His method ignores the women for whom the regulations are in fact burdensome.

nancies. The spousal notification provision penalized women who sought to exercise a constitutionally protected right, without the state intruding on their liberty to *decide* to have an abortion. Despite a waiver provision, the court of appeals concluded that the section could not survive strict scrutiny because it was not narrowly tailored to serve the state's interests in safeguarding the marital relationship or the father's interest in having children. The notification provision imposed an undue burden on women's liberty without expressing a sufficiently compelling state interest.[64] As the empirical evidence suggests, spousal notification is burdensome to significantly more women than the statute's other provisions.[65]

The conflicting opinions of the district court and the court of appeals posed several important questions for the Supreme Court. Was *Roe* still the law of the land? Is the right to decide in favor of abortion a fundamental right or merely a liberty interest? How should judges measure the burdens that various state regulations impose on pregnant women seeking an abortion? Could the Court develop a principled way to reconcile the competing private rights and public interests at stake in the abortion controversy? What is the impact of the lower courts' decisions on the evolution of substantive due process rights?

In a 5–4 decision, the Supreme Court sustained the court of appeals holding in *Casey*. A majority concluded that "the essential holding of *Roe v. Wade* should be retained and once again reaffirmed."[66] Nevertheless, a plurality consisting of Justices O'Connor, Anthony Kennedy, and David Souter sustained Pennsylvania's regulations of abortion, with the exception of the spousal-notification requirement. In balancing the competing private and public claims, the plurality employed a vague "unduly burdensome" yardstick rather than the more precise empirical standard that Circuit Judge Walter Stapleton had employed. The plurality also abandoned Justice Blackmun's trimester analysis and "compelling interest" standard.

64. *Id.*, 709–15.

65. As the Mansfield study indicated, while 70 percent of the women surveyed agreed that women should have a right to choose to have an abortion, 80 percent favored the parental-consent provision of the Pennsylvania law, 69 percent favored the spousal-notification requirement, 93 percent favored informing women about the alternatives to abortion, and 82 percent favored the twenty-four-hour waiting period. "The Public Mind," 18–22.

66. 112 S.Ct. 2791 (1992) (majority), 2804. The majority included Justices Blackmun, Stevens, O'Connor, Kennedy, and Souter. The opinion was authored jointly by O'Connor, Kennedy, and Souter, with Blackmun and Stevens concurring in part and dissenting in part with the judgment and decision of the Court. Chief Justice Rehnquist, joined by Justices White, Scalia, and Thomas, authored a separate opinion dissenting and concurring in part with the Court's judgment.

Searching for a pragmatic compromise, the Court articulated three "principles" in *Casey*. First, before viability, a woman has a right to decide whether to have an abortion and "to obtain it without undue interference from the State."[67] Prior to viability the state's interests in maternal health and potential life are not sufficient to prohibit abortions or pose substantial obstacles to a "woman's effective right to elect the procedure."[68] Second, the Court affirmed the state's authority to restrict abortions after viability, except when necessary to protect a woman's life or health. Third, a majority acknowledged the state's legitimate interest in safeguarding maternal health and potential life from the onset of pregnancy.

The Court used *Casey* to affirm its understanding of the Fourteenth Amendment's due process clause as a limitation on state legislative power. It explicitly recognized that due process has a substantive as well as a procedural component. Since *Mugler v. Kansas*, wrote O'Connor, Kennedy, and Souter, "the Clause has been understood to contain a substantive component as well, one 'barring certain government actions regardless of the fairness of the procedures used to implement them.'"[69] Specifically referring to the term "liberty" as the controlling element in *Casey*, the majority confirmed Justice Harlan's view that in the United States due process has become a bulwark "against arbitrary legislation."[70]

Although the majority acknowledged that "liberty" includes the specific protections of the Bill of Rights, it asserted that the due process clause protects all fundamental rights (both enumerated and unenumerated) from the states' invasion. Due process is a constitutional promise "that there is a realm of personal liberty which the government may not enter."[71] The Court denied that the framers' understanding of the Bill of Rights and the states' practices at the time of the Fourteenth Amendment's ratification established "the outer limits of the substantive sphere of liberty which the Fourteenth Amendment protects."[72] Not unlike Harlan and Stewart, the *Casey* majority argued that the courts should exercise "reasoned judgment" in determining the specific interests that the due process clause encompasses. The majority admitted the importance of constitutional tradition in defining these inter-

67. *Id.*
68. *Id.*
69. *Id.*
70. *Id.*, quoting from Harlan, J. (dissenting), *Poe v. Ullman*, 367 U.S. 497 (1961), 541 (quoting *Hurtado v. California*, 110 U.S. 516 [1884], 532).
71. 112 S.Ct. (majority), 2805.
72. *Id.*

ests but rejected the view that due process is a static concept, frozen "at some fixed stage of time or thought."[73]

In defining the "liberty of all," the Court attempted to link the right to decide in favor of abortion to a long line of precedents relating to marriage, the family, and reproductive freedom. As O'Connor, Kennedy, and Souter observed in their joint opinion:

> These matters, involving the most intimate and personal choices a person may make in a lifetime, choices central to personal dignity and autonomy, are central to the liberty protected by the Fourteenth Amendment. At the heart of liberty is the right to define one's own concept of existence, of meaning, of the universe, and of the mystery of human life.[74]

The plurality sought to protect the personal autonomy of women and their right to make intimate decisions affecting their future and their equal status and dignity in society. The joint opinion is consistent with the view of Brandeis that liberty and privacy are essential to individual autonomy, which the Constitution protects against governmental regulations that do not clearly serve a valid public purpose.

After affirming its commitment to substantive due process, the Court attempted to buttress its argument by appealing to the precedential value of *Roe*.[75] However, the majority's appeal to precedent seems fatuous. As Harry Blackmun conceded, the Court abandoned his trimester analysis and "compelling interest" standard, which was the analytical core of *Roe*.[76] The plurality chose viability as a pragmatic dividing-line concerning the scope of the state's regulatory power. Before viability the state can express its legiti-

---

73. *Id.*, 2806.
74. *Id.*, 2807.
75. *Id.*, 2810–16. Since *Roe* had not proven to be unworkable, the majority argued, there was no principled reason to abandon the central tenet of reproductive liberty. Indeed, a generation of women had come to rely on the decision in structuring their most intimate relationships. If the Court abandoned a valid legal principle in the face of political pressure, reasoned the majority, it would undermine its legitimacy as well as the value of precedent in establishing and maintaining a rule of law.
76. Despite his partial concurrence, Justice Blackmun criticized the plurality for abandoning *Roe*'s analytical core, the trimester approach and the compelling-interest standard. Only by abandoning this analytical tool could the plurality sustain regulations virtually identical to statutes that the Court previously had declared unconstitutional. *Id.*, Blackmun (concurring and dissenting in part), 2844–47.

mate interests in maternal health and potential life as long as its regulations do not unduly burden the woman's decisional liberty. After viability the state can restrict or even prohibit abortion, except when necessary to safeguard the woman's life or health.[77] While the Supreme Court affirmed that the due process clause contains a substantive component encompassing reproductive liberty, its appeal to precedent reads like an apologia to advocates of *Roe*.

Justice O'Connor's approach fared somewhat better than Blackmun's, even though the plurality diluted her standard by describing unduly burdensome legislation as any "state regulation [that] has the purpose or effect of placing a substantial obstacle in the path of a woman seeking an abortion of a nonviable fetus."[78] Thus the states can enact legislation that is designed to inform, even persuade, but not coerce a woman into childbirth as a means of promoting potential life. They can adopt regulations that are reasonably related to safeguarding women's health, as long as these requirements "do not constitute an undue burden."[79] Regulations that are coercive or that significantly increase the costs and risks or reduce the availability of abortions would constitute an undue burden. The plurality's definition gives the states significantly greater regulatory discretion than Blackmun's *Thornburgh* opinion.

In overturning the spousal-notification provision, the majority emphasized the requirement's burdensome effect on the small class of married women "who do not wish to notify their husbands of their intentions and who do not qualify for one of the statutory exceptions to the notice requirement."[80] For those women who fear physical abuse or economic and psychological coercion to bear children, the Court concluded that the notice requirement was tantamount to an impermissible veto over a woman's reproductive decisions.[81] If the conclusion of the majority is hardly more

77. *Id.*, 2816–17.

78. *Id.*, 2820. As Justice Scalia argued (concurring in the judgment in part and dissenting in part), the plurality eliminated "the more narrow formulations used in Justice O'Connor's earlier opinions. Those opinions stated that a statute imposes an 'undue burden' if it imposes '*absolute obstacles* or *severe* limitations on the abortion decision.'" *Id.*, 2878. See also O'Connor (dissenting), *Thornburgh*, 476 U.S. 747, 828.

79. 112 S.Ct. (plurality), 2821.

80. *Id.* (majority), 2829–30. As the Mansfield study indicated, 69 percent of the women surveyed agreed with the legal requirement that a husband "must be informed before his wife has an abortion." "The Public Mind," 20.

81. According to the majority, the spousal notification provision reflected a view "repugnant to our present understanding of marriage and of the nature of the rights secured by the Constitution." 112 S.Ct., 2831.

than a reflection of public opinion, there is little reason to believe that judges can read opinion polls better than legislators.

Both Chief Justice William Rehnquist and Justice Antonin Scalia aimed broadsides at the Court's decision and at the plurality's opinion. Rehnquist denied that abortion is a fundamental right under the due process clause. "Unlike marriage, procreation and contraception," he noted, "abortion 'involves the purposeful termination of potential life.'"[82] The abortion decision is *sui generis;* it is different from the other rights of "personal or family privacy and autonomy" that the Court has accorded constitutional protection.[83] Adhering to the plurality opinion in *Webster,* Rehnquist characterized abortion as a liberty interest rather than a fundamental right. Employing the minimum-rationality standard of *Williamson v. Lee Optical Co.,* the chief justice concluded that the states can regulate the performance of abortion "in ways rationally related to a legitimate state interest."[84] While Rehnquist came to a different conclusion than the majority, he employed a similar balancing approach to reconciling private rights and public interests.

In contrast to Rehnquist, Justice Scalia denied categorically that the Fourteenth Amendment affords any protection for abortion.[85] Scalia rejected the fundamental-rights argument "because of two simple facts: (1) the Constitution says absolutely nothing about it [the right to an abortion] and (2) the long-standing traditions of American society have permitted it to be legally proscribed."[86] Beginning with *Roe,* Scalia argued, the Supreme Court had imposed its will on the American people, displacing the political choices and value judgments of their elected representatives with the justices' personal preferences. In the absence of a constitutional mandate, he observed, the Pennsylvania law should be upheld as a rational exercise of the state's authority.[87] However, Scalia's analysis is also defective because he ignores the constitutional tradition that shaped the framing of the Fourteenth Amendment.

82. *Id.,* Rehnquist, C.J. (concurring and dissenting in part), 2859.

83. *Id.* Since a majority of states regulated abortion at the time of the Fourteenth Amendment's ratification, the chief justice noted, there is little support for the argument that the right is deeply rooted in the traditions or conscience of the American people.

84. *Id.,* 2867.

85. Given the basic conflict between Scalia's and Rehnquist's arguments, it is remarkable that both justices signed each other's opinion. It is also surprising that Justices White and Thomas concurred in the two opinions.

86. *Id.,* Scalia (concurring in the judgment in part and dissenting in part), 2874.

87. If the state's exercise of power is beyond the Court's judicial competence, one wonders why it is necessary to proceed any further. As Scalia's view implies, the Court should merely dismiss such cases for want of jurisdiction.

Attacking the plurality's version of the "undue burden" standard as "inherently manipulable" and "hopelessly unworkable in practice," Justice Scalia dismissed it as "unprincipled in origin."[88] The plurality's opinion was a "verbal shell game" that concealed "raw judicial policy choices concerning what is 'appropriate' abortion legislation."[89] In Scalia's judgment, the undue-burden standard is a meaningless extraconstitutional invention that "invites the district judge to give effect to his personal preferences about abortion."[90] Because Roe had been wrongly decided, it should be buried rather than resuscitated. After delivering the coup de grâce, Justice Scalia denied that Casey had resolved the conflict over abortion. By foreclosing the democratic resolution of the abortion conflict, the decision would merely prolong the controversy.[91]

Although Casey has not resolved the abortion controversy, the Supreme Court explicitly affirmed its commitment to the fundamental-rights, substantive due process jurisprudence that it has developed since the late 1880s. Beginning with Mugler v. Kansas, the Court employed the Fourteenth Amendment's due process clause to limit the exercise of state legislative power vis-à-vis the individual's economic liberty. Since Meyer v. Nebraska the justices have expanded this realm of personal autonomy to include decisions concerning marriage, the family, and procreation. In Griswold and Roe the Supreme Court enlarged the outer limits of personal liberty to encompass contraception and abortion. Justice Black's funeral oration to the contrary, substantive due process survives as a source of unenumerated rights and a limitation on legislative power.

Despite dire predictions that the Court would abandon the basic principle of Roe, the Casey majority stated explicitly that the due process clause protects a woman's decision to terminate pregnancy by abortion. As Justices O'Connor, Kennedy, and Souter noted in their joint opinion, women have an effective right to elect abortion "without undue interference from the State."[92] However, the Casey plurality also acknowledged that the reproductive liberty of women is conditional rather than absolute and that therefore at some time during pregnancy the state can express its legitimate interest in protecting the life or potential life of the fetus. Moreover, at viability the

88. Id., 2877.
89. Id., 2878.
90. Id., 2880.
91. Id., 2884, 2882.
92. Id., opinion of the Court, 2804.

fetus may even acquire independent rights that outweigh a woman's interest in obtaining an abortion for "financial or psychological reasons or convenience."[93]

The joint opinion leaves the states considerably greater discretion to regulate abortion than Justice Blackmun's opinions from *Roe* to *Thornburgh*. By abandoning Harry Blackmun's trimester analysis and limiting the use of his "compelling interest" standard, Justices O'Connor, Kennedy, and Souter have returned to state legislatures the difficult political task of protecting the reproductive liberty of women and the fetus's right to live. Prior to viability, the plurality leaves the states room to adopt laws that are rationally related to such valid public interests as protecting maternal health, regulating the medical profession, or ensuring that women make voluntary and informed decisions. However, the joint opinion prohibits the states from using their regulatory power to destroy or seriously impair the right of women to decide to have an abortion. From the time of fetal viability, the states can enact laws that restrict or even prohibit the performance of abortion in order to protect potential life unless these statutes burden women significantly by increasing the risks to their health and life.

Because *Casey* was a facial challenge to Pennsylvania's Abortion Control Act, the lower courts must determine the degree to which specific regulations burden the abortion decisions of women. As subsequent litigation indicates, trial judges have begun the arduous task of deciding whether abortion regulations impose minimal, substantial, or severe burdens on women seeking to exercise their liberty.[94] Given the Court's balancing methodology, trial judges must decide whether the states' alleged interests in regulating abortion outweigh women's interests in terminating pregnancy. Ultimately, the Supreme Court must determine whether the "unduly burdensome" standard leads to principled judicial decisions or, as Justice Scalia claims, is "inherently manipulable" and "hopelessly unworkable in practice."

93. Victoria A. Sackett, "Between Pro-Life and Pro-Choice," *Public Opinion* (April–May 1985), 52, quoted in Barbara Hinkson Craig and David M. O'Brien, *Abortion and American Politics* (Chatham, N.J.: Chatham House Publishers, 1993), 253.

94. See, e.g., *Ada v. Guam Soc. Obstetricians & Gynecologists*, cert. den., 113 S.Ct. 633 (1992); 766 F.Supp. 1422 D. Guam 1990 *Barnes v. Miss.*, 992 F.2d (5th Cir. 1993); *Sojourner v. Edwards*, 974 F.2d 27 (5th Cir. 1992); *Barnes v. Moore*, 970 F.2d 12 (5th Cir. 1992); *Herbst v. O'Malley*, 1993 U.S. Dist. Lexis 2479 (D. N.D. Ill.); *Fargo Women's Health Org., v. Sinner*, 819 F.Supp. 862 (D. N.D. 1993); *Benton v. Kessler*, 1992 U.S. Dist. Lexis 14747; *Jane L. v. Bangerter*, 809 F.Supp. 865 (D. Utah 1992); *Planned Parenthood of S.E. Ariz. v. Neely*, 804 F.Supp. 1210 (D. Ariz. 1992); *Preterm Cleveland v. Voinovich*, No. 92AP-791 (Ohio Ct. App. 10th App. Dist., July 27, 1993); and *In re Petition No. 349*, 838 P.2d 1 (Okl. 1992).

Casey is a course correction rather than a sea change in the Supreme Court's substantive due process jurisprudence. Despite Scalia's criticism that the plurality opinion interferes with the democratic process, *Casey* invites the states to explore the limits of their regulatory power.[95] In deciding whether the states have exceeded their police power, the plurality cautions the lower courts to exercise self-restraint. When entering this political thicket, the plurality reminds trial courts to pay careful attention to legislative fact-finding and judgment. In a representative democracy, the plurality implies, legislative policies are entitled to great respect unless they burden fundamental rights unduly. After almost two decades of wrestling with this intractable conflict, the *Casey* plurality has fashioned a pragmatic compromise that reflects the public mind—namely, that the Supreme Court should affirm *Roe*'s basic promise of liberty but grant the states greater discretion in regulating abortion.

Despite its Herculean effort, the *Casey* Court has failed to fashion a principled resolution to the basic conflict between liberty, conceived in terms of individual autonomy, and republican definitions of the public welfare. The Supreme Court's failure stems from its understanding of individual rights and of the public welfare. Implicitly, a majority of justices define personal liberty as an indivisible dignitary right to privacy and individual autonomy. Unless regulations and prohibitions clearly serve a public purpose, government cannot burden the exercise of personal liberty and privacy rights.

While dignitary rights are indivisible, they are transitive—they can be arrayed on an ordinal scale. Thus it is possible to develop a hierarchy of rights and, on that basis, to decide conflicts of rights among individuals. At the same time, the majority view the public welfare in utilitarian terms. In a republican society the legislature's function is to weigh competing interests, strike a balance, and allocate scarce values or resources—that is, to determine the public good in cost-benefit terms. In other words, public goods are divisible and transitive.

Although dignitary rights and public goods are both ordinal and transitive, they cannot be arrayed on a single scale, because the former are indivisible values and the latter are divisible values. Therefore, it is impossible to balance personal liberties (conceived as indivisible dignitary rights) and the public welfare (viewed as divisible goods) on the same scale. As long as the Supreme Court treats privacy as a dignitary right, it must restrain public

95. As Craig and O'Brien note, there is little indication that the abortion controversy will end. "The abortion controversy," they conclude, "will remain a driving force in and a reflection of American politics." Craig, *Abortion*, 359.

intrusions unless they advance a right that has a greater value in the transitive hierarchy—for example, a person's right to life. Thus the Court could take the position that at viability the fetus effectively acquires independent rights as a person, protected by the due process clause, that outweigh a woman's interest in terminating her pregnancy.[96]

Alternatively, the Court could adopt a utilitarian theory of rights, which would leave legislatures free to weigh "rights" as public goods in cost-benefit terms. This would undermine the Supreme Court's substantive due process jurisprudence, since the legislature is responsible for making calculations of the public welfare in a republican society. The Court would lose its claim as a guardian of rights based on principles of justice that the U.S. Constitution either explicitly or implicitly comprehends. Its role would be reduced to determining whether the legislature had followed constitutionally prescribed procedural rules in distributing public goods.

Conceivably, the Court could attempt to reconstruct Field's and Cooley's police-power jurisprudence to adjudicate contemporary liberty and privacy claims. Their approach left legislators free to balance competing interests, while the justices kept a watchful eye to ensure that regulations restricting due process rights served a public purpose rather than the interests of a particular class or group. Despite the difficulty of applying nineteenth-century jurisprudence to twentieth-century problems, the justices' current methodology simply does not permit a principled resolution of the controversy.

Judge Walter Stapleton's circuit court opinion in Casey is a useful starting point for reconstructing and applying police-power jurisprudence to contemporary problems. In attempting to determine whether Pennsylvania's abortion regulations substantially burdened the decisions of women or destroyed their right to decide,[97] Judge Stapleton turned to the empirical evidence.

---

96. In effect, the Casey plurality has taken this approach in fixing viability as the point at which government can preserve a viable fetus, unless the regulation jeopardizes the mother's life or health, which then has a higher value in the plurality's transitive hierarchy than potential life.

97. Judge Stapleton reasoned that a statute could infringe on the right by "(1) causing a delay before the abortion is performed; (2) raising the monetary cost of an abortion; (3) reducing the availability of an abortion by directly or indirectly causing a decrease in the number of legal abortion providers; (4) causing or forcing the woman to receive information she has not sought; (5) causing the woman to find the person or persons whom the state has required that she notify or obtain consent from; (6) causing the woman to endure any negative or hostile response from a person whom the state has required the woman to notify or obtain consent from; and (7) taking away the power to decide whether to have an abortion by giving another person, usually a parent or spouse, a veto power on the abortion decision." 947 F.2d, 698.

How many women does a specific regulation affect? Are the additional costs caused by delays, reporting requirements, and medical procedures significant? By increasing the exposure of abortion facilities to public hostility, do disclosure requirements inhibit a substantial number of women from obtaining abortions? Do the regulations significantly reduce the number of legal abortion-providers? In answering these questions, Judge Stapleton focused on the empirical evidence to decide whether the specific regulation was unduly burdensome to a significant number of women.[98]

Inasmuch as *Casey* involved a facial challenge to the statute's constitutionality, Judge Stapleton's approach provided an opportunity for both parties to present evidence in a new proceeding after the law had gone into effect. Women challenging the law would have ample opportunity to demonstrate that various provisions seriously burdened or destroyed protected rights. The Pennsylvania attorney general could defend the statute by demonstrating that it clearly served public interests that are within the state's competence. As Stapleton's opinion demonstrates, the courts can decide whether a policy is a purposeless restraint of liberty or a reasonable protection of the public health, safety, welfare, or morals, without intruding unnecessarily on the state's authority.

98. As the Mansfield study indicated, while 70 percent of the women surveyed agreed that women should have a right to choose to have an abortion, 80 percent favored the parental consent provision of the Pennsylvania law; 69 percent favored the spousal notification requirement; 93 percent favored informing women about the alternatives to abortion; and 82 percent favored the twenty-four-hour waiting period. "The Public Mind," 18–22.

Epilogue

Since the late 1880s the Supreme Court has been developing a jurisprudence of unenumerated fundamental rights based on the due process clauses of the Fifth and Fourteenth Amendments. In the thirty-five years following the Civil War, such jurists and legal scholars as Stephen Field, Joseph Bradley, Thomas M. Cooley, Francis Wharton, and John Norton Pomeroy have argued that the Fourteenth Amendment imposes substantive restraints on the police power and other powers of the states. From their perspective, due process protects the individual's life, liberty, and property rights against arbitrary and purposeless restraints. Due process is a constitutional limitation on the exercise of legislative power, as well as a guarantee of fairness in the judicial process.

While some scholars conclude that the framers of the Fourteenth Amendment embodied concepts of natural justice in the due process clause, others argue that they relied upon common-law principles. In fact, the amendment's authors derived due process rights from Anglo-American legal history, which comprehends both the positive and higher law traditions. They justified specific civil rights in terms of natural-law and social-contract theory as well as the common law, state laws and constitutions, and federal and state court decisions in the era before the Civil War. Justice Black's criticism to the contrary, late nineteenth-century substantive due process jurisprudence was not vague and it did not embody principles of Social Darwinism.

The contemporaneous drafting of the Civil Rights Act of 1866 also indicates that the amendment's framers viewed fundamental rights largely but not exclusively in economic terms. The act provided statutory protection for the common-law right to make and enforce contracts, to acquire, use, enjoy, and dispose of property, and to equal protection for property and personal security. The privileges or immunities, due process, and equal protection clauses of the Fourteenth Amendment gave constitutional protection to these fundamental civil rights. As a minimum, the amendment expanded national power to secure life, liberty, and property against the states' arbitrary deprivations.

Between 1866 and 1875 Congress adopted a series of civil rights and judiciary acts that expanded the authority of the federal courts to protect fundamental rights against class legislation. In this period, Republicans and Democrats disputed the authority of Congress to displace the states as the primary guardians of the individual's constitutional rights. But there emerged a consensus that the Fourteenth Amendment protected three core rights—life, liberty, and property—against burdensome governmental conduct. The legislative drafters believed that the amendment imposed an affirmative duty on the states to protect fundamental rights, which Congress could authorize the federal judiciary to enforce in the event that the states failed to meet their responsibility.

Although Congress intended that the freedman be the primary beneficiary of federal protection, in the era of laissez-faire constitutionalism Justices Field, Bradley, Harlan (I), and Peckham employed the concept of substantive due process to secure the individual's property rights and economic liberty against partial or class legislation. Field and Bradley, in particular, believed that property and economic liberty are among the most important rights that the framers of the Fourteenth Amendment and the Civil Rights Act of 1866 attempted to protect. In the Lockean tradition, as James Ely notes, post–Civil War constitutionalists regarded the protection of property and economic liberty as one of government's essential functions.[1] The due process clause created new possibilities for national oversight of state legislation affecting property and economic liberty.

The Fourteenth Amendment does not mention liberty of contract, but Bradley, Field, and Peckham argued that it is indispensable to securing every other right, since contracts are the basis of economic relationships in a free society. Without security for property and economic opportunity, individuals could not be free, independent, or happy. Moreover, Field believed that the individual's economic liberty and the society's collective welfare were congruent. Despite existing inequalities in the distribution of wealth, economic liberty encouraged investment, new industries, and transcontinental

1. Ely, *The Guardian of Every Other Right*, 82.

expansion. By facilitating the accumulation of wealth, liberty of contract permitted individuals to realize their human potential and promoted the collective welfare of society. But Field and Bradley failed to anticipate that the new corporations would restrict market freedom, undermining the very economic opportunity and equality that the framers of the Fourteenth Amendment attempted to protect.

Nevertheless, both jurists recognized that the due process clause was not intended to shield economic liberty and property rights against all state regulations. Field, Cooley, and other jurists believed that these rights were conditional rather than absolute. In a republican society, the legislature has the authority to restrain the exercise of rights in order to promote the public welfare. Both Stephen Field and John Appleton, for example, argued that the states could impose reasonable limitations—that is, regulations and prohibitions that are directly related to a valid public purpose.

However, the legislature cannot deprive a person of a liberty merely to promote the interests of a particular class or group, unless such legislation also serves a valid public purpose. Nor can the legislature transfer property rights from one person to another. Thus Justices Field and Bradley opposed monopolies as a deprivation of economic liberty and a forced transfer of private property. Nineteenth-century police-power jurisprudence limited the exercise of legislative authority to promoting *public* purposes, while recognizing that private rights can be subordinated to the public welfare.

Field and Appleton adhered to the Jacksonian democrats' belief that the state should remain neutral in the economic, political, and social struggles of the new industrial age. As a guarantor of neutrality, the courts could ensure that private interests would not pervert public authority and that government would not give an advantage to one group at the expense of another. The purpose of nineteenth-century police-power jurisprudence was to prevent the unreasonable exercise of government authority, not to prevent the states from accomplishing any public purpose within their competence. Field did not perceive the courts' role as balancing competing public and private interests, nor did he perceive the need for government intervention to preserve economic liberty in the face of concentrations of private power and market distortions. Rather, he sought to keep the public and private spheres distinct.

Despite claims to the contrary, during the Gilded Age the Supreme Court upheld the economic regulatory legislation of most states. The justices sustained regulations that were directly related to protecting the public health, safety, welfare, and morals. However, they struck down policies that redistributed wealth, favored one set of economic interests over another, or interfered with functioning markets. The Fuller Court required the states to justify the reasonableness of measures burdening economic liberty and vested property rights. But the evidence does not support the argument that the Court routinely employed substantive due process to overturn state economic regulations or to favor business over other economic and social interests.

Even during the apogee of liberty of contract (1897–1905), the Fuller Court acknowledged that property and economic rights are conditional rather than absolute rights. Although the Court regarded liberty as the norm, it recognized that property and economic rights can be limited to advance the public welfare. As the states and the national government flexed their regulatory muscles, the Fuller, White, and Taft Courts became skeptical of the government's intentions. Suspecting that state and federal regulatory measures were economic protectionism rather than legitimate police regulations, the Fuller Court inquired into the legislature's intentions. In *Lochner* v. *New York*, for example, Rufus Peckham concluded that the legislature's fact-finding was a sham to protect large bakeries at the expense of small, independent bakers. There was no direct relationship between the regulation and the legislature's stated objectives.[2]

Although the Taft Court was wary of governmental policies that interfered with market forces, it tended to sustain wartime emergency measures restricting the exercise of property rights. After the emergency ended, the Court struck down legislation that interfered with functioning markets, but it was more amenable to policies regulating monopolies, public franchises, and other businesses that were exempt from market forces. While the Taft Court generally deferred to legislative judgments concerning the necessity of police measures, it opposed minimum-wage laws and policies favorable to labor unions as burdensome interferences with liberty of contract that merely favored the interests of labor over those of business.

During the Great Depression, as the Roosevelt administration and the states expanded their powers to the limits of constitutional authority, the Hughes Court subjected economic regulatory policies to more searching judicial inquiry. Between 1933 and 1935 the Court's commitment to laissez-faire constitutionalism clashed with the emerging welfare state. Following the confrontation between Franklin Roosevelt and the Supreme Court, the justices retreated from the protection of property rights and economic lib-

2. 198 U.S. 45 (1905), 57–58, 64.

erty. But the Court did not abandon the concept of substantive due process that had informed its protection of liberty of contract.

Beginning in 1923 the Supreme Court expanded the concept of substantive due process to include other personal liberty and privacy rights. In *Meyer* and *Pierce*, Justice McReynolds, later a bête noire of the New Deal, argued that due process embraces all of those common-law rights that the framers of the Constitution, the Bill of Rights, and the Fourteenth Amendment regarded as "essential to the orderly pursuit of happiness by free men."[3] But he acknowledged that these new personal liberty and privacy rights were conditional. Nevertheless, he asserted the judiciary's duty to determine whether legislative regulations advance the public welfare or are unreasonable restraints. McReynolds's broad conception of liberty included all of the fundamental rights, both enumerated and unenumerated, that are requisite for personal security and fulfillment. However, McReynolds was not a systematic thinker who attempted to provide either a codex of unenumerated rights or a rationalizing principle for inferring new rights from the due process clauses.

Following the Supreme Court's *Carolene Products* decision, the justices continued to use substantive due process to protect noneconomic liberties from unduly burdensome governmental policies. However, Justice Stone's opinion signaled a new bifurcated approach to unenumerated due process rights. While the justices applied strict scrutiny in evaluating police measures that implicated privacy rights, they abandoned any serious effort to scrutinize regulations burdening economic liberty and property rights. Stone's opinion marked the devaluation of economic liberty as well as heightened judicial solicitude toward other personal liberty and privacy rights.

Beginning with Stone's tenure as chief justice, the Court employed a balancing approach to fundamental rights. The justices attempted to balance claims of personal liberty against considerations of the public welfare. While they treated privacy, for example, as an indivisible dignitary right, they viewed the public welfare in utilitarian terms, as the allocation of divisible public goods. Both private rights and the public welfare are transitive, but they cannot be arrayed on the same scale precisely because they are different kinds of "goods." Thus the Supreme Court's balancing approach is basically flawed, no matter which level of scrutiny or standard of judicial review particular justices employ.

3. *Meyer*, 262 U.S. 390 (1923), 399.

Since the 1940s the Court has expanded the concept of unenumerated personal rights to include most aspects of marriage, the family, reproduction, and sexual intimacy. But the Court has failed to provide coherent rationalizing principles for including some rights and excluding others. It also has failed to offer a convincing argument for granting unenumerated privacy rights greater protection than unenumerated economic liberties or explicit property rights. As the decisions of the Warren and Burger Courts on reproductive liberty demonstrate, the justices' articulation of substantive due process rights has been pragmatic if not entirely subjective.

Therefore, the Court's decisions provide little or no guidance to trial judges who must decide whether new claims deserve protection under the due process clauses. Nor do these decisions help trial judges decide how much protection to afford unenumerated rights against burdensome state and national policies. As Judge Charles Petree of the Ohio Court of Appeals observed recently, the U.S. Supreme Court's "newly minted undue-burden standard . . . provides no guidance on which abortion restrictions will survive judicial scrutiny."[4]

The Court's failure to develop coherent rationales for determining whether individuals' due process claims deserve protection sometimes leads to contradictory results, as its decisions on sexual intimacy and privacy demonstrate. Having disengaged intimate sexual relations and decisions from marriage and the family, the Burger Court's refusal to extend the protection of the due process clause to the intimate conduct of homosexuals is at odds with its protection of heterosexuals' private behavior. There may be important differences between the two, but the Court has failed to provide a reasoned explanation. Public morality and long-standing tradition do not distinguish *Bowers* v. *Hardwick* from *Loving* v. *Virginia*, *Eisenstadt* v. *Baird*, and *Roe* v. *Wade*. At the time of these decisions, neither history nor the public ethos supported homosexual relationships, interracial marriage, the distribution of contraceptives to unmarried persons, or abortion.

In the area of marriage, the family, sexual intimacy, and reproduction, the justices have molded the standard of judicial review according to the "importance" of particular liberty interests and the burdensome effects of public policy on individuals. Thus plaintiffs asserting parental liberty interests have received less judicial solicitude than persons raising reproductive liberty claims. While there may be some reasoned justification for varying

4. Petree, J., concurring and dissenting in part, *Preterm Cleveland* v. *Voinovich*, No. 92AP-791 (Ohio Ct. App. 10th App. Dist., July 27, 1993), 33. Judge Petree found the standard particularly troublesome since only a plurality of the Supreme Court accepted it.

the level of scrutiny and standard of review, the Supreme Court has not provided one. Consequently, the Court's decisions appear subjective and result-oriented.

Although the recent abortion decision, *Planned Parenthood of Southeastern Pennsylvania v. Casey*, demonstrates the Court's continuing use of substantive due process jurisprudence, it does not contribute much to the evolution of unenumerated fundamental rights. The plurality's "unduly burdensome" approach is too vague to identify when public policies are so intrusive that the states must express compelling reasons for restricting the exercise of unenumerated rights. In the absence of a clearly reasoned controlling opinion, the Court has sent the issue back to the trial courts without "any appropriate criteria against which abortion regulations should be judged."[5] When are the state's reasons compelling enough to outweigh the individual's claims?

Such vague opinions as *Casey* lend credence to Hugo Black's criticism that the Court's substantive due process jurisprudence is subjective.[6] As Potter Stewart observed in *Zablocki v. Redhail*, the time has come for a candid discussion of the Court's use of substantive due process to invalidate legislative decisions that implicate unenumerated fundamental rights.[7] Rather than abandoning the concept of substantive due process, the Supreme Court needs to clarify the nature of the liberties protected and the limits of governmental power to protect the public welfare. The failure to articulate principled reasons for its decisions undermines the Court's institutional credibility and the legitimacy of its jurisprudence of unenumerated fundamental rights.

As a first step, the Court should abandon its balancing approach to unenumerated due process rights. The method is hopelessly flawed, because it requires judges to weigh fundamentally different kinds of "goods" on the same scale. Furthermore, it invites judges to act as legislators. In a republican society, legislators, who are accountable to the people through the ballot box, are responsible for weighing competing interests and allocating scarce resources. The judicial function is to hold legislators and other public officials accountable to constitutional limitations.

A renewed police-power jurisprudence offers an alternative to the modern Court's balancing approach to substantive due process rights. Rather than attempting to weigh the relative importance of unenumerated private rights

5. *Id.*
6. Black, J., dissenting, *Griswold v. Connecticut*, 381 U.S. 479 (1965), 522.
7. 434 U.S. 374 (1978), 395, 396.

and public interests, judges should ask: Do public policies actually serve the stated objectives? What are the foreseeable consequences of the policy? Does the record support the legislature's judgment? Is the regulation or prohibition directly related to some objective within the states' competence? Alternatively, does the policy merely serve a particular group's interests or seek to impose its values on the public? As Appleton, Cooley, Field, and other advocates of constitutional limitations recognized, the best way to preserve a private sphere is to ensure that government policies "serve a public purpose."[8]

8. Gold, *The Nineteenth Century Legal Mind*, 139.

Table of Cases

Ada v. Guam Soc. of Obstetricians & Gynecologists cert. denied. 113 S.Ct. 633 (1992); 766
    F.Supp. 1422 (D. Guam 1990), 206 n. 94
Adair v. United States, 208 U.S. 161 (1908), 124, 125–26
Adkins v. Children's Hospital, 261 U.S. 525 (1923), 133 n. 18, 141–42 n. 66, 143
Akron v. Akron Center for Reproductive Health, 462 U.S. 416 (1983), 179–80, 189, 191–92,
    196
Allgeyer v. Louisiana, 165 U.S. 578 (1897), 117–18
Barbier v. Connolly, 113 U.S. 27 (1884), 106 n. 30
Barron v. Baltimore, 32 U.S. (7 Pet.) 243 (1833), 35 n. 17, 40, 49, 66, 69, 70, 82
Bartels v. Iowa, 262 U.S. 404 (1923), 159 n. 18
Bartmeyer v. Iowa, 85 U.S. (18 Wall.) 129 (1873), 104
Beal v. Doe, 432 U.S. 438 (1977), 188 n. 22
Bellotti v. Baird (Bellotti I), 428 U.S. 132 (1976), 161 n. 25
Bellotti v. Baird (Bellotti II), 433 U.S. 622 (1979), 189
Blake v. McClung, 172 U.S. 239 (1901), 117 n. 78
Booth v. Illinois, 184 U.S. 425 (1902), 123
Bowers v. Hardwick, 478 U.S. 186 (1986), 176–77
Buchanan v. Warley, 245 U.S. 60 (1917), 114–15
Budd v. New York, 143 U.S. 517 (1892), 115 n. 72, 116
Burns Baking Co. v. Bryan, 264 U.S. 504 (1924), 131 n. 8, 136
Butchers' Union Co. v. Crescent City Co., 111 U.S. 746 (1884), 105–6
Calder v. Bull, 3 U.S. (3 Dall.) 386 (1798), 21
Carey v. Population Services International, 431 U.S. 678 (1977), 197–98
Carolene Products Co. (II), United States v., 323 U.S. 18 (1944), 147
Carolene Products Co., United States v., 304 U.S. 144 (1938), 133–35, 146, 147
Chicago, Burlington, and Quincy R.R. Co. v. McGuire, 219 U.S. 549 (1911), 123
Chicago, Milwaukee & St. Paul Ry. Co. v. Minnesota, 134 U.S. 418 (1890), 116
Civil Rights Cases, The, 109 U.S. 3 (1883), 90 n. 53, 93
Cleveland Board of Education v. LaFleur, 414 U.S. 632 (1979), 166–68
Colautti v. Franklin, 439 U.S. 379 (1979), 194
Connecticut v. Menillo, 423 U.S. 9 (1975), 193 n. 41
Coppage v. Kansas, 236 U.S. 1 (1915), 121–22

Corfield v. Coryell, 6 F.Cas. (No. 3230) 546 (C.C. E.D. Pa. 1823), 7, 47, 72, 80–81 n. 15, 91, 92, 93

Cruzan v. Director, Missouri Dept. of Health, 110 S.Ct. 2841 (1990), 5 n. 17

Darby, United States v., 312 U.S. 100 (1941), 145

Dash v. Van Kleek, 7 Johns (N.Y.) 477 (1811), 24 n. 102

Day-Bright Lighting Co. v. Missouri, 342 U.S. 421 (1952), 148

Dobbins v. Los Angeles, 195 U.S. 223 (1904), 114

Doe v. Bolton, 410 U.S. 179 (1973), 186 n. 14

Dorchy v. Kansas, 264 U.S. 286 (1924), 140

Dorsey, In re, 8 Ala. 295 (1838), 24 n. 102

Dred Scott v. Sanford, 60 U.S. (19 How.) 393 (1857), 23, 49

Eisenstadt v. Baird, 405 U.S. 438 (1972), 159, 177, 185–86

Eubank v. City of Richmond, 226 U.S. 137 (1912), 114

Euclid v. Ambler Realty Co., 272 U.S. 365 (1926), 137

Federal Power Commission v. Natural Gas Pipeline Co., 315 U.S. 575 (1942), 146–47

Ferguson v. Skrupa, 372 U.S. 726 (1963), 1, 149–50

German Alliance Insurance Co. v. Kansas, 233 U.S. 389 (1914), 115–16 n. 72

Ginsberg v. New York, 390 U.S. 629 (1968), 161

Griswold v. Connecticut, 381 U.S. 479 (1965), 48 n. 73, 152–53, 155, 168 n. 53, 184–86, 205

Gundling v. Chicago, 177 U.S. 183 (1900), 113–14 n. 65

H.L. v. Matheson, 450 U.S. 398 (1981), 190 n. 31

Hammer v. Dagenhart, 247 U.S. 251 (1918), 124, 125–26

Harris v. McRae, 448 U.S. 297 (1980), 188 n. 22

Hodgson v. Minnesota, 110 S.Ct. 2926 (1990), 190 n. 32, 196 n. 55

Holden v. Hardy, 169 U.S. 366 (1898), 122

Hollenbaugh v. Carnegie Free Library, 439 U.S. 1052 (1978), 176 n. 95

Hurtado v. California, 110 U.S. 516 (1884), 201 n. 70

Jacobson v. Massachusetts, 197 U.S. 11 (1905), 156 n. 8

Jane L. v. Bangerter, 809 F.Supp. 865 (D. Utah 1992), 206 n. 94

Jones v. Alfred H. Mayer Co., 392 U.S. 409 (1968), 163 n. 35

Lawton v. Steele, 152 U.S. 133 (1894), 113

Lincoln Federal Labor Union v. Northwestern Iron & Metal Co. 335 U.S. 525 (1949), 147–48

Lochner v. New York, 198 U.S. 45 (1905), 1 n. 2, 2, 118–21, 214

Loving v. Virginia, 388 U.S. 1 (1967), 169

Lyng v. Costello, 477 U.S. 635 (1986), 174 n. 83

Maher v. Roe, 432 U.S. 464 (1977), 188 n. 22

Maynard v. Hill, 125 U.S. 190 (1888), 168

McCulloch v. Maryland, 17 U.S. (4 Wheat.) 316 (1819), 63

Meyer v. Nebraska, 262 U.S. 390 (1923), xv, 4, 156–57, 159, 160

Miller v. Schoene, 276 U.S. 272 (1928), 137

Miller v. Wilson, 236 U.S. 373 (1915), 122

Minnesota Rates Case, The, 230 U.S. 352 (1913), 116

Moore v. East Cleveland 431 U.S. 494 (1977), 173–75

Morehead v. New York, 298 U.S. 587 (1936), 131–32 n. 9, 133 n. 18, 141–43

Mugler v. Kansas, 123 U.S. 623 (1887), 107–8, 205

Muller v. Oregon, 208 U.S. 412 (1908), 122

Munn v. Illinois, 94 U.S. 113 (1877), 109–11, 116

Murray's Lessee v. Hoboken Land & Improvement Co., 59 U.S. (18 How.) 272 (1856), 22–23

National Prohibition Cases, The, 253 U.S. 350 (1920), 124 n. 108

Nebbia v. New York, 291 U.S. 502 (1934), 138–40

New York Life Insurance Co. v. Dodge, 246 U.S. 357 (1918), 118 n. 82

New York Life Insurance Co. v. Head, 234 U.S. 149 (1914), 117 n. 78, 118 n. 82

O'Gorman & Young v. Hartford Ins. Co., 282 U.S. 251 (1931), 138 n. 46

Ohio v. Akron Center for Reproductive Health, 110 S.Ct. 2972 (1990), 190 n. 32

Permian Basin Area Rates Case, 390 U.S. 747 (1968), 147

Pierce v. Society of Sisters, 268 U.S. 510 (1925), 157 n. 11, 159–60

Planned Parenthood Assn. v. Ashcroft, 462 U.S. 476 (1983), 189–90, 194–95, 196

Planned Parenthood of Missouri v. Danforth, 428 U.S. 52 (1976), 189

Planned Parenthood of Southeastern Pennsylvania v. Casey, 112 S.Ct. 2791 (1992), xv, 180, 182, 200–209, 217

Planned Parenthood of Southeastern Pennsylvania v. Casey, 947 F.2d 682 (3d Cir. 1991), 196 n. 55, 199–200, 208–9

Planned Parenthood of Southeastern Pennsylvania v. Casey, 744 F.Supp. 1323 (E.D. Pa. 1990), 198–99

Poe v. Ullman, 367 U.S. 497 (1961), 182–84, 186

Poelker v. Doe, 432 U.S. 519 (1977), 188 n. 22

Powell v. Pennsylvania, 127 U.S. 678 (1888), 108

Preterm Cleveland v. Voinovich, No. 92AP-791 (Ohio Ct. App. 10th App. Dist., July 27, 1993), 206 n. 94, 216 n. 4

Prince v. Massachusetts, 321 U.S. 158 (1944), 160–61

Prudential Insurance Co. v. Cheek, 259 U.S. 530 (1922), 141

Radice v. New York, 264 U.S. 292 (1924), 141

Roe v. Wade, 410 U.S. 113 (1973), xv, 6, 152–53 n. 114, 179, 186–88, 197–98, 202–5

Rosen v. Louisiana State Board of Medical Examiners, 419 U.S. 1098 (1975), 193 n. 40

Runyon v. McCrary, 427 U.S. 160 (1976), 162–63

Rust v. Sullivan, 111 S.Ct. 1759 (1991), 188 n. 22

San Mateo County v. Southern Pacific R.R., 116 U.S. 138 (1882), 37 n. 25

Simopolous v. Virginia, 462 U.S. 506 (1983), 196 n. 53

Sinking Fund Cases, The (Union Pacific R.R. Co. v. United States), 99 U.S. 760 (1878), 110–11 n. 56

Skinner v. Oklahoma, 316 U.S. 535 (1942), 165–66, 167

Slaughterhouse Cases, The, 83 U.S. (16 Wall.) 36 (1873), 7 n. 23, 90–95, 100–104

Snyder v. Massachusetts, 291 U.S. 97 (1934), 184 n. 9

Sojourner v. Roemer, 772 F.Supp. 930 (E.D. La. 1991), 206 n. 94

Soon Hing v. Crowley, 113 U.S. 703 (1885), 106

Sunshine Anthracite Coal Co. v. Adkins, 310 U.S. 381 (1940), 142 n. 66

Taylor v. Porter, 4 Hill (N.Y.) 140 (1843), 24 n. 103

Thornburgh v. American College of Obstetricians & Gynecologists, 476 U.S. 747 (1986), 191, 194–95

Truax v. Raich, 239 U.S. 33 (1915), 117 n. 78

Turner v. Safley, 482 U.S. 78 (1987), 171–72

Tyson & Brothers v. Banton, 273 U.S. 418 (1927), 131 n. 7

Union Pacific R.R. Co. v. United States (Sinking Fund Cases), 99 U.S. 760 (1878), 110–11 n. 56

Van Horn's Lessee v. Dorrance, 2 U.S. (2 Dal.) 304 (C.C. Pa. 1795), 20–21

Webster v. Reproductive Health Services, 109 S.Ct. 3040 (1989), 194 n. 45, 196 n. 55

West Coast Hotel Co. v. Parrish, 300 U.S. 379 (1937), 133 n. 18, 143–45

Westerfelt v. Gregg, 12 N.Y. (2 Keenan) 2 (1854), 24 n. 103

Williamson v. Lee Optical Co. 348 U.S. 483 (1955), 148–49

Wisconsin v. Yoder, 406 U.S. 205 (1972), 161–62
Wolff Packing Co. v. Industrial Court, 262 U.S. 522 (1923), 140
Wynehamer v. New York, 13 N.Y. (3 Kern) 378 (1856), 24–25, 32 n. 4, 104 n. 22
Yick Wo v. Hopkins, 118 U.S. 356 (1886), 106–7
Zablocki v. Redhail, 434 U.S. 374 (1978), 169–71, 217

Index

abolitionist movement, 33, 73–74
abortion, 3–4, 5, 6, 186–209
  in first trimester, 153 n. 114
  lack of guidance to trial judges, 216
  liberty-of-contract, xv
  minors, 161 n. 25
  personal liberty, 158
  private *versus* public interests, xviii–xix,
    181–82
  undue burden, 179–80
absolute rights, 26, 47
accommodations. *See* Public Accommoda-
    tions Act of 1875 (Civil Rights Act of
    1875)
Adams, John, 14
affirmative duties of the states, xvii,
    212
Agricultural Marketing Adjustment Act of
    1937, 138 n. 47
allegiance. *See* political obligation; recipro-
    cal rights and duties
Amish society, 161–62
Anglo-American legal tradition. *See also*
    Magna Carta (1215)
  Civil Rights Act of 1866, 47, 52
  due process and, 57–58
  English customary law, 3, 45
  English law tradition, 34
  Fourteenth Amendment, 211
  government limitation, 9
  personal liberty, 158
  substantive due process, 126
Antifederalists, 17–18
Appleton, John, 3, 126, 213

arbitrary government
  England, 13–14
  Fourteenth Amendment, 69
  guarantees against, 52
  legislation to prohibit, 60
  state regulation and, 42
Arkes, Hadley, 8
association, freedom of, 86, 89, 184 n. 8

balancing of public and private interests. *See*
    public and private interests, balancing of
Barron v. Baltimore, 32 U.S. (7 Pet.) 243
    (1833)
  Bill of Rights and the states, 35 n. 17, 40
  Fourteenth Amendment and, 66, 69, 70,
    82
  James Wilson and, 49
Beaney, William M., 155 n. 3
Berger, Raoul
  Civil Rights Act of 1866, 35
  procedural due process, xiii, 56–63, 73
  significance of Fourteenth Amendment,
    36
Bill of Rights, 16–20
  Barron v. Baltimore, 40
  congressional debates on, 20 n. 79
  enforcement by the states, 51
  as justification for Civil Rights Act of
    1866, 45
  limitation of Congressional power, 62
Bingham, John
  civil rights bill, 50, 51
  and due process, 60–61
  Fourteenth Amendment, 63–69

Bituminous Coal Conservation Act of 1935,
    xviii, 142 n. 66
Black, Hugo
    contraceptives, 155, 185
    defense of state legislation, 152
    demise of substantive due process, 146,
        149–50, 154–55, 156
    objection to vague right to privacy, 1, 2,
        29
    "preferred" noneconomic rights, 133 n.
        20
    substantive due process, xiv
    Supreme Court as subjective, 217
Black Codes, 40, 49
Blackmun, Harry
    compelling-interest, 189, 202
    fetal viability, 194–95
    Fifth Amendment and Fourteenth
        Amendment, xiii
    informed consent, 191
    Roe v. Wade, xviii–xix, 6, 179, 186–88
    spousal consent to abortion, 189
Blackstone, William
    influence on Civil Rights Act of 1866,
        46, 47
    influence on Public Accommodations Act
        of 1875, 87
    "law-of-the-land," 14
    procedural due process, 57, 58
    substantive due process, 10, 60
Blair, James, 89
Bond, James E., 140 n. 56, 157 n. 11
Bradley, Joseph P.
    economic liberty, 98–99, 111, 112
    Fourteenth Amendment, 3, 211
    fundamental rights, xiii, 126
    laissez-faire constitutionalism, 212
    liberty of contract, xviii, 120 n. 90
    monopolies, 213
    public purpose, xix, 103
Brandeis, Louis, 155–56, 202
Brennan, William
    compelling state interest, 197–98
    contraceptives, 185–86
    extended family, 174
    "girlie" magazines, 161
Brewer, David, 116, 122–23
British law. See Anglo-American legal tradi-
    tion
Broomall, John, 50

Brown, Henry, 113, 122
"bundle of rights," 159 n. 13
burden, undue
    attack by Scalia, 205
    of consent and notification laws, 189–90,
        191–92, 199–200
    on fundamental rights, 197–98
    regulation of abortion, 194, 203
    and right to decide, 208–9
    vagueness of, 217
Burger, Warren, 161–62, 191 n. 37
Burger Court, 192, 216
businesses. See monopolies; price-fixing;
    public interest businesses; rate-fixing of
    railroads and utilities
Butler, Ben, 81, 84
Butler, Pierce
    Burns Baking Co. v. Bryan, 136
    Carolene Products Co., United States v.,
        133 n. 20
    Morehead v. New York, 142
    Nebbia v. New York, 139
    substantive due process, 130

Campbell, John, 100 n. 7
Carpenter, Matthew, 100 n. 7
Charles I, 13
Chase, Samuel, 21
child labor, 125, 161
child-support, 169 n. 58
childbearing, 5, 164–68
children and nuclear family, 158–64
choice, freedom of, 186–209
citizenship
    definition by Trumbull, 46
    fostering of good, 159
    rights of, 49, 72
civil liberty, 14 n. 54, 41, 43–44. See also
    liberty
Civil Rights Act of 1866, 43–54
    as antecedent to Fourteenth Amendment,
        34
    congressional authority and, 70
    economic liberty, 55, 99 n. 3, 211, 212
    Enforcement Act of 1871 and, 80, 82
    fundamental rights, 85
    political considerations, 33
    school attendance, 163
    significance of, 35

Civil Rights Act of 1875 (Public Accommodations Act), 75 n. 1, 76–77, 86–94
civil rights acts, 52, 212
  framing of Fourteenth Amendment, 58–59
  Fuller and White Courts, 127
  Justice Field opposition to, 99, 100, 104
  labor contracts as, 140–41, 142, 150
  marine insurance contracts, 117–18
  public purpose and, xix, 113, 114, 213
  racial discrimination in housing, 114–15
  Waite Court opposition, 126
Civil War
  debt, 37, 67 n. 51
  resolution of problems, 32
class legislation
  bakeries, 118–20
  Chinese laundry cases, 107
Coke, Edward, 10, 12–13
  interpretation of due process, 28
  procedural due process, 57, 58
  quoted by James Kent, 27
collective-bargaining. See also labor unions
  government intervention in, 143
  laissez-faire constitutionalism, 126
  Taft and Hughes Courts, 131, 140, 150
collective welfare, 31, 103, 212–13. See also public welfare
Colorado, Territory of, 60
Commentaries on American Law (Kent), 26–28, 46
Commentaries on the Constitution of the United States (Story), 28–29
commerce, interstate, 98, 145, 151
commerce-clause, 124–26, 133–34
commodities, 138
common callings, 105 n. 26, 157
common law
  antebellum cases, 26
  Civil Rights Act of 1866, 45
  distinction from natural-law, 34
  due process, 2–4, 9, 28
  Fifth Amendment, 41
  Fourteenth Amendment, 38, 94, 211
  freedom of trade, 105 n. 26
  influence on Republican philosophy, 33
  king of England, 11–12, 58
  personal rights, 155–56
  police-power jurisprudence, xx

Public Accommodations Act of 1875, 94
  Virginia Declaration, 15
common-law rights, 215
compelling-interest standard of judicial review, 189, 196, 197–98
  abandonment of, 202
  fundamental rights, 180
  Hughes Court, 152
  privacy rights, xviii
compensation for property, 19–20, 21
  emancipation of slaves, 67 n. 51, 68
Comstock, George F., 24–25
conditional rights, 59, 179, 213–14, 215
confiscation of property, 19–20
Congress. See also legislative power
  Bill of Rights, 17
  breach between Johnson and, 22, 33 n. 6, 43
  civil rights legislation, 39–40, 45, 47, 51
  Fourteenth Amendment, 37, 62, 63–67, 67–69, 70
  fundamental rights, 75–96
  Hughes Court, 130, 132
  limitations on power of, xiii–xiv
  parental rights, 164
  public welfare, xvi
  state deprivation, 55–56, 73
  Thirteenth Amendment, 41, 42
Conkling, Roscoe, 37 n. 25
conspiracy, 79, 80, 81–82, 85
Constitution, United States
  arbitrary governmental power, 52
  Civil Rights Act of 1866, 45, 47–51
  due process clauses, xiv
  Fourteenth Amendment, 65–66
  Freedman's Bureau bill, 39–40
  fundamental rights, xv
  individual rights, 6–7
  limitations, 101–2, 106–7, 111, 112, 126, 127
  Murray's Lessee v. Hoboken Land & Improvement Co., 22–23
  Preamble, 6–7, 28
  substantive restraints on Congress, 62
Constitutional Convention, 15–16
Continental Congress, 27
contraceptives
  Griswold v. Connecticut, 2, 48 n. 73, 155
  personal liberty and, 5, 158

Supreme Court decisions, 165, 181–86
unmarried persons and, 177, 216
contract, obligation of, 20–21
contracts. *See also* labor
Freedman's Bureau bill and Civil Rights
Act of 1866, 53
regulation by states, 31–32
right to make, 41, 43, 211
Cooley, Thomas McIntyre
conditional rights, 213
due process, 3, 4 n. 13
Fourteenth Amendment, 28–29, 211
as Jacksonian Democrat, 12–13 n. 45
public purpose and, xix
core values, xiv, 1–30. *See also* fundamental-rights; unenumerated rights
Corfield v. Coryell, 6 F.Cas. (No. 3230) 546
(C.C. E.D. Pa. 1823)
as precedent of Civil Rights Act of 1966,
47
privileges and immunities, 7, 72, 80–81
n. 15
Public Accommodations Act of 1875, 91,
92, 93
corporations. *See also* monopolies; public interest businesses
abuse by, 128
industrial capitalism, 97
property rights, 37
Cortner, Richard, 116
Corwin, Edward S., 13, 101 n. 12
cost-benefit terms and public goods, 207–8
cost of living, 141–52 n. 66
criminal process
Bill of Rights, 19
Civil Rights Act of 1866, 52
fairness in, 18
prisoners' right to marry, 171–72
sterilization of criminals, 165–66
Curtis, Benjamin, 22
Curtis, Michael Kent, 32–33 n. 5, 35
Cushman, Robert, 101–2 n. 12, 113 n. 61,
136 n. 31
customary law, 3, 15. *See also* common law

Darwinism, Social, 98, 120
Davis, Garrett, 82–83
Dawes, Henry, 81
Day, William
Buchanan v. Warley, 114–15

Coppage v. Kansas, 121 n. 96
Hammer v. Dagenhart, 124 n. 111, 125–
26
decide, right to, 186–209
Declaration of Independence
Civil Rights Act of 1866, 45, 49
Fourteenth Amendment, 72
Public Accommodations Act of 1875, 92
depression. *See* Great Depression
deprivations, state
arbitrary, 55–56, 212, 213
deprivation of property, 104, 108, 115
Enforcement Act of 1871, 78–79
Fourteenth Amendment, 63–68, 69, 72–
73
dignitary rights, xix, 207, 215
distress warrants, 22
divisible public goods, xix, 182, 192, 207,
215
Dixon, Robert G., 155 n. 5
Douglas, William O.
Griswold v. Connecticut, 48 n. 73
minimum wage, 142 n. 66
presumptive validity, 152
rejection of substantive due process, 148–
49
reproductive liberty and privacy, 2, 168
n. 53, 183, 184
school attendance, 162
sterilization of criminals, 165
Durant, T. J., 100 n. 7

Easterbrook, Frank H., 18–19 n. 74, 29
economic liberty, 211–14. *See also* property
rights
abdication by Hughes Court, 130
as civil liberty, 41
Freedman's Bureau bill, 39 n. 32
legislative power, 133–35
substantive due process, xvi, 123–28
Supreme Court, 97–128
economic and social policies
Franklin Roosevelt, 151, 152
legislative power, xviii, 1, 4, 136 n. 31
liberty of contract and, xiv
Stone, Vinson and Warren Courts, 146,
147
Edmunds, George, 81–82, 84, 85
education, parents' direction of, 159–64
Edward III (1327–77), 11, 13

Eleventh Amendment, 95
Ely, James W., Jr.
    Great Depression, 151 n. 111
    justification of regulations, 113–14 n. 65
    laissez-faire principles, 117
    limitation of police powers, 111 n. 60
    property rights, 134 n. 24, 212
    public interest, 138 n. 46
Ely, John Hart, 153 n. 114
emergencies
    price-fixing, 139–40
    Taft and Hughes Courts, 151
    wartime restrictions, 131, 132
eminent domain power
    accommodation of growth and change,
        xviii
    conditional rights, 7
    limitations of, 95
    Waite Court, 104, 111–12
employment. See labor; wage-and-hours reg-
    ulation
Enforcement Act of 1870, 75 n. 1
Enforcement Act of 1871 (Ku Klux Klan
    Act), 75 n. 1, 77, 78–86
Engleman, Michael R., 177 n. 100
English language in schools, 159, 159 n. 18
English law. See Anglo-American legal tra-
    dition; Magna Carta (1215); Parlia-
    ment
equal access, 44, 87, 88, 91
equal protection
    Civil Rights Act of 1866, 46, 55, 56
    due process clause and, 38
    Fourteenth Amendment, 64–65, 68, 77,
        88
    Freedman's Bureau bill, 35
    marriage rights, 169–71
    privileges and immunities clause, 66
    sterilization of criminals, 165–66
Equal Under Law (Ten Broek), 36 n. 21
equality
    and Declaration of Independence, 42
    Public Accommodations Act of 1875, 86,
        93
    racial, 70, 86, 169

Fair Labor Standards Act of 1938, 145
fairness in judicial proceedings, 26, 31, 211
    Fourteenth Amendment, 52
    Magna Carta and, 11, 12

natural and common law traditions, 9
    reproductive liberty and privacy, 183
family
    personal liberty, 216
    privacy, 157–59
    relationships, 173–80
    right to establish, 164–65
Farnsworth, John, 71
federal government. See national govern-
    ment
federalism, 32, 63, 66, 69, 83
fetal viability
    physician's rights, 193–95
    rights of the fetus, xix, 205–6, 208
    state regulation of abortion, 202–3
Field, Stephen J.
    economic liberty and property rights, 98–
        105, 110–12, 213
    Fourteenth Amendment, 3, 91–92 n. 57,
        211
    fundamental rights, xiii
    individual rights, 95
    as Jacksonian Democrat, 12–13 n. 45
    laissez-faire constitutionalism, 212
    liberty of contract, xviii, 120 n. 90
    marriage as basic civil right, 168–73
    public purpose, xix
    substantive due process, 2, 126
Fifth Amendment
    Bill of Rights, 16–17
    case law, 21, 22, 23, 26
    Civil Rights Act of 1866, 49
    Fourteenth Amendment, 66
    Freedman's Bureau bill, 41
    fundamental rights, xiii, 4, 5–6, 37, 211
    Joseph Story, 28
    personal liberty, 154–55, 158
    substantive and procedural limits, 19
Filled Milk Act, 134
fire insurance, 115–16 n. 72, 138 n. 46
First Amendment, 158, 161–62
Flack, Horace E., 33 n. 6
Fourteenth Amendment
    Casey and limitation of state power, 201
    Civil Rights Act of 1866, 52
    contraceptives, 184
    core values, 6–7
    due process, 28–29, 126
    extended family, 173
    framing of, xvii, 29–30, 32, 55–74

fundamental rights, xiii, 4, 5–6, 211–12
interracial marriage, 169
liberty and pursuit of happiness, 117–18
marriage rights, 170
personal liberty, 154–55, 158, 182–83
state's power, 3
teachers' right to bear children, 166–67
Fourth Amendment, 19, 158
franchises. *See* monopolies; public interest
businesses
Frankfurter, Felix, 148 n. 95
fraud protection, 108, 117–18, 131
Freedman's Bureau Extension bill (1866),
38–43
as antecedent to Fourteenth Amendment,
34
contracts and, 53
political considerations, 33
significance of, 35
substantive due process, xvii
freedmen, 32, 76
"freedom of contract," 151
Frelinghuysen, Frederick T., 92
Fuller Court (1888–1910)
conditional rights, 214
economic liberty, 112–13, 116–17
laissez-faire constitutionalism, 98
public purpose, 127
fundamental-rights. *See also* core values; unenumerated rights
common law, 3
development of philosophy, xiii
early case law, 16
family privacy, 156, 157 n. 11
Fourteenth Amendment, xv
McReynolds' broad concept of, 215
noneconomic liberties, 5–6
not as absolute, 179–80
reproductive liberty, 183
substantive due process, 126

general welfare. *See* public purpose; public
welfare
"girlie" magazines, 161
Goldberg, Arthur, 2, 184
Graham, Howard Jay
due process, 36, 73
limitation on policymaking, 56, 57
substantive due process, 37, 101–2
n. 12

Great Depression, 129, 132, 151 n. 111,
214
Griswold v. Connecticut, 381 U.S. 479
(1965), 184–86
marriage, 168 n. 53
personal liberty, 152–53, 205
substantive due process and, 155
unenumerated rights, 48 n. 73

Hamilton, Alexander, 18, 36 n. 18
Hardwick, Michael, 176–77
Harlan, John M.
economic liberty, 111, 112
laissez-faire constitutionalism, 212
liberty in the marketplace, 125 n. 119
limitations on legislative power, 104
principles of judicial inquiry, 107–8
public health, 156 n. 8
rate-making authority, 116
union membership, 124
Harlan, John Marshall (II)
constitutionally permissible objectives,
150 n. 106
contraceptives, 184
Fourteenth Amendment, xiv, xv, 48 n. 73
fundamental rights, xiii
judicial *versus* legislative power, 178–79
ordered liberty, 2, 48 n. 73
public purpose, xvi
reproductive liberty and privacy, 182–84
resurrection of substantive due process,
154–55
health. *See* maternal health; public health
Henry, Patrick, 14 n. 52, 17 n. 64
Henry III, 13
hierarchy of rights, 207
Higby, William, 66
higher-law philosophy
Civil Rights Act of 1866, 45, 53
Fourteenth Amendment, 211
Public Accommodations Act of 1875, 92
Hoar, George, 81
Hoke v. Henderson (North Carolina), 27–28
Holmes, Oliver Wendell, 4, 120, 159 n. 18
homosexuality, 176–77, 216
hours of employment. *See* wage-and-hours
regulation
housing, 114–15, 173–75
Hovenkamp, Herbert
Civil Rights Act of 1866, 55

economic liberty, 76 n. 3, 99 n. 3
Fourteenth Amendment and substantive
    due process, 60 n. 24
monopolies, 101 n. 11
railroads and public utilities, 115 n. 71
Howard, Jacob, 45–46, 63 n. 34, 71–72
Howe, Lowell J., 20 n. 80
Howe, Timothy, 92
Hughes, Charles Evans, 121 n. 96, 123
Hughes Court (1930–41), 150–53
    business and public interest, 131, 138
    definition of public welfare, xviii, 128
    economic due process cases, 136
    Great Depression, 214
    New Deal and, 132
    opposition to labor policies, 140–44
Hutchinson, Thomas, 14 n. 52
Huyett, Daniel, 198–99

immunities. See also privileges and immu-
    nities clause
    freedman's rights and, 43
inalienable rights
    as absolute rights, 26
    Civil Rights Act of 1866, 46, 47, 50
    Fourteenth Amendment, 73, 82
"incidents of freedom," 45
individual autonomy, 157–59, 181–209
individual rights. See also privacy rights
    contraception, 182–86
    core values, 6–9
    individualism in conflict with regulation,
        32
    as natural and civil liberties, 14 n. 54
    police powers, 59
    in Reconstruction Era, 95
    substantive due process, 73
indivisible dignitary rights, xix, 182, 207,
    215
informed-consent, 188, 190–92
"inherent duty," 36 n. 21. See also recipro-
    cal rights and duties
inherent rights
    as absolute rights, 26
    as conditional rights, 59
    Fourteenth Amendment, 71, 73
    as justification for Civil Rights Act of
        1866, 45
    Institutes of the Laws of England (Coke),
        12

interracial marriage, 169
Interstate Commerce Commission Act
    (1887), 98
interstate-commerce power, 98, 145, 151

Jackson, Robert H., 151, 165–66
Jacksonian democracy
    belief in economic opportunity, 111
    Justice Field, 13 n. 45, 99
    influence on Republican philosophy, 33
    state neutrality, 213
Jaffa, Harry, 23 n. 99
James, Joseph, 68
James I, 12–13 n. 45
Jehovah's Witnesses, 160 n. 23
Jim Crow laws, 90 n. 50
Johnson, Andrew
    breach with Congress, 22, 33 n. 6, 43
    Civil Rights Act veto, 46, 54
    Freedman's Bureau Bill, 38 n. 31, 42–43
    Freedman's Bureau bill veto, 34
Joint Committee on Reconstruction, 53, 62,
    63–67
Judiciary Act of 1875, 44
jury trial
    English law, 11
    James Kent and, 27
    Public Accommodations Act of 1875, 87
    Virginia Declaration of Rights, 15

Kales, Albert M., 127 n. 122
Kauper, Paul, 159 n. 13
Kennedy, Anthony, xix, 178, 200, 202
Kens, Paul
    liberty of contract, 7–8 n. 24, 25–26 n.
        110
    property rights, 110 n. 53
    regulation of markets, 138 n. 45
    Slaughterhouse Cases, 101
Kent, James, 26–28
    influence on Civil Rights Act of 1866,
        46, 47
    influence on Public Accommodations Act
        of 1875, 93
    property rights, 24 n. 102
    substantive due process, 10, 60
Kerr, Michael C., 40
king of England, 9 n. 33, 10, 11–12, 58
Koppelman, Andrew, 187 n. 16
Ku Klux Klan, 83

Ku Klux Klan Act (Enforcement Act of
1871), 75 n. 1, 77, 78–86

labor
child, 125, 161
contracts, xviii, 98, 141–42, 143, 147–
48
disputes, 124–25
productivity, 142–43 n. 69
right to contract, 43, 46, 51, 102, 112,
121–22
labor unions. See also collective-bargaining
membership, 121–22
Taft and Hughes Courts, 140, 214
war against, 128
laissez-faire constitutionalism
collision with welfare state, 121–22, 150
Fuller Court, 98
Gilded Age and lack of unanimity, 117
in Progressive Era, 126
protection against class legislation, 212
Justice Sutherland, 143–45
"law-of-the-land"
Bill of Rights and, 17
Edward Coke and, 12, 22
Hamilton interpretation, 18
James Kent interpretation, 27–28
procedural due process, 28, 57–58, 59
Virginia, 15, 18
William Blackstone and, 14
lawful calling, 102, 103, 112
Lawrence, William, 49, 93 n. 62
legislative fact-finding, 141–42, 143, 150,
151
legislative power. See also state's power
balancing of public and private interests,
168–69, 178, 179
Justice Black, 1, 149–50
case law, 20–30
common law, 3
contraceptives, 184
due process and limitations, 16, 211
versus judicial power, 5
limitations on, 4, 10, 16, 19, 31, 59–60
New York bill of rights, 18
property rights, 22–23
Public Accommodations Act of 1875, 92
public welfare, 8
substantive due process, 123–28, 205
Supreme Court, 217

Taft and Hughes Courts, 151
Letter on Toleration (Locke), 9
liberty
Civil Rights Act of 1866, 47, 52
as core value, xiv, 1–30, 212
as fundamental right, xv
Planned Parenthood of Southeastern Pennsylvania v. Casey, 201
procedural due process, xiii
Public Accommodations Act of 1875, 91
n. 56
Reconstruction Era, 76, 77
liberty of contract, 117–23
contraception and abortion decisions, xv
demise of, 133
economic liberty, xiv, 212–13
Fuller and White Courts, 112–13
as fundamental right, xviii
interference with, 141–42 n. 66
limitations of, 25–26 n. 110
as qualified right, 143, 214
reproductive liberty, 181
Taft and Hughes Courts, 140–41, 150
Vinson Court, 148
West Coast Hotel Co. v. Parrish, 143–45
life
as core value, xiv, 1–30, 212
as fundamental right, xv, 64
and procedural due process, xiii
Public Accommodations Act of 1875, 91
n. 56
liquor sales, 24–25, 104, 107–8
Lochner v. New York, 198 U.S. 45 (1905),
118–21
noneconomic personal liberties, xviii, 2
regulation and objectives, 214
rejection of substantive due process, 1 n.
2
Locke, John
Letter on Toleration, 9
protection of property, 99 n. 3, 103 n. 18
Second Treatise on Civil Government, 8–9
locomotion, freedom of. See movement,
freedom of
Lowe, David, 81, 84
loyalty of citizens, 50, 53. See also reciprocal rights and duties

Macedo, Stephen, 152 n. 114
Madison, James, 18–19

Magna Carta (1215)
  evolution of due process, 10–14
  "law-of-the-land," 28
  positive law, 27
  substantive due process, 57–58, 59
Maltz, Earl M., 32 n. 5, 39 n. 32
Mansfield State University Rural Services
    Institute, 182 n. 2, 200 n. 65, 209 n.
    98
markets
  lack of interference in, 151, 214
  liberty in the marketplace, 125 n. 119
  order to the marketplace, 132
  regulation of, 31–32, 138
marriage
  changing definition of, 173
  right of, 5, 164–65, 168–73
  as unenumerated right, 158, 216
Marshall, John, 63, 69
Marshall, Thurgood, 169–70
Massachusetts Constitution of 1780, 15
maternal health
  abortion regulation, 187, 192, 193, 201,
    203
  parental consent to abortion, 189–90
maternity leave regulations, 166–67
Matthews, Stanley, 106–7
McCorvey, Norma, 187, 188
McDougall, James, 42
McHenry, Henry, 89
McKechnie, William S., 13
McKenna, Joseph, 114, 115–16 n. 72
McReynolds, James Clark
  education decisions of parents, 159–60
  emergencies and governmental power,
    139–40
  government interference, 140 n. 56
  noneconomic liberties, 156–57
  nuclear family role, 159
  personal liberty, xv, 4, 157 n. 11, 164
  substantive due process, 130, 215
medicine
  personal liberty and medical treatment,
    158
  public interests in regulating abortion,
    187
  regulation of medical practice, 193–96
Meyer v. Nebraska, 262 U.S. 390 (1923)
  law and purpose, 160
  noneconomic liberties, 156–57

nuclear family, 159, 160
unenumerated rights, xv, 4
military power
  Enforcement Act of 1871, 79
  and English law, 13
  Freedman's Bureau Bill, 42
Mill, John Stuart, 179 n. 107
Miller, Charles, 19
Miller, Samuel F.
  Filled Milk Act, 134 n. 21
  legislative fact-finding, 120 n. 90
  monopolies, 105
  Slaughterhouse Cases, 7 n. 23, 90 n. 51,
    91, 93, 95, 100–101
  vested property rights, 104
Mills, Roger, 93
minimum-rationality standard of judicial re-
    view
  abortion, 199
  Hughes Court, 144, 152
  privacy interests, 164
  Rehnquist Court, 150
  Stone, Vinson and Warren courts, 146
  Stone Court, 134 n. 25
  teacher's right to bear children, 167
minimum-wage laws. See also wage-and-
    hours regulation
  as interference with liberty of contract, 214
  Washington State, 143
  for women, 131–32 n. 9, 141–42 n. 66
minors and abortion, 161 n. 25
  parental consent, 188–92
Missouri Compromise, 23
Missouri's Service Letter Law, 141
monopolies. See also price-fixing; public in-
    terest businesses; rate-fixing of railroads
    and utilities
  abuse of economic liberty, 128, 213
  equal rights, 58
  Justice Field's opposition to, 99
  regulation of, 214
  Slaughterhouse Cases, 91–92 n. 57, 100–
    104
  Whig party opposition, 12–13 n. 45
Monroe, James, 81, 84
morals
  interstate commerce, 145
  legislative power, xiv
  police power, 104, 105
  regulations, 122, 127, 213

Morton, Oliver, 67
movement, freedom of
  Civil Rights Act of 1866, 46
  Congressional protection of, 76
  privileges and immunities clause, 91
  Public Accommodations Act of 1875, 87
  Thirteenth Amendment, 41

national government
  authority and Freedman's Bureau bill,
    39–40
  Bill of Rights, 17
  Civil Rights Act of 1866, 48, 49, 50
  civil rights protection, 33
  conditional rights, 7
  judicial and executive power expansion,
    76–77
  welfare state, 129–31
National Industrial Recovery Act of 1933,
  xviii
natural-law philosophy
  Butchers' Union Co. v. Crescent City Co.,
    105 n. 26
  Civil Rights Act of 1866, 45, 46, 47, 49,
    52
  common law, 26, 34
  core rights, 27
  Dred Scott v. Sanford, 23 n. 99
  due process, xv, xvii, 29
  Edgar Cohen and tradition of, 41
  Fourteenth Amendment and, 38, 73, 211
  government limitations, 9
  influence on Republican philosophy, 33
  Lochner v. New York, 2
  Public Accommodations Act of 1875, 94
  Second Treatise on Civil Government
    (Locke), 8–9
  unenumerated rights and, 3
natural-right philosophy
  Civil Rights Act of 1866, 47, 48, 52
  Corfield v. Coryell, 7 n. 22
  Van Horn's Lessee v. Dorrance, 20–21
  Wynehamer v. New York, 25
Nedelsky, Jennifer, 144 n. 76
Nelson, William
  fundamental rights, 33, 38, 53
  substantive due process, 62 n. 32
New Deal, 13 n. 48, 130–33
New Hampshire Bill of Rights (1784), 15,
  59

New Jersey Constitution (1844), 60
New York Declaration of Rights, 27
Ninth Amendment, 2, 184
Northwest Ordinance (1787), 15–16
Norwood, Thomas, 92

objectives, state. See public purpose
obligation, political. See political obligation;
  reciprocal rights and duties
obligation of contract, 20–21
O'Brien, David, 133 n. 18
obscenity, 161
O'Connor, Sandra Day
  abortion, 179–80, 195; and critical-care
    hospitals, 196; informed consent, 191
    n. 37; parental consent, 189–90; regu-
    lation, 197–98; waiting period, 191–92
  guarantee against government intrusion,
    xix
  Planned Parenthood of Southeastern Pennsyl-
    vania v. Casey, 178, 200–203
  prisoners' right to marry, 171–72
ordered liberty, 48 n. 73, 134
Otis, James, 14

Paludan, Phillip S., 77 n. 4
parental consent, 189
  H.L. v. Matheson, 190 n. 31
  Hodgson v. Minnesota, 190 n. 32
  Ohio v. Akron Center for Reproductive
    Health, 190 n. 32
  Roe v. Wade, 188
Parliament, 10 n. 14, 12–14, 27, 58
Paterson, William, 19–20
Peckham, Rufus
  laissez-faire constitutionalism, 212
  liberty of contract, 117–18, 214
  public interest, 113–14 n. 65
Pennsylvania Abortion Control Act, 182 n.
  2, 194, 198–99
Perry, Michael, 6 n. 19, 127 n. 122
personal liberty. See also privacy rights
  as civil right, 70
  due process, xv
  privacy, 158, 164
  rejection of freedom of contract, 40
  reproductive liberty, 183
personal security, 34, 45, 212
  Andrew Johnson, 43
  burdensome state action, 56

as civil right, 70
Civil Rights Act of 1886, 46, 47, 49, 52, 53, 55
Freedman's Bureau bill, 39, 53
physical security as core value, 6
Reconstruction Era, 76, 77
Petition of Right (1628), 10, 13, 14
Petree, Charles, 216
physical security. *See* personal security
physicians, 184, 193–96
Pitney, Mahlon, 141
police power
  accommodation of growth and change, xviii
  Butchers' Union Co. v. Crescent City Co., 105
  Chicago, Burlington and Quincy R.R. Co. v. McGuire, 123
  class legislation, 99
  common law rights, 156
  conditional rights, 7
  Coppage v. Kansas, 121–22
  Fourteenth Amendment, xv, 211
  Freedman's Bureau bill, 39
  Fuller and White Courts, 112, 113
  Fuller Court, 127
  Hammer v. Dagenhart, 125
  Holden v. Hardy, 122
  judicial authority, 25 n. 108
  limitations of, 95, 96
  Lincoln Federal Labor Union v. Northwestern Iron & Metal Co., 147–48
  Miller v. Schoene, 137
  Morehead v. New York, 143
  O'Gorman & Young v. Hartford Ins. Co., 138 n. 46
  Planned Parenthood of Southeastern Pennsylvania v. Casey, 207, 208–9
  regulation of contracts, 31–32
  reproductive liberty, 183
  Slaughterhouse Cases, 100
  Waite Court,. 104, 111
police-power jurisprudence, 192
  as alternative to balancing approach, 217–18
  common law tradition, xx
  legislative record and regulation, 158–59
  nineteenth-century legislative authority, 213
  protection of unenumerated rights, 192

regulation of marriage, 168
  substantive due process, 2–4
policymaking authority of the states
  family privacy, 178–80
  Hughes Court, 151–52
  Supreme Court interference, xvi, xx
political obligation, 7, 71, 72, 73. *See also* reciprocal rights and duties
political rights
  distinguished from civil rights, 35 n. 14
  Fourteenth Amendment, 64
  national government authority, 41–42
  Thirteenth Amendment, 40
Pomeroy, John Norton, 211
Populist Era, 115, 123
positive law, 14 n. 54
  Civil Rights Act of 1866 and, 49
  Fourteenth Amendment, 211
  traced from Magna Carta, 27
Posner, Richard A., 120 n. 91
potential life, 187, 189–90, 194, 201
Powell, Lewis
  abortion and minors, 161 n. 25
  abortion cost and risk, 191–92
  abortion in hospitals, 196, 196 n. 53
  extended family, 173–75
  judicial *versus* legislative power, 178–79
  teachers' right to bear children, 167 n. 51
Preamble, U.S. Constitution, 6–7, 28
preferred rights, 134–35, 153, 157
pregnancy termination. *See* abortion
price-fixing, 131, 138–40, 151. *See also* rate-fixing of railroads and utilities
prisoners
  right to marry, 171–72
  sterilization of criminals, 165–66
privacy rights
  abortion, 6, 186 n. 15
  compared with property rights, xviii, 181–82
  contraceptives, 184–85
  expanded concept of due process, xviii–xix, 4, 215–17
  marriage and family, 154–80
  reproductive liberty, 182–84
private and public interests. *See* public and private interests, balancing of
privileges and immunities clause
  Article Four, 6–7, 66

civil rights, 212
Civil Rights Act of 1866, 50, 51
due process clause, 38
Enforcement Act of 1871, 80 n. 15, 81
equal protection, 65
Freedman's Bureau bill, 35
fundamental rights, xvii
natural persons, 37
Public Accommodations Act, 88, 90, 91, 92
as self-enforcing provision, 56
state deprivation, 72
Privy Council, 13
procedural due process, 57–63
Bill of Rights, 17–19
Civil Rights Act of 1866, 46
Fourteenth Amendment, 36
government limitations, 13, 15, 201
James Kent, 27
John Sherman, 42
Joseph Story, 28
judicial fairness, xiii, 11, 12
law-of-the-land, 14
procreation, 5, 164–68
Progressive Era, 115, 123
prohibition, 24–25, 104, 107–8
property rights. See also economic liberty
abdication by Hughes Court, 130
Civil Rights Act of 1866, 44, 46, 47, 49, 50, 52, 55
class legislation, 115, 127
as conditional rights, 213, 214
constitutional protection of, xiii
core values, 1–30, 212
Justice Field and, 110–12
Fourteenth Amendment, 56, 74
Freedman's Bureau bill, 53
as fundamental rights, xv
legislative authority, 60
Powell v. Pennsylvania, 108
privacy rights, xviii, 181–82
real property, 70, 137
Reconstruction Era, 76, 77
social and economic policies, 151
substantive due process, 113–15
Taft and Hughes Courts, 150
Taft Court, 137
Wynehamer v. New York, 32 n. 4
Public Accommodations Act of 1875 (Civil

Rights Act of 1875), 75 n. 1, 76–77, 86–94, 91 n. 56
failure of Supreme Court, 172–73
Justice Field, 213
flawed methodology, xix, 182, 215
judicial versus legislative task, 178, 179, 197–98
as legislative function, xvi, 168–69, 184, 186
police-power jurisprudence, 217–18
reproductive liberty, 192, 206, 208
public goods, 207–8, 215, 217
public health. See also maternal health
Bartmeyer v. Iowa, 104
Chicago, Burlington, and Quincy R.R. Co. v. McGuire, 123
Darby, United States v., 145
Gilded Age, 213
Jacobson v. Massachusetts, 156 n. 8
legislative power, xiv
Lochner v. New York, 118–21
Radice v. New York, 141
Slaughterhouse Cases, 101
public interest businesses, 109–12, 115–17, 138, 151. See also monopolies; price-fixing; rate-fixing of railroads and utilities
public purpose, 218. See also public welfare
due process, xvii
education and parents' rights, 160
Fourteenth Amendment, xv
marriage regulations, 168
monopolies, 102–8
police power, 158–59
policy, xvi
privacy, 156, 157
regulations, xix, xx, 113, 213–14
reproductive liberty, 183
state's objectives, 167, 170
substantive due process, 139
Supreme Court support of, 151
Taft Court, 137
public safety
legislative power, xiv
protection during Gilded Age, 213
Slaughterhouse Cases, 101
state's power, 40
public utilities. See rate-fixing of railroads and utilities

public welfare. *See also* public purpose
  core values, 6–9
  Justice Field, 126
  Gilded Age, 213
  inherent rights, 59
  judiciary, 29
  legislative power, 5
  Preamble of the Constitution, 7
  private rights, 4
  property rights, 24–25, 158, 164, 214
  regulations, 122, 127
  state's authority, xvii, xviii
  Supreme Court and definition of, 136
  voting during the workday, 148

qualified rights, 143

racial discrimination
  class and race distinctions, 106–7
  Fourteenth Amendment, 67
  sale of houses, 114–15
  segregated private schools, 163
racial equality
  Fourteenth Amendment, 70
  interracial marriage, 169
  Public Accommodations Act, 86
Radical Republicans
  Enforcement Act of 1871, 82, 83
  Reconstruction policy, 33
  substantive due process, xvii
rate-fixing of railroads and utilities, 104,
    106, 109, 112. *See also* price-fixing
  Federal Power Commission authority,
    146–47
  judicial review of, 115–17
rational-relation standard of judicial review,
    167
Raymond, Henry, 70
reciprocal rights and duties, 46, 48, 50, 53,
    71
Reconstruction
  breach between Congress and President,
    22, 33, 43
  Fourteenth Amendment, xvii
  fundamental rights, 75–96
  James Wilson and support for, 48
  resolution of problems, 32
Rehnquist, William, 167 n. 51, 174, 204
Rehnquist Court, 150, 177

Reich, Charles, 129–30 n. 2
Reid, John Phillip, 3
religious liberty, 162
remedial legislation, 68, 94
Removal Act, 75–76, 95
reproductive liberty, 181–209
Republicans. *See also* Radical Republicans
  centrist-conservative, 72
  congressional authority, 76–77, 92–94
Revels, Hiram, 87
Richards, David A. J., 178 n. 101
Riggs, Robert, 13, 19–20
Riker, William, 135
Roberts, Owen
  Nebbia v. New York, 138–39
  New Deal support, 132–32
  substantive due process, 130
  West Coast Hotel Co. v. Parrish, 143
Roe v. Wade, 410 U.S. 113 (1973), 197–98
  commitment to substantive due process,
    152–53 n. 114, 202–5
  conditional rights and, 179
  personal privacy and, 6
  right to decide, 186–88
  state regulations and, xv
Rogers, Andrew J., 49 n. 76, 60–61, 70 n.
    67
Roosevelt, Franklin D., 151, 160–61, 214
Ruffin, Thomas, 27–28
Rutledge, Wiley, 160–61

safety. *See* public safety
Scalia, Antonin, 204–5
school attendance, 160–64
schools, equal access to, 87
Schwartz, Bernard, 14 n. 52
searches and seizures, 19–20
Second Treatise on Civil Government (Locke),
    8–9
security. *See* personal security
segregation of schools, 163
sexual intimacy
  and consenting adults, 178 n. 102
  contradictory Supreme Court decisions,
    216
  personal rights and, 5, 158, 165, 177
sexually-transmitted diseases, 185–86
Shapo, Marshall S., 78 n. 8
Sheldon, Lionel, 83–84

Shellabarger, Samuel, 80–81
Sherman, John, 42
Sherman Antitrust Act (1890), 98
slaves and slavery
    attempts to reenslave freedman, 76
    Civil Rights Act of 1866, 55
    compensation for slaves, 67 n. 51, 68
    interference with equal rights, 58
    slaves as property, 23
    Thirteenth Amendment as end of, 39
Smith, Adam, 102
social-contract philosophy, xv, xvii, 211
    Civil Rights Act of 1866, 49
    development of due process, 29
    Fourteenth Amendment, 73
    influence on Republican philosophy,
        33
    obligation of contract, 20–21
    property rights, 25
    Second Treatise on Civil Government
        (Locke), 8–9
    unenumerated rights, 3
Social Darwinism, 98, 120
social equality. *See* equality
social policies. *See* economic and social poli-
    cies
social rights, 35 n. 14
sodomy, 176 n. 96
Souter, David, xix, 178, 200, 202
spousal notification
    Planned Parenthood of Missouri v. Danforth,
        189
    Planned Parenthood of Southeastern Pennsyl-
        vania v. Casey, 198 n. 60, 199–200,
        203
    Roe v. Wade, 188
Stamp Act (1765), 14
standard of judicial review, xx, 215, 217.
    See also compelling-interest standard of
    judicial review; minimum-rationality
    standard of judicial review; public and
    private interests, balancing of; strict-
    scrutiny standard of judicial review
    and burden of state regulation, 170, 171–
        72
    double standard of, 173, 186
    protection of preferred rights, 153
Stapleton, Walter, 196 n. 55, 199–200,
    208–9

state's power. *See also* eminent domain
        power; legislative power; police power;
        tax powers
    abortion, 187, 192, 204, 207
    Bill of Rights, 17–19
    case law, 20–28
    Civil Rights Act of 1866, 47, 48
    compelling interest, 179–80
    contract regulation, 31–32
    criminalization of sodomy, 176 n. 96
    due process and limitation of, 4 n. 13
    family privacy, 178–80
    Fourteenth Amendment, 3, 59, 66–67,
        211
    Freedman's Bureau bill, 39–40
    Hughes Court and abdication to, 130, 132
    intrusion upon, xvi
    judicial power over, 34
    marriage rights and regulation, 168, 170
    military protection, 43
    personal liberty, 5, 6
    police power, 59, 156, 192, 211
    property rights, 21, 112–13
    protection of rights, xvii, 7, 8, 51, 59
    public purpose, 213–14
    reproductive liberty and privacy, 183
    substantive due process, 205, 206
    statutory law, 22–23, 58, 94
    sterilization of criminals, 165–66
Stevens, Thaddeus
    framing the Fourteenth Amendment, 67–
        68, 69–70
    life, liberty and property rights, 35 n. 17
    marriage rights, 170
Stevens-Owens plan, 67–69
Stewart, Potter
    contraceptives, 2
    definition of family, 174
    marriage rights, 170–71
    parental consent to abortion, 189
    school attendance, 162–63
    substantive due process, 217
    teachers' right to bear children, 166–67
Stone, Harlan F.
    abandonment of economic liberty, 133–
        35
    as chief justice, 145–46
    police power, 137, 143
    privacy rights, 215

protection of government policies, 152, 153
regulation and public policy, 143, 145
sterilization of criminals, 165–66
Stone Court (1941–1969), 130, 146–47
Story, Joseph, 10
  Commentaries on the Constitution of the United States, 28–29
  influence on Public Accommodations Act of 1875, 88, 93
  procedural due process, 57, 58, 59
  substantive due process, 60
strict-scrutiny standard of judicial review
  abortion regulations, 197
  contraception, 184
  fundamental rights, 180
  Hughes Court, 152
  privacy rights, xviii, 215
Strong, Frank R., 152 n. 112
Strong, William, 111, 112
substantial-relation standard of judicial review, 152
substantive due process, xiv, 57–63, 109–12
  Bill of Rights, 17–19
  Civil Rights Act of 1866, 44, 51
  demise of, 1, 129–53
  economic liberty, 123–28
  Enforcement Act of 1871, 81
  Fifth Amendment, 19
  Fifth and Fourteenth Amendments, 9 n. 33
  Fourteenth Amendment, 35, 36, 73
  government limitations, 201
  John Sherman, 42
  modern view of, 29
  privacy rights, 4, 5
  rise and evolution of, xvi–xvii, 10, 98, 100–108
  royal power, 11, 13
  unenumerated rights, 205
  William Blackstone, 14
sue, right to, 41 n. 40, 42
suffrage, 41–42, 50 n. 82
Sutherland, George
  congressional fact-finding, 141
  emergency powers, 139
  liberty of contract, 141–42 n. 66, 144–45
  police powers, 137

regulation of theaters, 138
substantive due process, 130
Swayne, Noah, 104, 111, 112

Taft, William Howard, 127–28, 140, 141–42 n. 66, 150
Taft Court (1921–30), 150–53
  economic liberty and property rights, 214
  opposition to labor policies, 140–41, 150
  restraint on legislative policymaking, 130
Taney, Roger B., 23
tax powers
  accommodation of growth and change, xviii
  class legislation, 99
  head taxes, 19
  Territory of Colorado, 60
  Waite Court, 104, 111, 112
  Justice Washington on, 7
teachers' right to bear children, 166–67
Tenth Amendment
  Civil Rights Act of 1866 as breach of, 49, 51
  Fourteenth Amendment and, 66
  state's powers, xvii, 39, 95
Thayer, M. Russell, 49
Thirteenth Amendment
  Civil Rights Act of 1866, 45, 47, 49
  Congressional power, 39, 41, 42
  Michael Kerr interpretation of, 40
  right to contract labor, 51
Thurman, Allen, 89–90
trade, freedom of, 105–6, 108
trade unions. *See* labor unions
transportation access, 76, 87, 88
travel, right to, 7, 47, 51, 91–92
trespass, law of, 88 n. 44
trial by jury. *See* jury trial
trimesters and abortion, xviii–xix
  Roe v. Wade, 187, 189, 202
  Rosen v. Louisiana State Board of Medical Examiners, 193 n. 40
Trumbull, Lyman, 46, 82

undeniable rights, 27 n. 113
unenumerated rights, 4. *See also* core values; fundamental-rights
  burden, 180, 197
  Chinese laundry cases, 106–7

constitutional protection of, xiii
contraceptives, 2, 184–86
family privacy, 164, 178–80, 216
Justice Field on, 101–2
Fifth and Fourteenth Amendments, 211–12
focus from economic rights to, 130–31, 153
liberty of contract as, 118, 123
natural-law and social-contract basis of, 3
reproductive liberty, 181
sterilization of criminals, 165–66
Union party, 33
unions. See labor unions
unmarried persons, 173, 176, 177, 185
utilitarian theory of rights, 207, 215

Van Devanter, Willis, 130, 133, 139
variable standard of review. See standard of judicial review
vested property rights. See property rights
Vinson Court, 146, 147, 148
violence against southern blacks and loyalist whites, 77, 79, 80, 82
Virginia Declaration of Rights (1776), 15, 59
Virginia Ratifying Convention, 18
vote, right to, 41–42, 50 n. 82

wage-and-hours regulation. See also minimum-wage laws
as exercise of police power, 123
hours of employment, 122–23, 140, 141, 145
Taft and Hughes Courts opposition to, 131, 140, 142, 150
wage regulation, 143–45
Waite, Morrison, 109–11
Waite Court (1874–88), 98, 104, 111
waiting period and abortion, 191–92
war power, 40, 131, 132, 214
Warren, Earl, 169
Warren, Samuel, 155–56
Warren Court
demise of substantive due process, 146, 147

economic liberty and unenumerated rights, 130
reproductive liberty, 216
Washington, Bushrod
influence on Public Accommodations Act of 1875, 93
influence on Slaughterhouse Cases, 102
life, liberty and property, 72, 85
public purpose, 7–8
welfare, public. See public purpose; public welfare
welfare state
conflict with laissez-faire constitutionalism, 121, 214
emergence of, 130–35
as temporary response to the depression, 129
Wharton, Francis, 211
Whig party, 12–13 n. 45
White, Byron
abortion, 195
contraceptives, 2, 184
definition of family, 174–75
homosexual couples, 176–77
informed consent, 191 n. 37
school attendance, 162
substantive due process, 154–55
White, Edward Douglas. See White Court (1910–21)
White Court (1910–21), 127, 214
Whitehall, Robert, 17
Wilson, James F., 47–49, 50
women, employment of, 122–23, 141–45
women, health of. See maternal health
Woods, William, 105
worker compensation, 141
world war, 130, 131
Writs of Assistance, 14

yellow-dog contracts, 121–22

zoning, 114, 137

About the Author

Edward Keynes is Professor of Political Science at The Pennsylvania State University. His previous publications include *Undeclared War: Twilight Zone of Constitutional Power* (Penn State University Press, 1982; reissued in paperback, with a new preface, 1991) and with Randall K. Miller, *The Court vs. Congress: Prayer, Busing, and Abortion* (Duke University Press, 1989). He has received Alexander von Humboldt Fellowships in recognition of his scholarly contributions.